TARGETED

CRITICAL CULTURAL
COMMUNICATION SERIES

General Editors: Jonathan Gray, Aswin Punathambaker, and Adrienne Shaw

Founding Editors: Sarah Banet-Weiser and Kent A. Ono

Dangerous Curves: Latina Bodies in the Media
Isabel Molina-Guzmán

The Net Effect: Romanticism, Capitalism, and the Internet
Thomas Streeter

Our Biometric Future: Facial Recognition Technology and the Culture of Surveillance
Kelly A. Gates

Critical Rhetorics of Race
Edited by Michael G. Lacy and Kent A. Ono

Circuits of Visibility: Gender and Transnational Media Cultures
Edited by Radha S. Hegde

Commodity Activism: Cultural Resistance in Neoliberal Times
Edited by Roopali Mukherjee and Sarah Banet-Weiser

Arabs and Muslims in the Media: Race and Representation after 9/11
Evelyn Alsultany

Visualizing Atrocity: Arendt, Evil, and the Optics of Thoughtlessness
Valerie Hartouni

Authentic™: The Politics of Ambivalence in a Brand Culture
Sarah Banet-Weiser

The Makeover: Reality Television and Reflexive Audiences
Katherine Sender

Love and Money: Queers, Class, and Cultural Production
Lisa Henderson

Cached: Decoding the Internet in Global Popular Culture
Stephanie Ricker Schulte

Black Television Travels: African American Media around the Globe
Timothy Havens

Citizenship Excess: Latino/as, Media, and the Nation
Hector Amaya

Feeling Mediated: A History of Media Technology and Emotion in America
Brenton J. Malin

The Post-Racial Mystique: Media and Race in the Twenty-First Century
Catherine R. Squires

Making Media Work: Cultures of Management in the Entertainment Industries
Edited by Derek Johnson, Derek Kompare, and Avi Santo

Sounds of Belonging: U.S. Spanish-language Radio and Public Advocacy
Dolores Inés Casillas

Technomobility in China: Young Migrant Women and Mobile Phones
Cara Wallis

Orienting Hollywood: A Century of Film Culture between Los Angeles and Bombay
Nitin Govil

Asian American Media Activism: Fighting for Cultural Citizenship
Lori Kido Lopez

Struggling For Ordinary: Media and Transgender Belonging in Everyday Life
Andre Cavalcante

Homegrown: Identity and Difference in the American War on Terror
Piotr M. Szpunar

Dot-Com Design: The Rise of a Useable, Social, Commercial Web
Megan Sapnar Ankerson

Postracial Resistance: Black Women, Media, and the Uses of Strategic Ambiguity
Ralina L. Joseph

Netflix Nations: The Geography of Digital Distribution
Ramon Lobato

Celebrity: A History of Fame
Susan J. Douglas and Andrea McDonnell

Fake Geek Girls: Fandom, Gender, and the Convergence Culture Industry
Suzanne Scott

Locked Out: Regional Restrictions in Digital Entertainment Culture
Evan Elkins

Beyond Hashtags: Racial Politics and Black Digital Networks
Sarah Florini

The Digital City: Media and the Social Production of Place
Germaine R. Halegoua

Distributed Blackness: African American Cybercultures
André Brock, Jr.

Wife, Inc.: The Business of Marriage in the Twenty-First Century
Suzanne Leonard

Race and Media: Critical Approaches
Edited by Lori Kido Lopez

Border Optics: Surveillance Cultures on the US-Mexico Frontier
Camilla Fojas

Dislike-Minded: Media, Audiences, and the Dynamics of Taste
Jonathan Gray

Digital Media Distribution: Portals, Platforms, Pipelines
Edited by Paul McDonald, Courtney Brannon Donoghue, and Timothy Havens

Digital Black Feminism
Catherine Knight Steele

The Identity Trade: Selling Privacy and Reputation Online
Nora A. Draper

Latino TV: A History
Mary Beltrán

The Digital Border: Migration, Technology, Power
Lilie Chouliaraki and Myria Georgiou

Digital Unsettling: Decoloniality and Dispossession in the Age of Social Media
Sahana Udupa and Ethiraj Gabriel Dattatreyan

Streaming Video: Storytelling Across Borders
Edited by Amanda D. Lotz and Ramon Lobato

Chinese Creator Economies: Labor and Bilateral Creative Workers
Jian Lin

Fandom Is Ugly: Networked Harassment in Participatory Culture
Mel Stanfill

Projecting Desire: Media Architectures and Moviegoing in Urban India
Tupur Chatterjee

After Mass Media: Storytelling for Microaudiences in the Twenty-First Century
Amanda D. Lotz

Social Media and Ordinary Life: Affect, Ethics, and Aspiration in Contemporary China
Cara Wallis

Targeted: Corporations and the Police Surveillance Economy
Kelly Gates

Targeted

Corporations and the Police Surveillance Economy

Kelly Gates

NEW YORK UNIVERSITY PRESS
New York

NEW YORK UNIVERSITY PRESS
New York
www.nyupress.org

© 2025 by New York University
All rights reserved

Please contact the Library of Congress for Cataloging-in-Publication data.

ISBN: 9781479829194 (hardback)
ISBN: 9781479829217 (paperback)
ISBN: 9781479829262 (library ebook)
ISBN: 9781479829255 (consumer ebook)

This book is printed on acid-free paper, and its binding materials are chosen for strength and durability. We strive to use environmentally responsible suppliers and materials to the greatest extent possible in publishing our books.

The manufacturer's authorized representative in the EU for product safety is
Mare Nostrum Group B.V., Mauritskade 21D, 1091 GC Amsterdam, The Netherlands.
Email: gpsr@mare-nostrum.co.uk.

Manufactured in the United States of America

10 9 8 7 6 5 4 3 2 1

Also available as an ebook

For Greg

CONTENTS

List of Figures	xi
Introduction: The Avalanche of Video	1
1. "Grainy to Guilty": Police Video Forensics on the Cusp of Cloud Computing	27
2. "A High-Tech Company Masquerading as a Retailer": Target's Video Infrastructure	52
3. "Storage Costs Set to Skyrocket": Camera-Mounted Cops and Police Migration to the Cloud	85
4. "Our Machines Watch So You Don't Have To": Video AI for Policing and Profit	118
Conclusion: Putting Policing in a Different Frame	144
Acknowledgments	157
Notes	159
Bibliography	177
Index	189
About the Author	197

LIST OF FIGURES

1.1 Surveillance video image of the Boston Marathon bombers (FBI)   28
1.2 U.S. Bureau of Justice Assistance, *Video Evidence: A Primer for Prosecutors* (BJA)   32
1.3 A video forensics lab in Pittsburgh, Pennsylvania, 2017 (Kelly Gates)   39
2.1 A security stand inside a "Target store in the '80s" (Getty Images)   59
2.2a A security stand inside the Target store in North Park, San Diego, 2021 (Kelly Gates)   60
2.2b Self-checkout stations in the Target store in North Park, San Diego, 2021 (Kelly Gates)   61
2.3 *Subject to Debate: A Newsletter of the Police Executive Research Forum* (PERF), December 2010   74
2.4 Inside an Apple Store in San Diego, 2021: "We collect your image while you are in the store for security and fraud prevention" (Kelly Gates)   80
3.1 Axon Enterprise headquarters in Scottsdale, Arizona, 2017 (Kelly Gates)   98
3.2 Inside Axon headquarters in Scottsdale, Arizona, 2017 (Kelly Gates)   100
3.3 Screenshot of a police bodycam video, March 24, 2017 (MLive on YouTube)   105
3.4 A bar graph from a press release, "Axon Reports Second Quarter Results," August 7, 2018 (Axon Enterprise)   108

Introduction

The Avalanche of Video

2012–2017

It is an early Monday morning in spring 2012, in a conference room at a hotel in downtown Indianapolis, and I am getting my first lesson on forensic video analysis, part of a weeklong course on "the scientific examination, comparison, and/or evaluation of video in legal matters."[1] Thanks to the spread of video surveillance, expertise in the forensic analysis of video is in growing demand. The instructor this morning is a foremost forensic video analyst whose experience stretches back to the old analog days of magnetic tapes and videocassette recorders. Although I have never met him, I recognize him from a promotional video from a software company that offers a suite of video forensics technologies called "dTective." When I requested information, someone from the company sent me a DVD as my first introduction to the field. The software runs on Avid hardware, the industry leader in media asset management and digital nonlinear editing systems, the kind used by Hollywood editors and other creative media professionals.

There are about a hundred of us assembled in the room for training, mostly cops but also some civilians who work for law enforcement agencies. The course is on "Forensic Video Analysis and the Law," and it is organized and taught by senior members of a professional association that has positioned itself as a go-to organization for training and expertise in digital multimedia forensics, offering the gold-standard professional credential. The course includes both hands-on technical training in the Digital Multimedia Forensics Lab at Indianapolis University, along with some regular classroom instruction on case law and issues surrounding the legal admissibility of video evidence. Sessions are titled "Principles of Video Security Technology," "Introduction to

Nonlinear Working Environment," "Proper Handling of Digital Multimedia Evidence," "Introduction to DVR Processing," "Introduction to Photographic/Video Comparison," and my personal favorite, "Ethics for Expert Witnesses."

My intention in taking the course is to find out more about how police make use of video surveillance systems in criminal investigations and to what extent computer vision is being integrated with those systems to automate the work of managing their output. I discover that police officers and other people working for law enforcement agencies are becoming experts in digital media, doing what looks like editing and postproduction work with surveillance video. I also learn that using closed-circuit television (CCTV) for this purpose still requires plenty of human labor specially trained for tedious and time-consuming perceptual work. The week is packed full of technical material about compression, interlacing, time codes, metadata, codecs, and the many challenges that a lack of standardized surveillance systems poses for the field acquisition of video.

A primary focus of instruction is how to extract image and audio files, along with relevant metadata, from the wide range of storage devices that one might encounter at a crime scene, without missing or accidentally destroying any important data in the process. The transition from analog to digital video is still underway, and the hybrid configurations of cameras and recording devices that one can find in any investigation are nearly limitless. Video recovery is a formidable process of media-archaeological excavation that involves locating cameras to identify their brand names, and even opening up digital video recorders (DVRs) to examine the hardware inside. A lack of knowledge and technical skill, we learn, could lead to mishandling of digital multimedia evidence, such as overwriting videos with more compressed versions, and failing to acquire audio files or other key pieces of data that could make or break a case. The instructors emphasize the need to approach this type of work as *science* and to see oneself as a *scientist*—a form of self-understanding that sometimes conflicts with being a cop. It is especially important, we learn, to resist the pressure to simply give detectives and prosecutors what they want, even while keeping in mind exactly what that is. Knowingly falsifying evidence, or making a crucial mistake, could ruin your career, not to mention somebody else's life.

Five years after taking the video forensics training course, I arrive in Scottsdale, Arizona, to 119-degree heat to attend "Axon Accelerate 2017," a conference sponsored by the company formerly known as Taser International. Inside the Westin Resort conference center, the word "AXON" is displayed in giant freestanding letters next to the check-in desk. Taser has just changed its name in a major rebranding effort to consolidate the shift in the company's signature product from less-lethal weapons to "the Axon Network." The term is meant to designate not just the company's body-worn cameras but an entire distributed infrastructure of mobile video and signaling devices, smart vehicles with roof-mounted drones, and cloud-based evidence and records management systems with machine learning applications for video and data analytics. This pivot from stun guns to video technology is a business strategy of diversification accompanied by a major rebranding campaign to portray Axon as a high-tech powerhouse—a digital platform for the police. At the check-in counter, I sign in on an iPad and receive some swag, including a very nice black backpack with "Axon Accelerate 2017" embroidered in yellow. I download the Axon Accelerate app to my iPhone, look through my options for the next two days, and have a hard time choosing which panels to attend. I start with a handful: "Fleet, Signal, and the Future of Evidence Capture," "Drone Disruption in Law Enforcement," "Public Safety and Machine Learning," "Intro to Axon Forensic Suite," and "Evidence.com 101."

The next day, the event kicks off in a giant ballroom that has the atmosphere of a concert, with club-style lighting and thumping music. A noticeable difference relative to the two previous Taser events I attended, in addition to the company name change, is the presence of a cadre of new tech talent. Axon recently acquired two startups in the machine learning space, including a computer vision startup called Dextro. The company also poached some people from Big Tech, including Tesla, GoPro, Google, Apple, and Microsoft. It is not hard to distinguish Axon employees—every one of them, including the CEO and other top-level executives, wears a black t-shirt with the same message in yellow and white letters: "Write Code. Save Lives," a slogan that is clearly geared toward Axon's new team of tech workers. The name of the conference itself, a double-gesture at both rapid technological change and fast-paced business strategy, captures the tenor and main theme of the event. On a stage flanked with a giant screen, a series of speakers introduce the conference in the style of Google's yearly I/O event for developers. Their speeches, and the two-day conference that follows, convey a sense of a company blazing forward on a mission to remake itself in the mold of Silicon Valley—in Axon's case, by capturing policing's evidence and records management systems and replacing them with the Axon Network platform.

These two events—a 2012 training course for police video specialists and a 2017 corporate event hosted by a police technology company—are my framing devices for conveying the focus and scope of this book: a study of the *avalanche of video* that has occurred in the domain of policing and security in the post-9/11 decades. Video production, analysis, and asset management have become major areas of attention and practice for the police, completely embedded in the ways police power is exercised, criminal law enforced, and spaces of human habitation securitized. At video forensics training in 2012, the amount of video in circulation already seemed staggering, but the course had very little to say about cell phones and made no mention at all of drones or body-worn cameras. Five years later at Axon's 2017 conference, the media landscape had changed, and the deluge of audiovisual content in circulation had grown substantially. Professionals tasked with handling digital media evidence had an expanding volume and variety of audiovisual material to manage, coming from a widening range of sources. The police themselves produced more video, especially after their adoption of body cameras, contributing to a media environment that seemed more saturated and chaotic than ever before. Video was becoming embedded in the logistical and sensemaking systems of policing and security, for reasons largely assumed to be self-evident.

This book argues that while critical scholars have rightly focused on the datafication of policing, it is also necessary to understand the avalanche of *video* and its role in the expansion and intensification of policing and security in the first decades of the twenty-first century. The chapters focus on four areas of significance for understanding the video avalanche: (1) the field of video forensics, also called digital multimedia forensics, (2) private video surveillance infrastructure development, (3) police body-worn cameras and video evidence management systems, and (4) video analytics for the automation of surveillance, or the application of artificial intelligence (AI) to process and analyze video. While providing far from an exhaustive picture, these four areas reveal some of the pivotal ways that video content, technologies, expertise, and infrastructures have been integrated into policing and security to expand their reach and power. They also reveal the role of video infrastructure development in the increasingly entangled relationship between the modern police and the modern corporation and the changing "dual structure" of public policing and private security in the long wake and ruins of neoliberalism.[2]

What Is Unique about the Video Avalanche?

There have been other media avalanches. In *The Taming of Chance*, Ian Hacking describes an "avalanche of printed numbers" that occurred across Europe in the nineteenth century: "an event so all-embracing that we seldom pause to notice it."[3] The circulation of numerical information on paper contributed to the way populations were understood and governed as social and political formations of growing scale and complexity. Probability thinking changed the way the emerging human sciences viewed causation, introducing new ways of analyzing information to predict and affect outcomes. Statistics became a new kind of evidence, and in the process, the belief in human nature was replaced by numerical distributions for charting normalcy and deviance.

Two problems that received a great deal of attention among the counters and analysts who invented modern statistics were suicide and *crime*. Crime statistics came into being in nineteenth-century Europe, shaping the foundations of statistics and probability theory. This included the effort to measure crime as a social phenomenon and also to measure the bodies of criminals—to identify them as individuals or to classify the criminal body as a biological type. Influential figures like the eugenicist Francis Galton developed statistical concepts like correlation and regression to classify criminal types.[4] Probability, according to Hacking, was "the philosophical success story of the first half of the twentieth century."[5] In a relentless recursive logic, the success of statistical probability as a form of sensemaking emerged out of, and in turn was applied to, the problems of crime and criminalization.

In the United States, the rise of crime statistics converged with and helped to enact evolving forms of post-slavery state racism. In *The Condemnation of Blackness*, Khalil Gibran Muhammad charts the historical relationship between the rise of crime statistics and deep-seated notions of Black criminality that shaped criminal justice policy and practice after emancipation, addressing white people's anxieties about the newly won freedom of former slaves.[6] Sociologists used statistics to "prove" that former slaves were a degenerate race inherently prone to criminality, using census data from 1890, for example, to show that "absolute and relative growth of the black prison population" was "definitive proof of blacks' true criminal nature."[7] The claim was that there was no racism in the Northern states, so the high incarceration rates of Blacks in the North proved that they were born with criminal propensities. This fraudulent use of statistics gave scientific weight to Jim Crow laws and sentencing practices that punished Black defendants more harshly than whites. Statistics and enumeration proved to give weighty authority, objectivity, and concreteness to faulty, recursive claims based in the belief system of white supremacy.[8] The avalanche of printed numbers transformed modern thinking about crime and criminality and lent scientific authority to the structural racism of the modern criminal legal system.

By comparing the twenty-first century avalanche of video to the earlier avalanche of printed numbers, I want to suggest that these two media avalanches are similar in scale and significance. Much like the avalanche of printed numbers, the video deluge has been "so all-embracing that we seldom pause to notice it."[9] I also want to underscore the ways that, in both cases, a discriminatory, racialized understanding of crime and criminality is designed into the epistemic machinery, despite the seeming neutrality of the media.

Video and printed numbers are, of course, fundamentally different media. They are different kinds of evidence, diverging significantly in the manner in which they represent reality and serve as the basis of truth claims. Thus far, video has not been used to measure crime *rates*, at least not to a significant extent, although it is certainly seen to offer this potential. Crime statistics measure aggregates and patterns, while the legal and criminalistic uses of video center more on direct forms of crime prevention, investigation, and prosecution. The criminal legal system marshals considerable resources to treat crimes as specific and singular acts of legal transgression, and video is now central to this approach, as I discuss in Chapter 1. At the same time, there is considerable effort underway to analyze video datasets on a larger scale, applying computational forms of analysis. As I will argue, the combined priorities of policing and profit-making are driving these efforts.

If the nineteenth-century avalanche of printed numbers underpinned the rise of probability thinking, can we point to another major epistemological shift occurring with the avalanche of video? It probably makes more sense to say that if probability thinking was the philosophical success story of the early twentieth century, *computational thinking* is the philosophical success story of the early twenty-first century. This dominant paradigm of computation remains heavily reliant on probability. Louise Amoore's analysis of "the cloud form of computation" in *Cloud Ethics* does the challenging work of theorizing this emergent computational epistemology, conceptualizing "the cloud as an analytic gathering of algorithms with data" that is now the dominant way the world is rendered "perceptible and analyzable."[10] For Amoore, visual vocabulary or methodology—visually mapping the locations of data centers, for example—does us little good in making sense of the cloud as "a novel space of calculative reasoning." This type of reasoning operates not "on the terrain of human vision" but instead on a subvisual level.[11] We cannot see its powerful effects by looking at images.

The centrality of computational epistemology in our digital age raises the question of whether video is still a unique or defining medium, worthy of specific attention. In fact, there is an argument to be made that there is no longer any meaningful distinction between video and data. "All forms of image, text, sounds, and video are just raw data for AI systems," as Kate Crawford has noted.[12] Video itself has become data, and in the process, it has become calculable, computational media no different from other forms of data. As much of the critical literature on datafied policing suggests, it makes more sense to consider the *data* deluge, as opposed to *video* avalanche per se, to understand the shifting ground of knowledge about crime and policing.[13]

While acknowledging the profoundly important ways that computational systems are transforming how the world is analyzed, perceived, and acted on, I nonetheless want to insist on the significance of video as a distinct medium for understanding the technological and epistemological transformations taking place. We are living in a moment of unprecedented video production and circulation. While digital technologies have enabled these conditions, it would be inaccurate to say that video is no longer primarily audiovisual because it is digital now, or that analog video and magnetic tape formats were audiovisual media while digital formats are not. All media formats have material and multi-perceptual qualities, and digital video formats are still *audiovisual* media, even if computational systems now process videos as numerical data. General and agnostic concepts of "data" obscure the unique epistemic, logistical, and aesthetic affordances of video and fail to acknowledge how audiovisual media are changing as the tech industry expands its computational power.

In fact, there is a more complex relationship between video and data than a linear notion of digitization suggests. The size of a single audiovisual file is orders of magnitude larger than most of the other files on our laptops (except for the apps, which grow larger with every "upgrade"). The size of digital video recordings and the scale of computing power needed to archive and process *catalogs* of digital video are enormous. The fact that videos require a lot of processing power has meant that the reverse is also true: video has played a defining role in the development of computational systems. Notably, the computing demands of video processing have driven the development of faster processors. In turn, these faster processors were made available for other computational tasks. The chip designer Nvidia Corporation developed superfast graphical processing units (GPUs) to power video games, which in turn gave computer infrastructures the speed needed to usher in a new wave of development in machine learning. What is now being called artificial intelligence has been made possible by these graphics-specific processors. In other words, the demands of video processing have shaped, at a technical and infrastructural level, developments in machine learning.

Video cameras and their output have proliferated in myriad forms; they are no longer primarily designed as stand-alone devices but instead are embedded with other technologies, from eyeglasses to automobiles, and integrated into platforms. Video is a container technology for time, space, motion, and sound, and this combination makes it especially useful as an evidentiary, aesthetic, and logistical medium.[14] Video is an audiovisual medium that provides a sense of temporal immediacy across distance, for *live* transmission of activities occurring in different places. Its recorded forms and the volume of those recordings also give it the capacity to serve as a repository for revisiting past activities. Like numbers on paper documents, video's reproducibility and mobility are key features of the medium. In Hacking's argument, it was not just numbers but *printed* numbers that were essential to the philosophical success story of probability thinking. All the counting would be far less impactful without the power of print to reproduce the numbers. In the case of the video, its reproducibility and mobility allow activities captured as video recordings to be experienced by people at different times and places, expanding the capacities of witnessing, from the most banal to the most dramatic events.

While video is often thought of as a visual medium, the medium specificity of video is not strictly visual. Not all video contains sound, but much of it does, and it is often the combination of what is both visible and audible that matters for its uses, interpretation, and aesthetics. In some cases, what is visible is far less meaningful than what is audible. Videos represent sight, motion, and sound, including *words*. And sounds and spoken words are often central to the meaning and aesthetics of both live video transmissions and recordings replayed later. Overemphasizing video as a visual medium risks diminishing what makes it such a ubiquitous and powerful medium of communication, evidence, logistics, and aesthetic and affective experience.[15]

Computers, chips, algorithms, and infrastructures—the technological conditions behind the video avalanche—matter a great deal. The origins of digital video stretch back to the 1970s, but it took several decades for digital to become the dominant video format. In the process, digitization transformed video and its capacities, expanding its quantity and its uses. While a large volume of analog video was created in the last half of the twentieth century, the amount of video production that digitization afforded is exponentially greater. Untold millions of webcams, dashcams, body cameras, security cameras, and camera-mounted drones now generate far more video than humans could ever watch or listen to in total.

To address the demands of managing the video avalanche, the drive to develop automated forms of video analysis is fully in motion. These efforts overlap with and inform other experiments with machine learning.

Computational technologies promise to do the watching and listening in place of human eyes and ears, raising the prospect of more and more video produced by machines, for machines. Developers claim that machine learning will allow the organizations amassing video datasets to analyze the *totality* of video in those catalogs. "Our machines watch so you don't have to," claimed the computer vision startup company Dextro. They described their "Sight, Sound and Motion" machine learning technology as "a powerful system that rapidly understands the totality of your video."[16] The company, acquired by Axon Enterprise in 2017, also described the usefulness of its technology for "security video monitoring": "Dextro's system turns hours of security video into meaningful data in a matter of seconds."[17] While this lofty declaration said more about the desire for automated video processing than what the technology could achieve, it spoke volumes about one of the primary use-cases driving the development of video analytics.

If cameras generate more video than humans will ever watch, nonetheless, a great deal of that video contains records of *human activities*. Video cameras record information that other sensors do not, expanding the range of surveillance coverage both spatially and temporally. While humans are at times conscious of having their activities recorded, video technology can transmit and record us even when we are not conscious of being recorded. We are at best only half-conscious of the ways that video technology has become embedded in perception, memory, and experience.

Because video is so embedded in human experience, it is challenging to notice, let alone understand, the implications of the video avalanche. The ubiquitous presence of video technology represents "the thoroughgoing permeation of reality with mechanical equipment," which, precisely because it is so permeating, seems to offer "an aspect of reality which is free of all equipment."[18] Video has flooded every domain of social life, from the most intimate to the most public. Not only has videography been democratized, but human experience and perception are enmeshed with video technologies and recordings. Our lives are *mediatized*, in ways that extend and differ in many ways from earlier forms of mediatization theorized in communication and media studies.[19] There is no boundary between mediated and unmediated perception, as scholars of posthumanism have argued. Katherine Hayles shows how biological and technical forms of cognition "interpenetrate one another" and form "human-technical cognitive assemblages."[20] Rather than drawing a sharp line between human and computer cognition, Hayles argues, a more important distinction is between conscious and nonconscious cognition. Consciousness also matters to media scholars Anthony McCosker and Rowan Wilken, who theorize a "new camera consciousness" in the conditions of visibility created by evolving configurations of human and machine vision.[21] If machine learning algorithms turn video into data, in the process video has become even more deeply embedded in human-machine perception.

Video surveillance systems, police bodycam and dashcam systems, smartphones, tablets, laptops, and drones generate content that circulates on screens as television. What we might call *televisuality*, borrowing a term from John Caldwell's study of television's production culture,[22] began as a twentieth-century mode of technocultural mediation, and its evolving audiovisual forms are fully sutured into modern experience and sensibility. It is no longer possible for screen people to see televisuality as strange because it is completely integrated into the way modern humans perceive the world and make sense of themselves. Writing in the 1970s, Raymond Williams coined the term "mobile privatization" to describe the technocultural form of television in its earlier analog and broadcast era, when television was part of the new suburban modernity. Today, televisuality has been mobilized and privatized in whole new ways, fragmented and digitally distributed, monetized and personalized, leveraged and operationalized.

If we were to take a broad and deep look at both the content and form of televisuality, the entirety of a "televisual field" something like what Pierre Bourdieu calls the "bureaucratic field,"[23] we would be remiss in not noticing how much of its design and production processes, themes and formal qualities, its symbolic content and logistical uses, are given over to policing and security. The massive televisual mediation of policing is implied by what Loïc Wacquant refers to as "the rampant gesticulation over law and order," which, like the spectacle of pornography is "conceived and carried out . . . *for the express purpose of being exhibited and seen*."[24] Like sex and sexuality, crime and policing have been completely mediatized in ways that are embedded in perception and experience.[25]

Video and the Logistical Mediatization of Policing

Media studies has long been interested in the relationship between crime, policing, and media. The rise of modern mass media and modern policing occurred in tandem, with crime coverage playing a central role in the history of print journalism and the newspaper and, later, radio and television news programming. The consolidated media industries of the twentieth century elevated crime dramas and true crime storytelling to the center of content production in the United States. Violent crimes committed by individuals against other individuals typically receive a great deal of airtime in public discourses about crime, from local news to true crime and crime fiction genres. The collective representation of crime and criminality as the main social problem facing modern societies has been a central storyline of popular entertainment media and news, especially dominating local news.[26] Print, cinema, radio, and television all have extensive genre histories of fictional and true crime dramas and police procedurals. The fascination with the drama of crime and its investigation, easily dismissed as lowbrow sensationalism, has shaped public knowledge and perception about crime and policing. How crime and policing are represented in and made real through media, full of variation and contrasts, is a vital and defining feature of U.S. culture and society.

Knowledge and perceptions about crime and policing circulate back and forth from media representations to the real-life politics of police power. Black studies scholar Jared Sexton has examined the "cinema of policing" for what it reveals about the cultural politics of Black masculine authority, as conveyed, for example, through the cinematic figure of the Black cop. Cultural criminologist Travis Linnemann has argued that a "methamphetamine imaginary," lionized in the television show *Breaking Bad*, has served as an ideological filter for popular sensemaking about the drug trade, addiction, and punitive law enforcement.[27] According to Linnemann, "The methamphetamine and drug war imaginaries are clearly at work within a reciprocal system of cultural production, where the screen actively scripts the actions of police and state power."²⁸ Christina Aushana has argued that the performance of policing has a decidedly cinematic aspect, with films like Antoine Fuqua's *Training Day* screened for police recruits at training camp.²⁹ These studies extend Christopher Wilson's study of "cop knowledge," which examined how dominant ideas, values, and assumptions about crime and policing circulated back and forth from police policy and practice, to crime reporting and the popular genres of crime fiction and true crime storytelling in twentieth-century America.³⁰

While the cultural production of crime and policing has received a good deal of attention in media and cultural studies, the field has been far less inclined to examine the *logistical* uses of media technologies in policing. Where Paul Virilio theorized the "logistics of military perception" in the relationship between cinema and war-fighting, we can also identify a related yet distinct *logistics of police perception* in the relationship between audiovisual media and policing.³¹ The term I use for the integration of media technologies into logistical operations of policing and security is *logistical mediatization.*

Logistical mediatization is a process whereby media devices and formats are mobilized to organize activities, and where media technologies are designed into systems for managing the distributed flow of people and things. Communication scholars have highlighted the logistical function of digital media as a feature that differentiates them from the representational and narrative forms of mass media. According to John Durham Peters, logistical media are used to organize and arrange people and property, coordinate activities, establish and enforce hierarchies between superiors and subordinates, and "set the terms in which everyone must operate."³² Ned Rossiter developed a "media theory of logistics," focusing on the logistical operations that support the global economy: "the logistical industries that drive supply chain capitalism."³³ Rossiter's central concern is in the relationship between logistics and labor control, or the biopolitical implications of logistics as it regulates labor. Though not always recognized as such, logistics are centrally concerned with labor management. As Chandra Mukerji has argued, logistical activity "shapes social life differently" than the strategic exercise of will for domination, "affecting the environment (context, situation, location) in which human action and cognition take place."³⁴ Mukerji defines *logistical power* as "the ability to mobilize the natural world for political effect," a form of power that is designed into built environments, technologies, and embodied activities in ways that make it very difficult to challenge or even recognize.[35] Logistical power is infrastructural, a means of automatically delegating patterns of thought and behavior and silently shaping forms of life in largely unnoticed ways.[36]

Media technologies have been instrumental to the logistical operations of policing. Jeremy Packer and Joshua Reeves have argued that media have been integral to police logistics throughout the development of modern policing, from police gazettes and rogues' galleries to two-way radios and then digital technologies.[37] Focusing on more recent developments, Aaron Shapiro has argued that the technologies used to organize urban space are "logistical urban media," including "predictive policing," which he argues is essentially the use of data analytics for the logistical governance of police patrols.[38] In his study of twentieth-century police communication systems, Peter Manning argued that police organizations were "meaning production machines."[39] His use of the term "machines" stemmed from the inescapable reliance on telephones, teleprinters, VHF and UHF radios, and computer-cathode ray tubes for displaying information encoded by 911 operators. According to Manning, police "reproduce their own metaphoric version or *map* of society by their encoding and decoding processes."[40] Through the encoding and decoding of the messages that flow through their communications systems, he explained, police organizations "maintain the dramatic importance of the police, their actions, and the centrality of myths that reify the notion that the police control and can control all that needs controlling society."[41]

If police organizations are "meaning production machines," as Manning argued, producing metaphorical and logistical maps of society, today they are making far more use of video than ever before to monitor, map, control, and especially to maintain the dramatic importance—and power—of the police. The evidentiary, logistical, and aesthetic uses of video cannot be sharply differentiated, and understanding the ways they overlap is key to understanding the significance of video's assimilation into modern policing. It is also key to understanding the way the logistics of police perception circulates beyond the criminal legal system into other domains of media use.

The Police Surveillance Economy

This book highlights another key historical difference between the avalanche of video and the avalanche of printed numbers: the role of modern corporations and the Silicon Valley business model in building and profiting from video infrastructures and the logistical mediatization of policing. In her theorization of *surveillance capitalism*, Shoshana Zuboff makes an important point about the way this economic form took hold in the post-9/11 context, which she refers to as "surveillance exceptionalism." Privacy and other data protections, already very weakly governed by the deregulatory dogma of neoliberalism, were further decimated by the intelligence demands of the "war on terror." The bursting of the dot-com bubble in 2000 combined with the 9/11 terrorist attacks created a perfect storm for the rise of the surveillance economy. According to Zuboff, the surveillance exceptionalism of the post-9/11 moment "favored Google's growth and the successful elaboration of its surveillance-based logic of accumulation."[42] But if the Big Tech companies became the reigning surveillance capitalists in the post-9/11 decades, many thousands of other companies got into the growing, multifaceted business of surveillance.

The surveillance-based logic of accumulation stretched beyond Google to include the private security industry and others supplying equipment and services to law enforcement.[43] It is not only that the work of public policing is being "privatized" or "outsourced." Instead, we are seeing digital platforms work their way into policing and security, reconfiguring these domains much as they have other systems of media and communication. As legal scholar Julie Cohen argues, platforms do not just enter markets, they replace them.[44] Understanding the changing "dual structure" of public policing and private security today requires examining their relationship to the platform economy.[45]

Critical scholars of policing have made important arguments about the changing relationship between public and private policing.[46] Steven Spitzer explains that private policing was the rule rather than the exception for much of human history.[47] Examples include the collective liability that occurred under early Anglo-Saxon kings and in China under the Ch'ing dynasty in the seventeenth and eighteenth centuries, where neighbors were made to spy on one another (not unlike the more recent picture of the United States that Joshua Reeves provides in his book *Citizen Spies*).[48] Entrepreneurial forms of policing that emerged in eighteenth-century England included "thief-takers" who were intermediaries between thieves and victims, "operatives on both sides of the law."[49] The use of mercenaries to govern and suppress local populations was also common, although the absence of a legitimate foundation for their role as managers of domestic populations "meant that this form of policing frequently proved unstable."[50] Then there were the "company towns" that rose in the post–Civil War period in the United States, defined largely by paternalistic relations between workers and "captains of industry." The latter hired private police to preserve their hegemony and economic dominance of the towns. Spitzer refers to this as a "big stick" system, which declined as company towns were "gradually engulfed by and absorbed into the increasingly atomized and impersonal society of twentieth-century corporate America."[51] Other factors that contributed to the decline of private policing in the United States were "the 'socialization' of the costs of labor control," "the increased power of organized labor," and "major changes in the economic infrastructure itself."[52]

If private policing has a very long history, the "economic infrastructure" of the twenty-first-century capitalist economy is without question in a different phase of development. Driven by the demands and logics of finance capitalism, corporations are embedding themselves in police work and taking on more police functions, whether for their own security or to extract data, revenue, and market value from police budgets and labor. Such as it always was, perhaps, but not at the scale or to the extent that we see today. Today's private security industry is a sprawling sector with indistinct boundaries.[53] It encompasses everything from home security systems (such as ADT and now also Google Nest and Amazon Ring) to the ubiquitous guards-for-hire employed by companies like Allied Universal, to major in-house security operations of corporations, universities, and the paramilitary companies that provide private security to economic elites.

Notable for the argument that I make in this book, the private security sector is a major force in video infrastructure development. Corporations contract with government agencies and other companies to build large-scale video infrastructures for monitoring spaces, properties, and logistical operations. Far from one-time, fixed-cost procurements, these video infrastructures are costly ventures requiring perpetual investment, maintenance, and upgrading. Surveillance equipment and video asset management companies have become major global enterprises.

In the 1990s and early 2000s, surveillance studies scholars were paying close attention to the diffusion of video surveillance. Likewise, actors in the privacy policy community were advocating for regulation and oversight of the uses of these systems. But by 2009, there were references to CCTV as a "baroque arsenal," an expensive capital investment not living up to its promises to reduce crime.[54] Scholarly and other critical attention to video surveillance began to wane along with the rise of Big Data and related developments: smartphones, social media, smart cities, cloud computing, body-worn cameras, the Internet of Things, and artificial intelligence (many of these terms originating as marketing language). The banality that video surveillance achieved by the early 2000s perhaps also helped to render it less attractive as an object of study.[55]

But the construction of video surveillance infrastructures has continued unabated. According to one industry report, the U.S. video surveillance market was worth $10.99 billion in 2020 and expected to grow to $22.04 billion by 2029.[56] Another industry report valued the global video surveillance market at $36.89 billion in 2018, with an expected valuation of $83.3 billion by 2028.[57] The latter report predicted that countries in the Asia-Pacific, especially India and China, would see the largest growth. Industry reports described the video surveillance market as fragmented, but it was also clear that consolidation was occurring. For example, in 2014 and 2015, the Japanese conglomerate Canon Inc. acquired Milestone Systems and Axis Communications, both major video surveillance technology companies. Milestone was "among the world's leading providers of open platform video management software."[58] Axis was "the world's largest supplier of network cameras." The company initially built network printers in the 1980s and later introduced the first network camera for monitoring offshore oil drilling.[59] Canon acquired Axis for $2.83 billion and Milestone for an undisclosed amount. When announcing its acquisitions, Canon released a boilerplate yet revealing statement: "In recent years, the video surveillance system market has continued to realize rapid growth. Canon views its network surveillance camera business as a promising new business area and positions the business as a driving force for future growth within the Canon Group."[60] CEO Fujio

Mitarai described video surveillance as a market having "limitless possibilities for growth."[61] The point should not go without emphasizing: video surveillance was deemed a "driving force for future growth" of this multinational company because it saw that future growth as "limitless."

Another source of future limitless growth of great corporate interest and relevant to the video avalanche are police *records management systems* (RMS), which I discuss in Chapter 3. Police RMS are the "information heart" of police operations, informing the way police "operate spatially as a sovereign network."[62] While not typically associated with video, these systems are becoming large video repositories, especially with police adoption of body cameras. In a company brochure, Motorola Solutions notes that "the definition of a police record is changing. A complete law incident includes more than just forms and reports. It requires body-worn and in-car video recordings, audio files, images and other data collected over the course of an investigation."[63] The company implores its police customers: "Your agency needs a next-generation records management solution designed for this new reality."[64]

Motorola Solutions and its competitor Axon Enterprise are envisioning the information management and logistical needs of law enforcement as an expansive domain for revenue recognition. Of course, they are not the first companies to seek revenues from policing's bureaucratic and logistical systems. Notably, the modern corporation made a decisive appearance in police recordkeeping starting with the introduction of computers in the 1960s. As law enforcement and federal agencies began to adopt computers, IBM developed the Law Enforcement Manpower Resource Allocation System (LEMRAS), which was billed as a means of applying mathematical models for police managerial decision-making.[65] Police RMS have been irresistible sources of data for the purposes of crime analysis and law enforcement resource allocation (police logistics). Datafied crime analysis, or what was cleverly branded "predictive policing" in 2008, was a statistical endeavor for generating probabilities about where crimes were likely to happen and who was likely to commit them.[66] It also informed the managerial oversight of police rank-and-file and automated some police patrol functions.[67]

If "the definition of a police record is changing," the fact that Motorola Solutions is making this declaration suggests that there is financial value to be realized from police recordkeeping, crime analysis, and resource allocation. Computational capacitates are expanding in part to address the volume of video being produced by and for policing. Police video storage, once a local matter, has migrated onto proprietary data infrastructures. Police body-worn cameras, dashboard cameras, and their backend media management systems are the latest stage in the logistical mediatization of policing. This form of mediatization, where video is embedded in the logistical systems of policing and security, is posited as directly serving the specific needs of the police. However, it is a mistake to understand it narrowly in these terms. The adoption of bodycams by police has been a major impetus driving policing's recordkeeping systems onto corporate-controlled, proprietary computing infrastructures. In the process, police records management—the "information heart" of police operations[68]—has become a competitive site for corporate capture. Companies are competing to replace the logistical and bureaucratic systems of policing with a proprietary digital platform.

This is not to suggest that the corporate capture of police IT systems is a frictionless process. There is a fundamental structuring tension between corporate strategies and the social functions of policing as defined by the police themselves. In other words, the interests of these firms do not always align with the police, and police agencies are not without agency in these contractual relationships. The historian Stuart Schrader makes an important argument about the rise of the police as an autonomous political force during the Cold War (along with the transnational diffusion of the U.S. model of policing as a part of its political strategy of counterinsurgency).[69] If police used to pay allegiance to politicians as their patrons, by the time Bill Clinton was elected president in 1992, politicians were the ones paying allegiance to the police. The U.S. institution of law enforcement continues to exercise its own political power in the current era, but it is also the case that corporations exercise significant powers of policing. They also leverage the political power that has accrued to the police to serve their own powerful interests. In this book, I argue that we learn a great deal about the evolving entangled relationship between the modern corporation and the modern police—and how their expansive impulses feed and depend on each other—by turning a lens on the avalanche of video.

Video Activism

If video technologies are embedded in policing and security, they are also woven into struggles to resist and challenge over-policing and state violence. In its totality, the avalanche of video circulating across the world's media infrastructures includes cop-watching, eyewitness video, and human rights video activism. It is in many ways its own video avalanche, with no shortage of injustices and atrocities to document.[70] A wide range of actors with varying degrees of agency, intentionality, and expertise use video technology in the fight against police violence and the struggle for human rights.

As a relatively inexpensive and adaptable form of media, video has been used as a technology of activism and struggle since its inception. These uses have been wide ranging, from organized forms of participatory video beginning in the 1960s and 1970s to the more ubiquitous use of smartphones to capture eyewitness video. Allissa Richardson explains that the use of mobile phones and social media by Black folks in the United States to witness, document, and challenge police brutality and white vigilantism has a genealogy that extends back to the Black press of the civil rights movement and to slave narratives in the fight for emancipation.[71] But if "bearing witness while black" has a long history, media technologies are always at the center of political struggle, as Olga Kuchinskaya argues, and media-technological changes have important effects on the pace, scale, and pattern of that struggle.[72]

The widespread use of video-enabled cell phones to record the police was a dramatic and unforeseen development in the practices of vernacular videography. Despite a long history of cop-watching, not to mention the enormous cultural impact of the Rodney King beating, pent-up demand to document police violence was not likely on the radar of Apple and the other smartphone companies. Nor did the tech companies that launched video-sharing platforms like YouTube (in 2005) or Facebook Video (in 2007) anticipate the use of social media for distributing videos of police violence. Perhaps they were unaware how much there was to document, since it was far less likely to be happening in their neighborhoods. Seemingly overnight, many more people became cop-watchers, video activists, or bystander eyewitnesses, using their cell phones to capture very different perspectives of policing than those that typically circulated on television. Embedding video technology into mobile phones converged with a deep social need to document and share these incidents from perspectives other than police themselves. If there was nothing new about the amount of police violence against Black folks in the United States, smartphones and the capacity to share video online made the extent of the problem more apparent to much wider publics.

The activist response to the increased visibility of police violence was also distributed to broader audiences using the sharing capabilities of social media sites. Livestreaming became an important means of disseminating protest actions aimed at resisting police repression. The scholar, activist, and journalist Chenjerai Kumanyika was among the "unpaid local livestream journalists" who livestreamed the Black Lives Matter protests, participating in a wave of "DIY Black Liberation politics" that arose after the police killings of Eric Garner and Michael Brown in the summer of 2014.[73] Livestreaming apps launched in 2015—namely, Periscope and Facebook Live—helped fill a void in both media coverage and the capacity for networked participation.

The increase in video of police activities and new avenues for sharing and watching it online suggested that a more level playing field of surveillance was taking shape. Andrew Goldsmith called it "policing's new visibility," arguing that the police were losing their ability to control the narratives of crime and policing and becoming more accountable to the public.[74]

Without a doubt, activists have made the most of video, from analog camcorders to smartphone cameras and social media. Yet it is hard to say to what extent video activism has succeeded in bending the arc of the moral universe toward justice.[75] The promise that eyewitness and police bodycam video would reduce police violence was soon challenged by the relentless barrage of more video of police violence. Instead of spurring systemic change, the videos fed into competing narratives and widely divergent views about crime and policing. The police quickly became more adept at manipulating the conditions of their "new visibility." The criminal legal system repeatedly dismissed video of police violence as offering only a partial perspective, pointing to important differences between popular and legal conceptions of photographic evidence, as Jennifer Petersen explains.[76] In the case of police bodycam video, videos would mysteriously go missing at key moments, or police decision-makers would withhold it, citing privacy concerns. As the legal scholars Laurent Sacharoff and Sarah Lustbader argued, as long as body cameras were controlled by the police themselves, they would have little to no effect on police accountability.[77] Police body cameras became another tool for helping police to manage their image, as Bryce Newell has argued, selectively using the video to control representations of policing.[78] At best and in highly circumscribed cases, body cameras helped to individualize responsibility for police violence, which has long been a convenient way of circumventing the problems of structural racism and inequality in the criminal legal system.

Video recordings of brutal police violence, including extrajudicial killings, also circulate in a highly fragmented environment of online media reception. As legal scholar David Owens argues, the proliferation of these videos has become a spectacle of Black death reminiscent of the spectacle of the scaffold in medieval Europe and the circulation of lynching photographs in the Reconstruction and Jim Crow eras.[79] Video of police violence has fed into a powerful strand of white cultural allegiance to the police and long-standing racist beliefs in inherent Black criminality. Efforts to record video evidence of police misconduct have been repeatedly hindered by the police's political power and media-technological capacities, which are now amplified by corporations seeking to extract revenues and other financial value from policing.

My focus on policing and industry makes me more skeptical of the power of video to level the playing field between the police and overpoliced people. The chapters reveal what the struggle for a more equitable world is up against: the combined power of the police and the security and tech industries to build infrastructures and imaginaries to serve their aims. I want to suggest that there are reasons that video has failed to move the needle in the direction of less police violence, reasons that we can understand better by examining the way the criminal legal system has acquired the epistemic machinery to make use of the video avalanche and the way private companies have become more embedded in the media infrastructures of policing.

Outline of the Chapters

This study of the avalanche of video in policing and security begins with the field of *video forensics*, also known as *forensic video analysis* and now *digital multimedia forensics*, a field that got started in the analog days of video and well before smartphones, social media, or body-worn cameras. The use of surveillance video as legal and public evidence extends at least as far back as the Patty Hearst kidnapping and bank robbery in 1974, and it has become a far more developed field of technical practice since then. In the 2000s and 2010s, video became one of the most prolific forms of evidence in the criminal legal system. But while the evidentiary status of video seemed self-evident, making recorded video useful as evidence was far more challenging than most people realized. It took a considerable amount of effort to develop techniques and protocols of video evidence recovery, handling, analysis, and presentation, and the expertise and epistemic machinery has been far from evenly distributed or applied. In addition, as video technology has changed, new challenges have arisen that require new kinds of technical and epistemic competency. In Chapter 1, I provide an account of video forensics that reveals some of the complicated entanglements between human perception and media technologies that have taken shape for producing and interpreting video evidence. Looking inside the black box of video forensics challenges the assumption that the analysis of video can be readily automated by machine learning algorithms, or that artificial intelligence can provide complete analytics of large volumes of video.

Chapter 2 focuses on one of the major sources of the video avalanche: private security, including the in-house private security operations of major corporations. Focusing on Target Corp., the U.S. retail giant, I examine how corporations built proprietary security infrastructures that rivaled and even surpassed the surveillance systems operated by cities and police departments, contributing to the shaping and workings of surveillance capitalism. Contracting with global surveillance equipment suppliers like Axis Communications and media asset management companies like Milestone Systems, Target built a massive video surveillance system throughout its retail infrastructure. The scale of this infrastructure and its vast output of video led the company to develop its own proprietary forensics operation to make effective use of the video for asset protection and store security. In addition, the company formed public-private partnerships with police departments in the cities and municipalities where it located its stores. It also developed an approach to corporate philanthropy-for-policing that included grant-making to police departments as well as in-kind donations of security expertise and surveillance equipment. In the chapter's final section, I discuss the repurposing of video surveillance systems for retail analytics, which represents the complete integration of security and marketing and a kind of holy grail for the construction of the *securitized brandscape*.[80]

Chapter 3 shifts the focus from video infrastructure development in retail to the mobile media infrastructures of police body-worn cameras. It also shifts the lens from the retail giant Target to the company Axon Enterprise (formerly Taser), a leading supplier of police body cameras in the United States. Among the promises that Taser/Axon made to its police customers was that body-worn cameras would be labor-saving technologies, initially suggesting that bodycam video could replace the police report and eliminate the heavy bureaucratic burdens of police work. But the reality was that as police officers attached cameras to their bodies to record their work, they were also tasked with managing the video output. In turn, police adoption of body cameras, and the avalanche of police video it produced, was a major driver accelerating the migration of police IT systems onto cloud-based software-as-a-service platforms. Companies began competing to build platforms that would allow them to capture the data, labor, and information flows of the criminal legal system, turning them into direct revenues and other forms of financial value. If Axon's investor communications were any indication, the company viewed the body camera not primarily as a tool for police accountability or reducing workloads but instead as a market device for leveraging surplus value from police labor. While police departments have always been business customers (e.g., for equipment like guns, radios, and cars), becoming customers of digital platforms was a fundamentally different proposition. It meant changing the scope of work that police performed while also giving tech companies greater material interest in the growth of police budgets. In Chapter 3, I show that despite the big promises that Axon makes to their police customers, their corporate interests diverge quite far from the organizational interests of police departments (and from the tax payers funding the police).

Chapter 4 focuses on another so-called labor-saving technology: video AI. The development of computational technologies for processing and analyzing video was an overdetermined moment in twenty-first century video infrastructure development. Massive volumes of video created the need for scaled-up, content-based image retrieval—i.e., the ability to search the "essence" of image and audio files, rather than solely the attached metadata. Image search is hard enough with still photos. It is infinitely more challenging with video. And the more video that accumulated, the greater the perceived need for automated ways of searching, sorting, listening to, and watching it. To an extent that is difficult to measure, video AI has been driven and shaped by the expanding video infrastructures of policing and security, and the challenges of making use of their voluminous video output, both live and recorded. The video infrastructures of policing and security produce valuable datasets for training machine learning algorithms, which benefit from large amounts of labeled, domain-specific video data. At the same time, the quantity of video being generated by video devices and infrastructure is fueling the demand for more automation. Chapter 4 argues that, like AI in general, video AI is both technological infrastructure and technocultural imaginary, a combined technological project and work of cultural production. One does not function without the other, and in both cases, video AI has been dominated and defined by the tech industry's powerful claims on the future. Embedded in the infrastructure of video AI are the fused priorities of policing and profit-making, especially their respective growth imperatives.

Finally, in the book's conclusion, I revisit some of the issues raised in the chapters that would benefit from more attention, including the overlapping aesthetic, evidentiary, and logistical uses of video evidence; the challenges of analyzing the scale of surveillance infrastructures adequate to the stakes; the influence policing has on video analytics; and the relationship between the police surveillance economy and the prison-industrial complex.

Now, a note about my positionality. My father died at a young age and my mother remarried my stepdad when I was still a small child, so I had three sets of grandparents. My maternal grandparents were economic migrants to the United States from Ireland, and they settled in Pittsburgh, in the company town of Turtle Creek. I grew up in the postwar suburb of Monroeville, and my mother, siblings, and I identified as Irish Americans. All three of my grandfathers worked as laborers in steel mills, and all three also died relatively young, so I never knew them (two were gone before I was born). After my biological father died, my mother worked as a secretary for US Steel, and the man she remarried, for full discloser, was a Pennsylvania State Trooper. One of his main duties was to patrol the Pennsylvania Turnpike, which, according to its website, was "America's First Superhighway."[81] Since both my parents had jobs, they were much better off financially than their parents had been, but to me it never felt stable. No doubt because my real father had died, I would lay in bed worrying that my stepfather would get shot on the job that night. I did not understand that his job was relatively safe, especially compared to my grandfathers' jobs.

In a debate with "Maoist militants" in 1971, the philosopher Michel Foucault was trying to convince them that the idea of a "proletarian counter-justice" was a contradiction and there could be no such thing as "popular justice."[82] In the eighteenth and nineteenth centuries, Foucault argued, penal law was developed "as an important tactical weapon" to create a system of divisions between workers and peasants. One of the main functions of the penal system was "to make the proletariat see the non-proletarianised people [i.e., the jobless poor] as marginal, dangerous, immoral, a menace to society as a whole, the dregs of the population, trash, the 'mob.'"; "All the literary, journalistic, medical, sociological and anthropological rhetoric about criminals" also helped to create this system of division.[83] According to Foucault, "the bourgeoisie offered [the jobless poor] the following choices: you can go to prison or join the army, you can go to prison or go to the colonies, you can go to prison or you can join the police."[84]

1

"Grainy to Guilty"

Police Video Forensics on the Cusp of Cloud Computing

Introduction

On April 15, 2013, two bombs exploded in the crowd of spectators near the finish line of the 117th Boston Marathon, killing three people and injuring over 200 others. The ensuing investigation and manhunt can only be described as a forensic-media spectacle, with the effort to identify and capture the bombers playing out live on news and social media. It was immediately obvious that investigators would be searching through video from security cameras and cell phones to identify suspects.[1] In what seemed like record time, the Federal Bureau of Investigation (FBI) released images of two men three days after the bombings (see Figure 1.1), but not before "digilantes" had combed through images posted on social media and misidentified two other men as bombing suspects.[2]

While the search for Boston bombing suspects appeared to take place on live television, what transpired in the FBI's investigation—"poring over mountains of footage and still imagery"[3]—happened off-camera and behind closed doors. The speed with which the FBI produced images of the two men gave the impression that locating these images was virtually automatic, but the process was a labor-intensive undertaking. FBI investigators worked around the clock in multiple locations: at the blast sites and surrounding areas, at FBI headquarters in Quantico, Virginia, where evidence was flown in daily, and at a lab set up by a computer analysis response team at the Boston division of the FBI.[4] Cameras that may have captured relevant footage had to be located, and video files had to be recovered from their storage media, a more time-consuming and complex undertaking than most people realize. Segments of video had to be identified and then studied closely to locate relevant information. FBI investigators had a difficult time spotting relevant details in

Figure 1.1. Surveillance video image of the Boston Marathon bombers, released by the Federal Bureau of Investigation on April 18, 2013. Photo credit: FBI. Reprinted under fair use.

the crowded and chaotic scenes captured on video. Among the video recovered from the scene was a segment from a camera mounted in front of a restaurant called Forum, located immediately behind the second explosion. Multiple analysts watched the segment over and over, slowing it down, zooming in on details, rewinding and watching again. Despite multiple viewers and repeated viewings, no one was able to see a person planting a bomb.

A break for the FBI came when a marathon spectator managed to get through to investigators with a cell phone photo he had taken from across the street, showing the location from the opposite perspective. Examining this image closely, analysts were able to spot a backpack, partially visible on the sidewalk behind the barricade separating the crowd from the runners. Only at that point were they able to spot a suspect among the crowd, a young man wearing a white ball cap, first in the cell phone image and then in the surveillance video from the restaurant. They then were able to follow him backward in time and space, tracing his steps in reverse through recorded footage from other security cameras on the same block: a Walgreens drugstore, a Bank of America ATM, and another camera at a bar called Whiskey's on the corner of Boylston and Gloucester Streets. Whiskey's camera, which was pointed out onto the sidewalk, captured footage of a second suspect walking a few paces in front of the young man in the white hat. This suspect was a taller man wearing a black ball cap.

As this account of the FBI's investigation suggests, by the time the Boston Marathon bombings took place in April 2013, the state's investigative apparatus was more media-centered and effective than ever before. The Boston bombings occurred at a unique historical and media-technological conjuncture, at a specific stage in the spread of video surveillance, smartphone capacities, and social media. Michiko Kakutani, a journalist and media critic, referred to the Boston bombings as "America's first fully interactive national tragedy of the social media age."[5] The eruption of violence, and the subsequent investigation, also happened at a specific moment in the development of video forensics, a set of techniques and field of expertise for transforming raw video footage into usable evidence. The unique media-technological conjuncture helped create the conditions in which the violence was experienced, investigated, and covered as a media event.

And yet, while video seems to afford the capability, it is not possible to rewind reality. Nor is it possible to fully experience the media environments of the past. It is not only that media technologies have changed; our modes of perception have also changed in lockstep with media. To paraphrase the philosopher Langdon Winner, as society invents new technologies, it also invents the kinds of people who will use them.[6] Our deep entanglement with media makes it particularly challenging to understand what is historically unique about our current media-technological conditions.

In this chapter, I argue the field of video forensics represents a special site for understanding the entangled relationship between media and perception precisely because its techniques are attuned to what is perceivable in media recordings. The people who perform this type of work develop ways of seeing and listening to recordings with a deep sensitivity to their digital formats. As the work of video forensics suggests, *computational perception* is not performed exclusively by machines or algorithms but in the entanglement of human perception with digital media.

My argument challenges a number of assumptions about video evidence and the persistent belief that video "speaks for itself," effectively and objectively capturing what happened in front of the camera.[7] Given the central role that video recordings now play in criminal investigations, the evidentiary value of video is presumed to be self-evident. However, what a video record shows and does not show is rarely a simple matter. Instead, transforming video into evidence involves a complex and evolving set of technical, perceptual, and discursive practices that must be developed and learned. Trained professional video analysts spend their working hours enmeshed with video data, devices, and infrastructures. They direct their perceptual capacities to acquiring, examining, and working with media recordings to interpret what they show and do not show, attempting to reconstruct events as they unfolded in time and space. As the workings of this field suggest, the evidentiary status of recorded video is the result of an interpretive process and, often, a process of media production.

My analysis of video forensics also challenges the assumption that the transition to digital video has led directly to the automation of video analysis. The reality is that the avalanche of video did not lead immediately or inevitably to large-scale systems for automated video processing or video artificial intelligence (AI). The embodied perceptual capacities of trained human beings remain central to processing and analyzing video, and in fact, if computers are learning to see the world like humans do, the reverse is also true—humans are learning to see like computers. The people acquiring specialized skills in media forensics are not the only ones who engage with video recordings and infrastructures in ways that deeply entangle their embodied perceptual capacities with those technologies. But the work that they do, and the way they learn to do it, challenges facile assumptions about the inevitable or expeditious rise of what Google calls "video AI."[8]

To support these claims, I first discuss the unique epistemology of video forensics starting with the analog origins of video. Here we begin to see the perceptual, interpretive work involved in transforming video recordings into evidence. I then explain how digitization changed the analysis and evidentiary uses of video, giving special attention to the *temporal indexicality* of video recordings, or the need to establish their direct link to past moments of time. Timelines and time-date stamps are central to the evidentiary status of video. Third, I discuss the work of image comparison, focusing on a murder investigation that became an important instructional test case for forensic video analysts in training. In this murder case, like the Boston Marathon bombing investigation, video forensics also became the focus of news coverage, publicizing forensics as a form of sensemaking about the event. Next, I discuss how the expanding workload challenges and time-consuming work of video forensics inevitably means that the epistemic machinery gets selectively applied—a problem that is equally if not more significant than the outright falsification of evidence. Finally, I discuss the migration of video storage onto proprietary computing infrastructures and the call for more automation to manage the video avalanche. These developments entangle police *media work* more tightly with tech companies and the surveillance economy. Recent developments in forensic video analysis reveal the "blurring of public and private boundaries in surveillance activities" and the "collaborations and interdependencies between state security authorities and high tech firms."[9]

Video Evidence and Forensic Sensemaking

As a media technology invented in the middle of the twentieth century, video has not always been part of the investigation of crime. It was put to use for this purpose as soon as it was technically feasible, but much like photography, video's evidentiary usefulness took time and effort to negotiate.[10] Today, video has become one of the most prolific forms of evidence in the legal system. A 2016 document from the U.S. Bureau of Justice Assistance (BJA), *Video Evidence: A Primer for Prosecutors*, declared that there was a "staggering abundance of video" flooding criminal investigations and the courts (see Figure 1.2). While ten years prior it was rare for a court case to feature video evidence, it was "becoming unusual to see a court case that does not."[11] Five years later, a 2021 industry survey estimated that 85 percent of criminal cases included video evidence.[12] The abundance of video means that the investigation of crime now frequently involves the specialized media work of video forensics.

Video forensics is both like and unlike other forensic sciences. In forensic analysis, everything is media: a drop of blood, a piece of clothing, a bullet hole, a tire streak. But recorded video is a different type

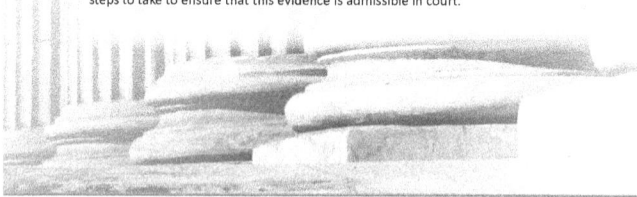

Figure 1.2. U.S. Bureau of Justice Assistance, *Video Evidence: A Primer for Prosecutors*, October 2016. Photo credit: BJA. Reprinted under fair use.

of media and a different type of forensic evidence than other material forms. This is because it represents those other forms both iconically, as a resemblance, and indexically, as a physical trace. Understanding how video represents things like fabric, skin color, light, time, and spatial dimensions is central to forensic video analysis. Video forensics treats the materiality of video recordings as part of the basis of interpreting what the video represents. Thus, even if all forensics involves some form of mediation and translation of material traces into representations, video forensics is a unique type of forensics.[13]

The *forensic sciences*, along with *crime statistics*, are two forms of "cop knowledge" that are understood to be more scientific than the street knowledge that cops claim and wield.[14] And yet, both these sciences are deeply intertwined with the day-to-day workings and sensemaking practices of policing. Police reporting generates crime statistics; these numbers measure crime only when the police intervene in lawbreaking activities and document them. Where crime statistics are used to make general statements about the social prevalence of crime and its spatial and temporal distribution, the forensic sciences make individualizing claims about specific crimes and criminals. Media scholar Greg Siegel has argued that as modernizing forms of transportation led to disastrous high-speed accidents, "forensic mediation" became the preferred means that the modern world devised to make sense of those accidents.[15] The same holds true for intentional, individualized acts of lawbreaking. The focus of forensic investigation is a specific act of legal transgression, the effort to reassemble it with materials, identifying the individuals involved, including perpetrators, witnesses, and victims. Forensics has a precision-oriented epistemology that individualizes crime, and the history of forensics reflects the effort to establish a scientific basis for the investigation of crimes and the identification of criminals.

The criminal legal system's need for forensic expertise in video analysis initially grew in tandem with the proliferation of video surveillance systems and efforts to use surveillance video as evidence in the days of analog cameras and magnetic tapes. Analog systems posed plenty of problems for recovering video and making it usable as evidence. The video was typically of low quality and therefore of questionable value as evidence. Magnetic tapes were often physically degraded from repeated use. Playing, fast-forwarding, and rewinding further damaged the tapes, reducing the quality of the recordings in the process of analyzing them. Videocassette recorders also had a tendency to "eat" videotapes, their magnetic strips getting mangled up in the machine.

A major challenge with making use of analog video as evidence was *multiplexing*, an analog way of economizing storage, where video feeds from separate cameras were fed to a single recording device and inscribed onto a single tape. The replayed recording would flip through the different video feeds from one moment to the next, skipping moments of time from each camera feed, making it difficult to see and examine details and establish continuous sequences of time. As I learned in video forensics training, multiplexed systems were terrible to try to recover evidence from. *Interlacing* was another form of inscription that scrambled the visual information. Many other factors could affect the appearance and sound of recorded video, including lighting, camera angles, and internal design features of cameras and recording devices (all still true of digital).

The transition to digital formats did not solve all the problems of quality or storage. The U.S. Federal Communications Commission forced the transition to digital in the early 2000s with the promise that digital video would have advantages over analog, including better quality. However, as we learned in video forensics training, digital video was initially of very poor quality and would frequently get tossed out of court (i.e., ruled inadmissible by judges). In video forensics, the term "quality" refers mostly to *definition* or *fidelity*, what is visible and audible in a video recording, but it also suggests aesthetic concerns. The promise that digital video would be of better quality than analog did not go as planned. In fact, the challenges of making use of video as evidence multiplied and became more complex, requiring more technical knowledge, more time, and more people to perform the media work.

One of the aims of video forensics is to correct and compensate for the lack of fidelity to reality inherent in media recordings—the altered, distorted, or illegible way that bodies, objects, motion, sounds, spaces, and times get recorded (or not) as media. Both analog and digital recording technologies offer highly imperfect traces of material reality. This is in part because they are *compressed*, in multiple senses: as *sampled* versions of original signals and as *framed slices* of spatiotemporal ranges of perception. Digital compression, the rate a signal is sampled for recording, became a source of new problems for making evidentiary use of video. Compression reduces the amount of data contained in a video file to economize storage. Live video feeds may look like high-resolution images with an enormous amount of detail, but what is being recorded is only a sampling of that information—a compressed version. For obvious reasons, compression creates problems with a recording's fidelity to reality, problems that must be corrected or at least explained if they cannot be fixed. The higher the rate of compression, the more likely that key objects and sounds fall below the "threshold of detectability": the pivotal line between what can be perceived and not perceived in media recordings.[16]

Making invisible details visible in an image is what most people associate with the investigative analysis of images. A technique that can sometimes be used to enhance images is called *frame averaging*. This technique was used to produce an image of the hijackers passing through airport security to board their flight in Boston on the morning of September 11, 2001. A 2002 article in *Wired* magazine, "Video Forensics: Grainy to Guilty," noted that "the famous shot of Atta and Aziz Al-Omari whisking through the Portland Airport security checkpoint was made using a technique that combines seven video frames into one high-resolution image."[17] The surveillance still shot, which became an iconic piece of 9/11 photojournalism, was a type of composite image produced using the video forensics technique of frame averaging.

We learned the basics of frame averaging in video forensics training. In one hands-on exercise, we were given a video of a car with a license plate that was unreadable. With guidance from the instructor, we used a software program to separate the video frames and then imported them into a separate video forensics software program. We then manually selected the frames from a compressed video file that contained the most visual information, called the I-frames, or intra-coded pictures. I-frames are fully specified pictures that look like regular photographs. The frames in between I-frames are the P-frames, or "predicted pictures," and contain data representing only what has changed since the previous frame. Each frame represents a fraction of second, with the length of that fraction depending on the frame rate. A higher rate of compression, we learned, means that there are more P-frames in between the I-frames. After selecting the I-frames, we selected the region within one of the frames that contained the information we wanted to clarify—the license plate. Next, we applied a software filter that averaged the I-frames into a single image. The license plate's numbers and letters, which were unreadable when watching the video, came into view.

Forensic video analysts refer to the successful use of image enhancement to make invisible details visible as "CSI moments," after the popular television crime drama *CSI: Crime Scene Investigation*. In video forensics training, we learned that CSI moments happen only rarely. In most cases, you cannot make a license plate, a face, or other detail more visible from a recording. It often is not possible to get any more information from compressed video because the pixels are simply not there. But if actual image enhancement work is only an option in certain limited cases, there was still plenty of work to be done to transform video into usable evidence. A key point that our instructor emphasized in the first lesson was that most of the work did not involve clarifying images to bring out hidden details. Instead, most of the work of video forensics involves using one's own perceptual capacities and trained judgment to determine what can and cannot be stated about objects and activities recorded on video based on exactly what information is there.

Digital compression became a dimension of video recording that analysts had to learn to understand intuitively to adequately conduct an analysis. Acquiring expertise in media forensics meant, among other things, learning to recognize the ways that compression algorithms can change how recordings look and sound. A logo on a sneaker can easily disappear in a compressed video file. An artifact produced by a compression algorithm can look like an object in a person's hand. If you do not understand compression, our instructor explained, you cannot accurately interpret what a video does and does not depict. Another problem that digital imaging intensified was the ease with which aspect ratios (the proportional relationship between width and height of the image frame) could be altered. An altered aspect ratio distorts the dimensions of the scene and all bodies and objects in it—for example, making a person appear taller and thinner or shorter and heavier than they are. With digital video, aspect ratios are always suspect.

Forensic video analysis often involves performing the perceptual work of *image comparison*—that is, comparing videos and still images of places, bodies, or objects taken at different times, to discern similarities and differences that have evidentiary value. Again, this type of comparison work requires trained perception, knowing how to look for slight, almost imperceptible visual traces that a lay observer might not notice. Tattoos, for example, have become a major focus of forensic image analysis and the subject of their own dedicated training sessions. A forensic video analyst could be tasked with comparing an image of a tattoo on a suspect's arm with a tattoo on the body of a person who appears in a recorded video. Other common objects of image comparison include clothing, cars, faces, and weapons, as well as buildings and other location markers. Subtle lighting differences can indicate different times of day or the movement of objects. Identifying individual people, objects, places, and times is the essence of forensic work, and image comparison is an essential method. A great deal can ride on the integrity of image comparison, and it is an area of considerable focus for both establishing and challenging the epistemic authority of video forensics.

Often the most important task that forensic video analysts must perform in any specific case is not visual but temporal. Analysts must establish the *temporal indexicality* of video—its direct connection to a precise moment of measured time.[18] One of the first steps of forensic video analysis, after the video is acquired, involves placing recordings on a timeline to precisely locate their place in time. Creating a timeline is essential for establishing the evidentiary status of video. This is done using metadata, recorded audio streams, knowledge of encoding and playback, and cross-referencing video segments with other recordings and with testimony. Analysts must be extremely attentive to the construction of timelines because timing can be a decisive factor in an investigation. They need to determine not only what happened but *when* events occurred and *for how long*.

While modern societies have accepted a system of measurable, chronological time as normal, reconstructing past time from video is not as straightforward as it would seem. As a time-recording and time-shifting medium, video is fully embedded in what Sarah Sharma calls the "temporal infrastructure" of modernity.[19] The perceptual and technical work of video analysis is *time-consuming*. It is also work that involves the analysis of time. Matching video recordings to past moments of time can be an object lesson in the strange physics of time and temporality, raising puzzling questions about "real time" versus "mediated time." The construction of timelines from video is a type of editing work that requires an allegiance to precision—an alignment with a precise moment and chronological sequence of past time. Precisely aligning video recordings with past times and temporal sequences can be especially challenging given that the surveillance cameras and recording equipment are not standardized and can be cheaply produced. Frame rates can vary, and frames can be dropped in the recording process, altering recorded time by mere fractions of seconds that nonetheless disrupt precise synchronization. Dropped frames can also distort the appearance of motion, making the movement appear faster, which is a problem when you want to know the speed of objects. For example, it is not always possible to measure precisely how fast a car was moving from a video recording alone. The recording process can distort time.

The temporal indexicality of video becomes a *visual* matter with the insertion of the time-date stamp on the images as commonly found on surveillance video. The banality of the time-date stamp belies its significance in providing a visual indicator of a video recording's temporality, including the exact time the scene occurred and the amount of time that elapsed while it unfolded. Typically, a time-date stamp is imprinted automatically by the camera or recording device. In video forensics training, we learned that time-date stamps could be extremely unreliable temporal indicators. Different sources of video were often set to different times, so one needed to time-calibrate different videos to a trusted clock. We learned how to use software to insert a time-date stamp on a video when the original did not have one or to change one that was deemed to be inaccurate. The question of temporal accuracy was posited as a matter of verifying the time and date that appears on the image against another source. The time of a 911 call to dispatch, for example, was one suggested source of "ground truth" for time calibration. Even when a measurement of time was stamped on the video feed automatically, trust in a recording's temporal indexicality should not be automatic. Like the video on which it was printed, the time-date stamp is not *in itself* reliable, truth-telling media.

What I have described thus far are only some of the very basic tasks and technical knowledge required to adequately perform the work of forensic video analysis. What more experienced analysts observe while examining a video is very different from untrained observers. These analysts acquire a distinctive form of professional vision, including a more developed perceptual acuity for the technical process of inscription.[20] Those who acquire this trained perceptual capacity become more attuned to the way the world gets captured and recorded in a format that can be replayed. They have a keen sense for the distortions and omissions that the recording process creates. The lead instructor of the

Figure 1.3. A video forensics lab in Pittsburgh, Pennsylvania, 2017. Photo credit: Kelly Gates.

training course that I took, for example, had the kind of trained perception and tacit knowledge that comes from years of working with video, developing new techniques for analyzing video as media technologies changed, and understanding the investigative questions, legal issues, and wide range of cases that one might encounter. The special technical and perceptual skills of digital multimedia forensics constitute a form of *computational perception* that trained analysts use to make sense of digital video recordings. (For a view of a video forensics lab where analysts do this work, see Figure 1.3.)

Forensic analysts have varying levels of training and skill in computational perception and the analysis of video. They also face considerable pressure to produce results that will win legal cases. In video forensics training, instructors emphasized that being a qualified and ethical forensic scientist meant resisting those pressures, whether they came from one's superiors or one's own desire to provide the decisive evidence. If the status of video as evidence is the result of a process of production, as I argue in this chapter, then it would seem to follow that video evidence can be falsified with alarming ease. However, it is also true that the epistemic authority of video forensics depends on preventing both intentional falsification of evidence and the mistakes that result from the unconscious cognitive bias that analysts bring the work. Of course, efforts on the part of this professional field to prevent the production of fraudulent evidence does not prevent it from happening.

The Bento Case

A murder investigation in the United Kingdom from the early 2000s illustrates some of the thorny issues of trust and epistemic authority that have haunted the field of forensic video analysis. In December 2005, a young Polish immigrant, Kamila Garsztka, disappeared from the town of Bedford. The first evidence about her disappearance came when a passerby found women's clothes neatly folded by the edge of Bedford's Priory Lake. Later, Garsztka's boyfriend, a young Portuguese immigrant named Nico Bento, reported her disappearance to the police. He was concerned, he said, because she left his flat without warning, leaving behind her handbag, cell phone, and identification. Seven weeks after her boyfriend reported her missing, Garsztka's body was pulled from Priory Lake.

In their investigation of Garsztka's death, the Bedford Police discovered surveillance video that apparently showed Garsztka walking along the embankment of Priory Lake on the night of her disappearance. And thanks to the analytical work of Casey Caudle, a forensic video expert from the United States, this video ended up being a key piece of evidence. Working for the Bedford Police, Caudle analyzed the video and determined that it showed Garsztka carrying the handbag that was later found in her boyfriend Nico's apartment. Armed with this forensic video evidence, the police charged Nico Bento with the murder of Garsztka. With Caudle's expert testimony, Bento was convicted of killing her and sentenced to life in prison.

What Nico Bento's defense counsel was not aware of, according to a *BBC Newsnight* report, was that the Bedford Police had engaged in what is sometimes called "expert shopping."[21] Before enlisting the help of Caudle, the police had sought out a number of forensic scientists in the United Kingdom, all of whom told investigators that they could not establish that the woman was in fact carrying her handbag in the video.

One expert, John Kennedy from the U.K. Forensic Science Service, reportedly advised the Bedford Police "to exercise caution in relying on such poor-quality [video] evidence."[22] In a BBC interview, Kennedy said that he had told the police "the only scientific process [he] would recommend so as to provide authoritative opinion" about whether the woman was carrying a handbag in the video "would be to undertake a reverse projection."

Reverse projection is a forensic technique that involves reconstructing a scene captured on surveillance video, under the same lighting conditions, using the same cameras and recording devices and the actual physical evidence. Once the new, reconstructed video is produced, the original recordings are compared with those produced in the reconstruction. Software can be used to overlay the images to display differences between the original and the reconstruction, but much of the comparison work involves an analyst manually examining the videos and identifying differences using their own trained perception.

The forensic video analyst who testified in this case, Casey Caudle, had not conducted a reverse projection in his analysis of the video of Kamila Garsztka. Instead, Caudle claimed to have "enhanced" the images in a way that appeared to show the handbag on Kamila's shoulder as she walked along the lake. The evidence that her handbag was on her shoulder in the video depended largely on the authority of Caudle's expert testimony.

Luckily for Nico Bento, his case was not over. Thanks to Grant Fredericks, a leading forensic video analyst in the United States, a second analysis of the video evidence was conducted that challenged the prosecution's case. When Fredericks learned about the outcome of the Garsztka murder case, he asked Caudle, who was his former student, to share the images so that he could use them for instructional purposes. When Caudle failed to do so, Fredericks became suspicious. He eventually got ahold of the video evidence and quickly determined that the way to analyze it properly was to perform a reverse projection, just as Kennedy, the U.K. forensic examiner, had recommended. Fredericks traveled to the United Kingdom and staged a reconstruction of the scene depicted in the video, at the exact location and time of night, using both the material evidence and a stand-in for Kamila Garsztka. The woman wore Kamila's clothing and carried her handbag. Using the reverse projection technique to compare the new video with the original one of Garsztka, Fredericks determined that she was not carrying a handbag in the original video, as Casey Caudle had testified. The earlier expert testimony in this case was exposed as fraudulent. After serving two years and four months of his life sentence, Nico Bento's conviction was overturned based on the fraudulent forensic evidence, and he was released from prison.[23]

I first learned about the Bento case in the training course I took in 2012. It was a cautionary tale against which video analysts-in-training were encouraged to define their own professional ethics and identities. Both in forensics training and in the news coverage this case received by the BBC, Casey Caudle was portrayed as a flawed and unethical professional. The ultimate correction of the record, and overturning Bento's conviction, was presented as the result of the proper workings of the criminal legal system and the diligence and professional ethics of well-trained forensic analysts. This case of wrongful conviction shows that forensic analysis of video can and does produce falsified evidence at times, and that forensic video experts are concerned with rectifying these cases in order to gain and maintain the epistemic authority of their field. Notably in this case, video forensics itself became a central part of the story, and the cautionary tale about video expertise extended beyond analysts-in-training to a wider public audience.

If Nico Bento's conviction in the U.K. courts initially seemed important for the field of video forensics, the exposure of Caudle's testimony as fraudulent carried even more weight. Even as it highlighted what can go wrong, the story ultimately helped to establish the legitimacy of the field by showing that it could regulate itself and its boundaries of expertise. And yet, the reversal of Nico Bento's conviction did not completely settle the matter of what should count as a credible forensic video analysis. The *BBC Newsnight* report concluded with a brief comment from the chief of the Bedford Police. When asked why the police had not staged a reconstruction, the chief replied that he was advised that a "reconstruction shouldn't be done and wouldn't be of value," and he added that "the reconstruction that has been done, I think, is of questionable value."[24] This explicit challenge to the authority of the reverse projection suggested a selective interest in the forensic techniques that can be used to produce video evidence. Consistent with how forensic evidence often gets leveraged in the criminal legal system, the Bedford Police were willing to make use of forensic video analysis as long as the results supported the case against their suspect. Believing that justice was served in this case would also require ignoring the two years and four months that Nico Bento spent in prison, not to mention the experience of being charged and tried and the lasting impact that incarceration has on a person's life. As a working-class immigrant, Nico Bento would never be deemed innocent enough to be free from of suspicion of criminality. As prison abolitionists have argued, the virtue of innocence is a trap that stands on the always-shifting ground of carceral logic.

The Selective Use of Video Forensics

Although the falsification of video evidence is certainly possible and concerning, an equally significant problem stems from the time-consuming work of video forensics. In any specific case, analysis involves watching video recordings repeatedly, often frame by frame, for hours. More experienced analysts spend less time on tasks than novices, but it takes a long time to acquire the expertise. The ever-growing quantity of video multiplies the labor-intensive nature of the work. In the aggregate, there are massive volumes of video to search and analyze for potential traces. By economizing storage, digital compression expanded the volume of recorded videos available for investigations, creating a much heavier labor burden for analysts. According to the BJA, "the transfer, storage, redaction, disclosure, and preparation of video evidence for evidentiary purposes can stretch the personnel and equipment resources of even the best-funded prosecutor's office."[25]

Along with the expanding number of investigations that involve video, the labor needed to do this work has also grown exponentially. Video forensics training emphasized that by acquiring more knowledge of digital video, especially compression and sampling, forensic analysts would learn to economize their time and avoid wasted effort. Still, the problem of workload has continued to haunt those tasked with the labor-intensive work of video analysis. At a video forensics conference that I attended in Florida in 2015, analysts described work overload as one of the biggest challenges they faced. There was too much information to absorb in training and too much work to manage in their jobs. The overwhelming caseload was a recurring theme, especially when this community of experts was anticipating a new flood of video to analyze from police body cameras.

The fact that video forensics was and remains labor-intensive and time-consuming work inevitably means that investigative resources are devoted to certain cases and not others. A forensic video analyst I spoke with in 2015, who had decades of experience, insisted that *every* investigation could include video, provided one was willing and able to take the time to locate and acquire it. He told me about a sexual battery case he once worked on that illustrated what was possible with enough time to do the work. The detectives had a video showing a suspect running from the scene, and they requested his assistance in getting an image of the man's face from the video. He took one look at the video and knew that he could not get an image of the face. But he saw the direction the suspect was running, and because he knew the area, he knew that there were buildings in that direction that would likely have additional cameras.

The analyst's demanding workload would typically prevent him from doing the time-consuming work of going out to look for cameras, acquiring the video, and searching through recordings for more potential evidence. But he had been tasked earlier with taking photographs of the injuries to the victim's face, and his sympathy for her, he said, motivated him to want to help identify and prosecute the man who attacked her. So, he went out to the area and found cameras in the direction the suspect was running. He was able to gather additional video and eventually identify the suspect by piecing together traces of the man in videos from multiple sources. Using cameras at an adjacent residential building, he found images of the suspect moving in and out of the building at the time of the attack and earlier that day. He also traced the man back in time to a store where he had purchased alcohol. From the store video, he was able to get a clear image of the suspect's face. Had the analyst simply told the detectives that he could not get an image of the man's face from the video and let that be the end of it, this suspect probably would not have been identified in this case. It is, of course, always possible for analysts to misidentify people in video, and this risk can increase when videos are assembled from multiple places and times of day. This makes it extremely important not to rely exclusively on video evidence. (The analyst noted that there was also DNA evidence in this case.)

One imagines that for every case pursued, there are endless numbers of cases not pursued, footage left undiscovered, and relevant video overwritten with new recordings. In fact, the selective application of forensic investigation is one way that criminal law reproduces and amplifies structural inequalities in the distribution of punishment. Systemic inequities in the legal system are well documented, and they extend to the forensic sciences and the application of their findings. A 2009 U.S. National Academy of Sciences report on the state of the forensic sciences, produced at the request of the U.S. Congress, identified major problems, including "great disparities among existing forensic sciences operations . . . with respect to funding, access to analytical instrumentation, the availability of skilled and well-trained personnel, certification, accreditation, and oversight."[26] On top of this, as Gary Edmond's research has shown, judges tend to apply a much lower threshold for the admission of forensic evidence in criminal cases than for the admission of scientific evidence in class-action lawsuits against companies.[27]

Which cases get investigated and which do not is inescapably tied to the relative value placed on different crimes and different victims. Notably, violent sexual offenses are often used to justify more surveillance and a well-heeled prosecutorial arsenal. But as instruments of law enforcement, the forensic sciences have not been particularly effective at addressing the social problem of gender violence. In 2022, there was a backlog of at least 25,000 untested rape kits in the possession of U.S. crime labs, for example.[28] This problem extends to the evidentiary uses of video in cases of sexual violence where the victims are not deemed to be as worthy of the time-consuming and labor-intensive work of an investigation. In a study of sex workers' experiences with video surveillance, for example, researchers found that the women they studied could not trust or rely on the police to use the video to protect them from harm or to prosecute crimes against them.[29] The use of video only served to police their activities and their exchanges with johns in ways that made their work more dangerous—for example, hindering their efforts to screen their customers by forcing those screenings to be done quickly and out of view of the cameras. Given constraints on investigative resources in many legal jurisdictions, the likelihood of investing significant time and effort into searching, acquiring, and analyzing video no doubt depends on the social standing and perceived moral worth of victims.[30]

The selective use of forensic video analysis can have compounding effects. It has especially grave consequences for poor Black communities, which are disproportionately targeted by policing and the criminal legal system. Policing and police surveillance are deeply racialized and racializing processes, as Simone Browne and others have shown.[31] In addition, the workload challenges of video forensics predictably feed into the drive to automate, including applications of machine learning for *video analytics*. But while automation may speed up certain tasks involved in processing and producing video evidence, it is unlikely to solve the problems of workload in an absolute sense. "Labor-saving" technologies are not primarily designed to lessen the burdens of labor; instead, they often end up creating more work (for less pay). And unfortunately, technologies of automation consistently prove adept at reinforcing and intensifying the structural racism of policing and surveillance.[32]

From Proprietary Formats to Proprietary Platforms

In video forensics training in 2012, we learned that one big challenge that forensic video analysts often faced when acquiring video to analyze for an investigation was the problem of proprietary formats. A lack of technical standards for video surveillance technology meant that video recorded in different formats was often unplayable without the original equipment and software. Most methods for working around this problem by converting the digital files into a playable format altered the original recordings, which could mean losing relevant data. The efforts of companies to lock their customers into proprietary products and services meant that surveillance technologies were not interoperable and thus poorly suited to evidentiary uses. The BJA's 2016 primer on video evidence for prosecutors highlighted two problems associated with the "staggering abundance of video" in the legal system: "handling the large file sizes of video evidence" and "dealing with the wide variety of video formats, each with its own proprietary characteristics and requirements."[33]

Analysts were still dealing with the problem of proprietary surveillance technologies when I attended a video forensics training conference in San Diego in October 2022. A decade had passed since the training course I took in Indianapolis in 2012, and much had changed in the field, including a whole new set of challenges posed by eyewitness video and police bodycam footage. In addition, a new and formidable problem had emerged for accessing and analyzing video recordings: video storage and the computing power for processing video was shifting from local devices to remote storage in the cloud. The shift to cloud computing promised to make surveillance systems interoperable, but cloud data storage was compounding rather than resolving the problems of analyzing and making use of video as evidence.

In short, the migration of video software and storage to the cloud meant that the problem of proprietary *formats* was morphing into the problem of proprietary *platforms*. The rise of cloud computing was leading to a shift across industrial and service sectors to subscription-based software and data storage business models. As IPVM, an independent research firm covering the video surveillance industry, noted in its blog in 2019, "The video surveillance market has changed significantly since 2000, going from VCRs to an emerging AI cloud era."[34] There was widespread recognition among video experts that the move in the direction of video platform services represented a major power grab by companies maneuvering to lock customers into proprietary systems, in turn extracting higher and higher rents. This new business model was being called *video surveillance as a service*.[35] John Honovich, CEO of IPVM, called it "hostage as a service," a trend in which users of video surveillance systems have to make ongoing payments to stream video from the cameras they have already purchased.[36] Honovich predicted that video surveillance as a service would be dominated by "mega cloud providers" by 2030, and these "emerging mega cloud physical security providers will be larger, more profitable, and more powerful than any today."[37] The mega cloud physical security providers aiming to become more profitable and powerful include Google and Amazon, which have moved into the business of home security by acquiring Nest and Ring, in the process allowing them to acquire video and other data about the activities of the home.[38]

Another company making a claim to the video flooding onto the cloud is the body-camera company Axon Enterprise, which I discuss in Chapter 3. At the video forensics training conference in 2022, I learned that Axon had just acquired Occam Video Solutions and its flagship video forensic software called iNPUT-ACE, rebranding it "Axon Investigate."

In Axon's announcement of its new acquisition, the company made big claims about software's labor-saving benefits. Investigators spend "an average of 83 minutes" searching the Internet for conversion tools they can use to play videos recorded in proprietary video formats, the announcement said.[39] Other problems can arise from there. Conversion tools can alter video files in a way that destroys or undermines their evidentiary value. Not so with Axon Investigate; the company promised that the software would convert thousands of video formats into perfectly viewable media. If there was any question about the business model that would govern how forensic analysts accessed Axon Investigate, the company dispelled it by offering a premium version: Axon Investigate Pro. This costlier version provided more functionality "for video-centric investigations."[40] In other words, investigators (or rather, their agencies) would have to pay more to access features like video enhancement, multi-clip time syncing, as well as tools for creating narrative reports and demos for courtroom presentation.

Once again, not all forensic video analysts were excited about the "hostage as a service" business model. At the same conference session where I learned about Axon Investigate, I also observed a lively discussion among analysts about the escalating costs of software and storage. Those in the room expressed palpable frustration with tech industry profiteering. Someone mentioned their sense that police leadership was being influenced by lobbyists for these companies, and someone else commented that it was all going to boil down to monopolistic ownership of this space. There seemed to be general agreement that there should be options available other than an increasing dependence on tech companies and being forced to pay a premium for the data storage and software they needed to perform their investigative work. After all, many of them worked not for profitable businesses but for strapped state and municipal agencies that are funded by the public purse.

Conclusion

Along with the video avalanche, video forensics has grown in significance. In any specific investigation that involves video, there is often an extensive amount of work involved in transforming the footage into usable evidence. This is true of cases involving one piece of video evidence, as in the Bento case, and in investigations that involve a large volume of media, as in the Boston Marathon bombing investigation. In both of these cases, the epistemic authority of video forensics had to be negotiated, and the forensic investigations were publicized beyond the legal system in ways that subtly treated forensics as a popular form of sensemaking.

As these examples suggest, video forensics is enmeshed in battles for epistemic authority playing out in and beyond the criminal legal system—anywhere that video is used as evidence to make claims about real events. Video forensics now plays an important role in the efforts of law enforcement to build and control the epistemic machinery for producing video evidence in the criminal legal system and beyond. The field has developed techniques that enable practitioners to speak with scientific certainty about video evidence in an intensively mediatized environment. This environment is characterized by vastly expanding surveillance infrastructures, built and operated by both public and private entities, along with untold millions of mobile cameras recording ever-expanding volumes of data and audiovisual content. It is also characterized by intensified media and political fragmentation and deep distrust in institutions. While societies of consensus have never existed, the epistemic chaos of the early twenty-first century has erupted at a distinct media-technological conjuncture.

Under contemporary conditions of epistemic turmoil, it is perhaps unsurprising that the techniques of video forensics have found alternative uses. Forensic techniques are being adopted by media artists, human rights activists, open-source investigators, and video journalists, all of whom work in domains of activity that have been profoundly affected by the video avalanche. As Sandra Ristovska has argued, the massive increase in eyewitness video from conflict zones has prompted human rights activists to acquire expertise in verifying and analyzing videos of atrocities.[41] "Open-source investigation" is a term of choice to designate the analysis of eyewitness video and other information from social media platforms and other publicly available sources, and using those materials to assemble accounts of events. The work of open-source investigation resembles the forensic investigation of crime in the legal system, especially in its focus on media evidence, but the investigative methods typically employed *by* the state are turned *on* the state and other powerful actors to document and expose their wrongdoing. Eyal Weizman has used the term "counterforensics" to invoke the oppositional orientation of this work.[42] Video forensics is also finding a place in changing forms of television news. As online video journalism has burgeoned, so has journalism's use of media forensics as both a journalistic method and a mode of address, applying forensic sensemaking to produce an aesthetically compelling and dramatic form of audiovisual storytelling.[43] This *forensic turn* in video news production is a means of claiming epistemic authority under contemporary conditions of media and political fragmentation.

While these alternative uses are notable, the historical development of the forensic sciences in service to the criminal legal system makes them precarious methods for activism. As Weizman has warned, efforts to challenge "officially sanctioned truths" using the tools of media forensics "is not a guarantee of progressive politics."[44] It is also the case that the extension of media forensics into broader spaces of sensemaking feeds into a cultural desire for conviction that is uncomfortably wedded to carceral logics. And given the limited resources available for alternative uses of forensics, it remains important to understand how choices are made about which cases to investigate. As I have explained in this chapter, extensive training and expertise is needed to do this type of media work proficiently. In addition, the precision-oriented epistemology of forensics means that it can be applied only on a case-by-case basis, and it offers a very narrow approach to understanding "the crime problem." Like the nineteenth-century epistemic virtue of "mechanical objectivity," the forensic sciences purport to jettison interpretation, staying tightly wedded to the material facts.[45] Forensic sensemaking reduces the analysis of lawbreaking to specific questions about the who, what, when, and where of specific incidents. It has little or nothing to say about why.

The labor-intensive nature of the work of video forensics and the growing volumes of video to analyze are among the problems driving the demand for automation. In the process, automation is providing further inroads for companies to embed their proprietary technologies into the logistical systems of policing. Companies have long been involved in the work of video forensics, including companies that provide forensics services for-hire as well as companies that sell proprietary surveillance equipment and software applications. Some companies have even built their own in-house capacity to conduct forensic investigations of activities that occur on their properties. One notably example is the U.S. retail giant Target Corp. As I discuss in Chapter 2, to make use of the enormous video surveillance infrastructure installed across its distributed network of retail outlets, Target established an in-house private crime lab specializing in video forensics. The company's expertise in video forensics for "loss prevention," in addition to its industry-leading retail analytics, points to the expanding surveillance capacities of twenty-first-century corporations and the extent to which they influence the prosecutorial work of the criminal legal system. In the process of building a video surveillance infrastructure that rivaled and surpassed those of most police departments, Target became a company in the business of private policing.

2

"A High-Tech Company Masquerading as a Retailer"

Target's Video Infrastructure

Introduction

In 2012, a news magazine story by Charles Duhigg revealed "How Companies Learn Your Secrets," explaining how the retail giant Target Corp. used data analytics techniques to predict people's buying behaviors.[1] One of the most unnerving revelations was that by analyzing purchasing data, Target's market research machine could determine when women were pregnant even before they told their family members. This story became an oft repeated example of the predictive capabilities of so-called Big Data. It was not only the Big Tech firms that were harnessing large volumes of data to gain deep insights about people in an effort to predict and influence their behavior. It was also the big box, brick-and-mortar stores like Target. In an interview with the *Washington Post* six years earlier, Target's vice president for governmental affairs was already describing Target as "a high tech company masquerading as a retailer."[2] As this quip intimated, even companies selling actual stuff were trying to cash in on behavioral data, portraying themselves (especially to investors) as "high tech" companies in the business of data analytics. Target stores and the goods for sale on their shelves became a front for a far more lucrative backend Big Data influence machine.

If it quickly became legend that Target knew when women were pregnant, another aspect of the company's surveillance operations received less attention: the massive video infrastructure that extended across its physical properties, which by 2010 contained upwards of 75,000 cameras.[3] Target's claim to being a "high tech company" came not just from the volumes of customer data it collected or the company's capacity to crunch the data to determine intimate details about people's lives. It also derived from the way it designed the physical space of its stores as securitized "brandscapes," integrating an extensive security apparatus into its retail infrastructure and into the branded "Target experience." Target had gained a reputation as a trailblazer in retail security, with a security infrastructure that was the envy of the industry.[4] Store cameras were connected to a centralized corporate command center in the company's home city of Minneapolis, referred to by one industry insider as "the Mecca of loss prevention."[5] For Target, being a high tech company meant not only growing its expertise in predictive analytics for individualized customer targeting. It also meant developing the technological capacity for physically monitoring its stores and operations and for intervening in the activities taking place on those properties.

The tightly intertwined relationship that Target built between security, policing, corporate philanthropy, and retail analytics is the focus of this chapter. By building extensive video surveillance infrastructures, corporations like Target contributed significantly to the video avalanche. In the process, they also contributed to the morphing dual structure of public policing and private security, taking on policing functions that public police departments were not equipped for and tuning those functions to the needs of the firm. As Target illustrates, the private security operations of modern corporations have come to occupy significant ground in the broader landscape of policing and security, performing police functions and exercising police powers.

Target's extensive and proprietary video surveillance infrastructure provided the site and source materials to produce video evidence in the investigation and prosecution of retail and other crimes against Target. Most notably, the company decided in the early 2000s to develop its own capacity to make evidentiary use of its surveillance infrastructure by establishing an in-house crime lab that specialized in fingerprint analysis and video forensics. With this move, Target stepped further into the territory of law enforcement instrumentation and procedures, taking on the work of investigations and evidence assembly for prosecutions. Target was not alone in developing its own internal capacity for forensic investigations. In the first two decades of the 2000s, forensic labs "popped up in big companies across industries," including at other retailers like Walmart as well as banks, utilities, and tech firms, with these private labs "more likely than police labs to have high-tech tools and the latest forensics software."[6] The move of modern corporations into the business of forensics was an outgrowth of the expansion of their proprietary security infrastructure. It also compensated for the limited capacities of public police departments to investigate and prosecute retail theft and other crimes against capital.

In addition to its private video surveillance infrastructure and in-house forensics labs, Target Corp. formed relationships with local police departments in areas where its stores were located, developing public-private partnerships that aimed to influence the work of those agencies. Target engaged in a form of corporate "philanthropy" focused on its security priorities, an approach to philanthropy-for-policing that included actual grant-making to police departments as well as in-kind donations of security expertise and surveillance equipment. The company also helped build a nationwide infrastructure to facilitate philanthropy-for-policing, assisting in the formation of local police foundations across the country. These police foundations in turn created funding channels that allowed corporations and wealthy elites to direct resources to the police, without the need to go through official procedures for public oversight and approval. While the actual financial support has been minimal relative to police budgets, these police foundations have served as avenues for peddling influence through police foundation boards.[7]

Target has always been a retail company first and foremost, and as Charles Duhigg's famous 2012 story revealed, the company by then had become an industry leader in retail analytics. In the chapter's final section, I discuss the repurposing of video surveillance systems for retail analytics, using security systems for the analysis of shopping behavior at scale and more fully integrating loss prevention, labor management, and consumer targeting. To explore these developments, I look beyond Target to companies like Milestone Systems and Axis Communications, both major video surveillance technology providers that supply the equipment and software that outfit Target's stores. If video infrastructures can be used for both security and retail analytics, they become much more valuable to these firms. It gives retailers greater capacity to analyze patterns of behavior in their stores, while investing surveillance technology providers with a means of generating recurring revenue from systems they have already sold.

The materials that I use to assemble this Target story offer only a partial view. They include local and national press coverage, industry materials, Target corporate communications, and reports on public-private partnerships with police that the retailer sponsored in collaboration with the Urban Institute Policy Center and the Police Executive Research Forum. I also mine my own experience. Like millions of other people, I have been targeted by Target's marketing campaigns for years while purchasing toiletries, household items, clothes, food, and other goods at their stores and having the banal, sometimes annoying and sometimes mildly pleasant "Target experience." But the epistemic asymmetries of surveillance capitalism are formidable.[8] Target Corp. has a significantly greater capacity and wealth of data to study me, and everyone around me, than I have to study the company and its practices.

Securitized Brandscapes

The Target discount chain began with three stores in 1962, as one of many ventures of the Dayton Company, a Minneapolis-based business that included jewelry stores and the bookstore B. Dalton.[9] In the span of 15 years, Dayton Company became Dayton Hudson Corporation, and the Target chain grew spectacularly, becoming Dayton Hudson's largest source of revenue by 1977. Over the next two decades, Dayton Hudson worked hard to make Target an iconic American company, deeply embedded in U.S. culture and society. After two more decades acquiring other retail companies, constructing new stores, and building the Target brand, Dayton Hudson began the new millennium by changing the parent company name to Target Corp.

Target is one major retailer among many, and it has long operated in the shadow of Walmart, a company that sat at the very top of the Fortune 500 for ten consecutive years (as of 2023), above Apple, Amazon, Alphabet, and ExxonMobil. Yet Target's position was far from weak. Ranked at number 37, Target's 2023 revenues were $107.4 billion, up from $60 billion in annual sales in 2005. By 2023, the company had 1,956 stores, almost double the 1,000 stores it had in July 2001.[10] It is a company that has left an imprint on American culture. It is precisely its everyday presence in

American life and its seemingly less significant role in the surveillance economy that makes Target an important company to consider.

Target sells its own branded products, but its main brand is the store itself and the experience of shopping there. According to one Target executive, "We try to create a shopping experience that's not just commodity exchange.... We want to be a lot more like Disney World and a lot less like a flea market."[11] One way of conceptualizing the efforts of commercial designers to create curated, branded spaces is the "brandscape." For surveillance studies scholars Kirstie Ball and David Murakami Wood, the brandscape concept refers to an encompassing marketing strategy for reordering space and remaking the subjective experience of shopping.[12] The brandscape extends beyond conventional marketing, combining it with architectural design, urban planning, and data analytics. The aim is to create immersive experiences that engage individuals with brands at an affective, sensory level. Disney World has long been the quintessential brandscape. Others have included Nike Town and every casino resort in Las Vegas. The modern brandscape has taken its place in the longer history of "dream worlds of consumption,"[13] but as Joseph Turow notes in his study of recent transformations happening in the retail industry, "the world of physical retailing is a radically mutating place."[14]

Underestimated in common understandings of branding and shopping is the important role that perceptions of safety play in the curation of the retail space. Brandscapes are spaces that must be "intensely monitored and policed," so much so that "brandscapes must also be securityscapes, in order to provide material shape to dreams of safety and risk-free living."[15] Constructing the securitized brandscape is partly a matter of managing the perceptions of shoppers. Target's annual reports, for example, explicitly state that "guest perceptions regarding the cleanliness and safety" of the stores is one of the risk factors affecting the company's ability to compete with other retail businesses, including those online.[16] How safe shoppers feel going to a Target store does not depend solely on what happens inside the stores; it is also tied to shoppers' perceptions of where the stores are located. For Target, this has meant that constructing the securitized brandscape has required not just focusing on making the stores appear clean and safe; it has also meant extending its vision of security into the communities where the stores are located, including an increasing number of smaller format stores in urban areas.

Although the design of brandscapes has focused intensively on shoppers' perceptions, retail security is also concerned with the material problem of shoplifting and other sources of inventory "shrinkage." In the aggregate, shoplifting adds up to significant losses for retail firms. The stores are places where people are supposed to purchase goods with money earned from wages, but the act of taking the goods without paying also occurs with great regularity. Shoplifting has no doubt always been a problem for merchants, but the twentieth-century expansion of the retail firm came with more systematic efforts to intervene on this form of inventory shrinkage. The larger the retail company, the greater the concentrated revenue loss from the regularity of shoplifting. This is not to suggest that small businesses experience less harm from shoplifting, only that the losses grow in absolute terms the larger the firm, making the threats and stakes also seem larger.

The growth in the scale of corporate retail came with a parallel growth in the scale of the problem of shoplifting. Shoplifting occurs with enough frequency that its prevention, investigation, and prosecution cannot be fully managed by the socialized system of public policing. Investigating and prosecuting the full extent of these legal infractions is far beyond the capacity of police departments and the criminal legal system. It is for this reason, as much as perception management, that large companies like Target have invested in their own proprietary security systems for "loss prevention."[17] The loss prevention operations of major retail firms have involved the development of video surveillance infrastructures, making them ubiquitous in the spaces of market exchange.

In-Store Video Surveillance Systems

The origins of video surveillance for retail security stretch back to the analog days of broadcast and closed-circuit television, but much has changed over time in these systems and their role in the business of retail, including the extent of video surveillance coverage. As retail video surveillance has become ubiquitous, it has also become increasingly banal. The criminologists Benjamin Goold, Ian Loader, and Angelica Thumala refer to "the banality of security" to describe the power that has accrued to the uses of video surveillance as these systems are deployed extensively in everyday environments.[18] Video surveillance has become "so all-embracing that we seldom pause to notice it."[19]

Video surveillance has existed in Target stores for decades. A press photograph of a "Target store in the '80s" shows a television monitor mounted in plain view (see Figure 2.1) and a dome camera mounted to the ceiling behind a security guard. The press photographer saw fit to capture the elements of the store's security system design, which, except for the human security guard, were probably state-of-the-art, suggesting that audiovisual systems were being integrated into market spaces as a form of built-in security as early as the 1980s.

A visit to one of Target's newer small-format stores in North Park, San Diego, in 2021 illustrates how much the "banality of security" had taken root and how intensively integrated the securityscape was with the brandscape (see Figure 2.2a). Playful murals on the walls serve as the backdrop to the aisles of merchandise and other experiential dimensions of the space of the store. While store visitors may or may not notice the surveillance cameras mounted to the ceiling, there is no corner of this store that is not within the field of view of the security cameras. But if the ceiling-mounted cameras blend into the retail atmosphere, the small monitors at each self-checkout station are situated at eye level to show shoppers their own images as they scan their items and pay for them. These monitors are meant to deter people from taking advantage of the depersonalized checkout experience to take products without paying. Other visible signifiers, like the security stand at the store entrance, seem purposefully placed. On the day I visited this store and snapped a few pictures with my cell phone, no actual security person was seated at the stand; instead, a reflective vest was draped over an empty chair (see Figure 2.2b).

All these elements blend together in a way that might fall below the threshold of awareness, intentionally designed to create a kind of pleasant, passive experience of safe and secure shopping. If store visitors are supposed to notice certain indicators of security, like the subtle suggestion of a guard and the monitors at the self-checkout stations, they are supposed to barely notice, to register these features as normal. People have grown quite accustomed to seeing themselves on surveillance video monitors, for example, as well as on their own computer screens at home. As the image from the 1980s in Figure 2.1 suggests, the video monitor displaying live feeds, mounted inside the store for customers to see, is a common design practice dating back to the original installation of private security cameras. It is a form of "ambient television" that U.S. cities and suburbs started making space for in the twentieth century, much like they did with television and its circulation of commercial culture.[20]

Figure 2.1. A security stand inside a "Target store in the '80s. Bill Johnson/Getty." The surveillance monitor is framed with a placard that alerts shoppers to "Smile. You Are on TV." A domed camera casing is mounted to the ceiling. Photo credit: Getty Images. Reprinted under fair use.

Figures 2.2a & 2.2b. A Target store in North Park, an urban neighborhood in San Diego, California, from August 2021, a year after the store opened. In the above image, a reflective vest is draped over the chair behind the security stand, in place of an actual security guard. Photo credit: Kelly Gates.

Figures 2.2a & 2.2b. In this image, self-checkout stations have monitors displaying images of shoppers as they swipe their purchases. The domed camera casings mounted into the ceiling are placed throughout the store to cover the entire space. Photo credit: Kelly Gates.

Retail firms have had no legal obligation to reveal anything publicly about their video surveillance infrastructure development, but fragments of information about the expansion of Target's security operations are archived in press and security industry sources. A 2011 article in the *Boston Globe* described Target as operating "one of the largest and most advanced networks of cameras," not a separate, siloed CCTV system at each store, but an interconnected network that extended across its retail operations.[21] A 2012 article in *Security Technology Executive* magazine reported that each of Target's security cameras—numbering over 75,000 devices by 2010—was a node in a distributed video infrastructure that spanned across Target's properties.[22] Target's video surveillance system had gone through different iterations, "from analog and eventually to IP," and different configurations of "audio communication devices."[23] The company also developed a distributed network of "investigation centers" that "served as monitoring posts for multiple stores."[24] According to the *Boston Globe* report, one node in the network was the Target Investigations Center located in the Boston neighborhood of Westborough, at the time one of 14 regional centers.[25] Target's regional investigation centers had access to multiple stores' video systems and were in turn linked up to a corporate command center in Minneapolis, Minnesota. Referred to in-house as "C3," the command center was using "cutting-edge technology to assist with crisis preparedness and response, including satellite imagery and remote surveillance of stores and distribution centers."[26]

Target's assets protection team saw its centralized video surveillance system as a labor-saving technology for security and loss prevention. One executive explained that Target's integrated investigation centers allowed the company's security teams "to coordinate activity to use video as a force multiplier—to look at multiple stores at once so that the staffing model by store doesn't have to be as robust."[27] Target also experimented with technologies for automatically processing the volumes of video generated across its properties. In 2011, Target's system reportedly was equipped with anomaly detection technology that worked algorithmically to alert security staff "when shoppers dwell too long in front of merchandise or roam outside stores after closing time."[28] Large-scale video infrastructures like Target's—consisting of thousands of cameras—pose challenges for the human labor of monitoring them. Predictably, companies have experimented with the automation of video analysis for detecting such nefarious activities as lingering in aisles or walking around outside the stores at night. The company's large-scale video infrastructure provided an ideal laboratory for experimentation, but it had no legal obligation to disclose the full range of its uses of "anomaly detection" and other technologies of surveillance automation. As I will discuss later in this chapter, there are other ways that retail firms like Target are making use of their video surveillance systems, including the application of automated video analytics to analyze the behavior of shoppers, which takes the securitized brandscape to another level by seamlessly integrating security with marketing.

Integrating Store Security with Law Enforcement

As Target's proprietary surveillance operations grew, so did its relationships with law enforcement and criminal justice programs in the United States. These efforts extended the reach of Target's security operations—its expertise, personnel, and tech infrastructure—beyond the territorial boundaries of its properties and into the communities where the stores are located. Target framed these efforts as a form of corporate responsibility for community safety, leveraging relationships with law enforcement to support the securitization of its retail infrastructure and directing resources to the police in the form of grants and security expertise. As the *Washington Post* put it, Target "replaced the concept of 'assets protection' in its stores with crime prevention in the community."[29]

The Target concept of crime prevention included relationships the company established with law enforcement in its headquarter city of Minneapolis. In 2003, Target gave Minneapolis seed money to support the purchase and installation of 30 cameras, launching the SafeZone program that was later rebranded "Safe City." Minneapolis would be the first test case, but the aim was to extend the program to localities across the United States, wherever Target stores were located. Modeled after a crime prevention program in North Hampton, England, the project would lend Target's security expertise to law enforcement agencies and enlist those agencies to support the company's vision for a retail environment that would be more attractive to its customers. Later, after the 2008–2009 financial crisis, Target began positioning its Safe City program as a form of assistance to police departments hamstrung by reduced public budgets. According to a former president of the New York Police Foundation, Target's Safe City program was "a boon to police departments nationwide as they face shrinking budgets and can't afford to keep up with the latest technologies."[30]

Target also shared the expertise it acquired in video surveillance systems with police agencies, some of which were behind the curve. In 2012, the deputy police chief of Minneapolis, Rob Allen, explained how much his agency relied on Target's expertise in video surveillance system design when it came to implementing a police system in downtown Minneapolis:

> I knew nothing about video systems, and it didn't make sense for me or the police department, which knew nothing about video, to try to develop a video system . . . so we worked very closely with Target—which is headquartered downtown and has been a great crime-prevention partner with us—to identify how to build a video system. They have 1,500 stores, and every store has 70 to 90 cameras—that's a lot of cameras. They understand video systems, so they helped us design the system. Their legal department helped us get the clearances to install cameras.[31]

The command center for the video surveillance system that the Minneapolis Police created in close partnership with Target was depicted in a series of images for *Security Technology Executive* magazine. (Each of these photos was labeled "Photo courtesy of Target Corp.")[32] The photos offered various views of desktop and wall-mounted monitors displaying surveillance camera feeds. One photo caption read, "Minneapolis Police works hand-in-hand with dispatchers in the Fusion Center," under an image of a Minneapolis police officer and a woman seated at a desktop monitor, wearing a shirt labeled "Fusion Center Dispatcher."

The police surveillance system staged in these images was only minimally funded by Target Corp. According to *Security Technology Magazine*, Target provided $200,000 in seed money, a nominal amount given the total cost of such systems (actual dollar amounts are harder to unearth). The Minneapolis SafeZone project started out as a nonprofit 501(c)(3) and was later supported with commercial property taxes collected to fund the Minneapolis Downtown Improvement District.

The companies that supplied the technology were identified in the caption of another photo showing a man seated at monitors with surveillance feeds: "A video management system from Milestone helps the Minneapolis Police monitor cameras from Axis Communications that have been strategically placed in the downtown area." Milestone Systems makes video management software for large-scale surveillance systems, designing software that could be integrated with a wide range of proprietary hardware. Axis Communications was by then a leading surveillance equipment provider; its proprietary video surveillance technologies were being used to monitor retail centers and other spaces throughout the world. (As noted in the Introduction, in 2015 both companies were acquired by Canon, Inc., which viewed the network surveillance camera business as a "driving force for future growth.")[33]

The partnership between the Minneapolis Police and Target was the first of multiple public-private initiatives. The Minneapolis SafeZone project was followed by "23 or 24 [similar projects] around the country, from Hawaii to Compton [Los Angeles] to Columbia Heights, British Columbia," which, according to the Target executive in charge of these projects, all had "the same premise to use technology as leverage and use that almost to bring people together."[34] From Target's perspective, the

SafeZone project "transformed from a crime-control measure to basically, in our terms, almost a business growth driver."[35]

CSI: Target

The growing network of cameras in Target stores created the problem of how to monitor and make use of the video they produced. As a representative from Target put it, the company "had a volume of evidence from our cameras but no expertise" in video handling.[36] It was also the case that the public police departments in most jurisdictions had limited resources and, again, limited expertise to devote to investigating retail crimes that companies like Target deemed necessary to their bottom lines. Companies thus developed their own instruments of law enforcement, including not just security personnel and video surveillance systems but also the capacity to investigate crimes and assemble the evidence to secure convictions.

In 2003, a year that began with U.S. publicly funded crime labs reporting a backlog of over 500,000 requests for forensic services,[37] Target Corp. created its own in-house crime lab. The lab staffed by a team of full-time forensic experts and located at the company's Brooklyn Park campus in Minnesota.[38] Two years later, the company opened a second lab in Las Vegas, "to help with the caseload."[39] Target's crime labs specialized in latent fingerprint and forensic video analysis and soon became accredited through the American Society of Crime Laboratory Directors/Laboratory Accreditation Board (ASCLD/LAB), the official accrediting body for forensic labs in the United States. By 2008, the Target forensics labs had a team of seven investigators, most of whom had formerly worked for law enforcement agencies.[40] By 2011, forensic specialists employed by the Target lab had appeared as expert witnesses in court, including at least one murder case.[41] In 2012, Target posted an article on the corporate pages of its website promoting the lab to people interested in "An Unexpected Career: Target's Forensic Services Laboratory." The article noted that "team members hail from all areas of criminal justice."[42] Target tapped some of the leading specialists in the emerging field of digital multimedia forensics. One came from the Oklahoma State Bureau of Investigation, two were members of scientific working groups sponsored by the Federal Bureau of Investigation

(FBI), and the lab director was "a Target 'lifer,' having worked in assets protection and other leadership roles at Target for more than 16 years."[43] Another was "a former criminal investigator with the U.S. Army who had retrieved and analyzed evidence in the abuse of detainees at the Abu Ghraib prison in Baghdad."[44]

The Target forensic lab soon established a reputation among law enforcement agencies. The lab was considered better equipped for forensic work than many municipal and state-run crime labs, especially for forensic video analysis. Target's lab became "best known for its ability to pick up details from surveillance camera footage," according to *Forbes*.[45] Target's forensic specialists began assisting police agencies with criminal investigations beyond retail theft. The Target team lent a hand in some high-profile cases, including an arson investigation in Houston, Texas, where they retrieved images from a damaged videotape showing kids buying gasoline. The video evidence led to their conviction. "Requests for help soon became overwhelming," according to a *Washington Post* story.[46] *Forbes* reported that Target's crime lab became "inundated with requests to restore and review tapes, track cell phones and pick up and analyze fingerprints."[47]

In Minneapolis, the police department relied on the Target crime lab, especially in cases where they got video from outside sources but lacked the necessary technology to analyze it.[48] The challenge was the wide variety of compression schemes and codecs used by different surveillance systems. As the Minneapolis deputy police chief put it, "It's impossible for our crime lab to have all those different codecs. . . . Target typically has all those, so when we are using other people's video, they have programs that sometimes can enhance it better than our folks can."[49]

Target positioned its pro bono forensic work for the police as corporate philanthropy and good corporate citizenship, serving the greater good of communities. But Target's move to set up its own in-house forensic labs was part of a broader effort to build surveillance and security infrastructure that supported its private, commercial model of spatial development. Having its own video forensics labs would allow the company to make productive use of the video being generated by its extensive video surveillance system. The firm had its own internal needs for the video, and these needs required technologies and expertise in video forensics. Establishing an accredited lab would also allow the company to produce legally credible evidence (i.e., evidence that it could transfer to the legal system in support of prosecutions). If the police were unable to devote enough resources to investigate the crimes against Target, the company's own in-house forensic experts would perform the work instead.

Although Target was doing pro bono work for the police on arson and murder investigations, a good deal of its own forensic investigations no doubt focused on shoplifting and employee theft. In the framework of the retail firm, the investigation, prosecution, and conviction of shoplifters was conceptualized as a form of managing inventory. The Target assets protection team approached shoplifters the way they approached the processing of goods. The effort to prevent loss from shoplifting was something like "reverse logistics." According to this logic, identifying shoplifters and moving them into the legal system was just like moving inventory through stores. Target's vice president of government affairs stated this most explicitly: "It struck me that following repeat criminals was really an inventory management problem."[50]

Because its crime labs and security operations are proprietary, not public, the full extent of Target's forensic investigations are unknown. However, anecdotal evidence suggests that Target has experimented with approaches to shoplifting that extended the investigations over time, rather than intervening in every single theft. They allowed people to get away with shoplifting, waiting until they became repeat offenders, amassing offenses that would lead to stiffer legal penalties. For example, a 2016 story that was verified by Reddit's Upvoting moderators involved an addict caught shoplifting at Target. The Reddit user, who went by the alias StiggyPop, explained how he had stolen about $15,000 worth of Blu-Rays from a single Target store over a four-month period to pay for his drug habit.[51] He simply walked in, filled up a basket, and walked out, not bothering to disguise himself and even driving away in his own registered car. He would sell the stolen merchandise to a resale store. When he was finally apprehended, it was by two men from "higher level Target loss prevention."[52] They not only knew his name but where he lived, who else lived there, and the store where he sold the discs. Although StiggyPop expressed gratitude for the relatively respectful treatment the Target security people gave him, they could have easily apprehended him sooner, before allowing him to rack up more serious charges that would more likely include jail time.

As the anecdote suggests, rather than intervening only on individual crimes, Target assets protection group sought to elevate its investigations to higher levels of crime severity. The retail industry in general has also focused on what it sees as more systematic forms of illegitimate market activity—namely, the industry-defined problem of "organized retail crime," a grave problem of "national retail security."[53] In 2021, the *Wall Street Journal* reported that organized retail theft was reaching a boiling point, with alleged networks of organized professional shoplifters, known as "boosters," brazenly shoplifting in groups and making off with enough merchandise to cost the retail industry an estimated $45 billion in annual losses.[54] The article described the practice as "a menace that has been supercharged by the pandemic and the rapid growth of online commerce," with chain-drugstore CVS reporting an increase of 30 percent in reported theft between the beginning of the pandemic and mid-2021. As the *Wall Street Journal* explained, based on information from sources including Ben Dugan, director for health retail crime and corporate investigations at CVS Health Corp., "Boosters, often drug addicts targeted by crime rings, typically sell their goods for about 5% to 10% of retail value to a street-level fence, who then sells them to a larger-scale distributor." Other companies engaged in a battle with the rising tide of organized retail crime included Target Corp. as well as Home Depot, Publix, Ulta Beauty Inc., Walgreens, Walmart, and TJX Companies, the parent company of TJ Maxx and Marshalls.

Notably, the goods stolen from these retailers were often being sold on Amazon, yet another way that the online retail giant was cutting into the revenues of brick-and-mortar retailers. In other words, if the competition from Amazon was coming from online sales, additional unfair competition came from an illicit market that offloaded goods on Amazon that were stolen from retailers like CVS and Target. Investigators and law enforcement officials described Amazon as "one of the biggest outlets for criminal networks" and notoriously hard to deal with when it came to obtaining information about sellers on its platform, claiming that it does not share information without a subpoena because of privacy concerns.[55] According to the *Wall Street Journal*, Amazon lobbied against legislation that would require e-commerce sites to do more to verify third-party sellers and make information about them public. According to an Amazon spokesperson, "We believe the most effective way to stop fraud and abuse is for Congress and the states to increase penalties and provide law enforcement with greater resources."[56] In other words, Amazon advocated for larger police budgets and more prosecutions rather than policy that would require the company to do more to make sure stolen goods were not being sold on its platform.

If organized retail crime seemed like a growing drug-related and COVID-induced plague on society, it was arguably just a trumped-up construction of the retail industry's imagination. Jerry Iannelli, an editor for a nonprofit news outlet called *The Appeal* that advocates for police reform, has argued that the big retail chains were manufacturing the shoplifting crisis, much the way Stuart Hall and his colleagues argued that the media created a moral panic about muggings in the United Kingdom in the 1970s. "While 'organized retail theft rings' do exist in some form," Iannelli wrote, "there is little evidence to support the idea that they're driving an unprecedented wave of shoplifting."[57] The FBI's Uniform Crime Reporting data showed no evidence of a steep increase in shoplifting. In addition, a 2023 industry survey by the National Retail Federation showed that "the effect of theft on retailers' bottom lines [was] about the same as it has been for years."[58] Rather than reflecting a real increase in theft, trumped up claims about an epidemic of organized retail crime were being used by national retail chains and law enforcement officials to push for more resources for policing and harsher sentences for shoplifting offenses.

In general, shoplifting is studied only to the extent that the analysis aids in prevention and prosecution, in the interests of business owners, which are equated with those of society. But shoplifting is a more complicated social problem than is usually acknowledged. Notably, studies have found that adolescents are overrepresented in the groups identified as shoplifters.[59] Adolescents are bombarded with commercial messages, including messages crafted by a marketing apparatus that uses applied adolescent psychology and now "predictive analytics" based on intimate data gathered about their behavior from their use of social media. Inundated with this messaging and spending much of their time in groups of other adolescents being targeted by the same digital influence machine, adolescents face significant pressures to accumulate things. Yet because they often do not have the money to purchase those things, adolescents sometimes resort to shoplifting.

Another category of shoplifters are people with addiction problems. A 2014 study of a large U.S. supermarket chain found that products that played a role in illicit drug use were stolen at a significantly higher rate than other products.[60] And while shoplifting is defined and treated as a form of property theft, at least one study of shoplifters found that some of those who do it see it as a form of work.[61] It goes without saying that many people who shoplift belong to the ranks of unemployed surplus labor. There are a wide range of reasons for shoplifting, among them people's need for basic goods when they do not have the means to pay for them. Nonetheless, the primary "solution" advocated for, again and again, is more policing, prosecution, and incarceration. Terms like "organized retail crime" serve to further vilify the people caught up in these illicit economies.

Corporate Philanthropy and Police Foundations

When private companies form "public-private partnerships" with public agencies, these relationships are typically framed as a better alternative than government programs and a form of charity that offers broad public benefits. Yet they typically serve the interests of corporations or align with the ideological beliefs of wealthy elites rather than serving the public. In Target's case, the company developed a model of corporate philanthropy that integrated a program of grant-making and in-kind consulting to police agencies with its security strategy. Target described its partnerships with police, including its support for police video surveillance systems and its pro bono forensic work, as part of its philanthropic mission. In an interview with Michigan Public Radio in 2011, Target's vice president of assets protection said that the relationship that Target was building with police departments was part of its "broader policy on charitable giving."[62] But while Target claimed to be engaging in charitable activity as an ethically motivated company, this activity served the company's direct needs for assets protection, store security, and the construction of a securitized brandscape. Making contributions and creating partnerships with police departments allowed Target to influence police department agendas, expropriating the public resources of the police and even at times making the police accountable to Target for their prosecutorial outcomes.

Target branded its philanthropic, public-private partnerships with police departments as "Target & BLUE." A 2007 document published by an organization called the Security Executive Council described Target & BLUE as "a multifaceted program that provides national and local law enforcement with investigative and forensic support and services, as well as technology donations, financial grants, and information sharing."[63] Various efforts fell under the Target & BLUE umbrella—for example, assisting in police investigations into "not just retail-oriented crimes . . . but violent crimes like arson, assault and homicide"; "forensic services"; "the Safe City Program"; and grants "for such equipment as patrol bicycles, child identification kits, steering wheel locks, and awareness literature" as well as donations of technology, "including surveillance equipment and lightly used laptops and PCs."[64] Listed under Target & BLUE's other programs were Target's consulting services to police agencies: "Sharing insights and best practices for recruitment, employee retention, business finance and numerous other business-critical processes," according to the report, "can provide great value at little cost to the company."[65] Target & BLUE was the name used to encompass corporate-wide efforts to build relationships with the police in areas where Target stores were located, integrating the company's security operations with law enforcement and incorporating perceptions of safety into the Target store brand.

Through corporate-wide Target & BLUE initiatives, personnel from assets protection at individual Target stores were authorized to initiate relationships with police and make contributions to "community safety" programs. Local stores could make their own grants to police municipalities through their police foundations, based on local relationships between Target employees and the police and their sense of local needs. According to the description of Target Public Safety Grants at the company's corporate information pages, these grants were "managed locally by our Target store and distribution center Assets Protection teams"; local Target security personnel took the lead on decisions about awarding grants "to eligible organizations across the country" and choosing funding recipients for "crime prevention programs, community safety or youth engagement activities."[66] Descriptions of grant-making to law enforcement agencies repeatedly tacked on references to funding for youth programs, which were common recipients of early police foundation giving.

Local grant-making to municipal police departments was a way of building relationships between Target stores and local police, but Target's funding initiatives and influence in criminal legal practices went beyond grants to community safety and youth programs. According to the *Washington Post*, the company was also "paying for a lawyer and a paralegal in the Minneapolis prosecutor's office through its charitable foundation, with an emphasis on prosecuting repeat criminals"; furthermore, a county attorney noted that the Target funding came with "huge strings attached. . . . We were expected to routinely communicate how the money was used and what kind of results we'd gained."[67] Once the Minneapolis prosecutor's office was "working with Target," this attorney explained, they were expected to track not only how many criminals were charged but the number of convictions they achieved each year. With the additional resources from Target to support legal efforts, the prosecutor's office increased convictions of repeat offenders from about three cases per year to 90, according to a *Washington Post* source.[68] Target also worked with Minnesota law enforcement agencies to develop their criminal records systems and bring different agencies together to address impediments to information sharing across jurisdictions. Target donated technology as well as employee expertise and labor time to create a better infrastructure for sharing information among police agencies. In addition, Target's collaborative activities with state security entities included activities at the federal level aimed at protecting its supply chain. As the *Washington Post* reported, Target "helped coordinate national undercover investigations and worked with customs agencies on ways to make sure imported cargo is coming from reputable sources or hasn't been tampered with."[69]

It is significant that, as a condition of support from Target, the Minneapolis prosecutors' office was required to report back to the company on their results. It meant that Target was leveraging its "philanthropic giving" to push for more prosecutions.[70] Target's so-called philanthropic activities extended the reach of the company's governing functions beyond its own employees or labor force and into the criminal legal system. A philanthropic program that channeled small amounts of funding to police agencies allowed Target to transfer its security agenda onto recipients of Target giving, delegating roles to those actors in ways that served the company's interests. The grant-making process made recipients accountable to Target for outcomes. As a condition of receiving funding, grant recipients are often responsible for not only spending the money on the program as outlined in their grant proposals but also reporting back to grant makers on the outcomes of the grants. In this way, corporate philanthropy becomes a form of corporate governance of the police. It is also a way of expropriating the public resources of the police, making actors in the criminal legal system partly accountable to grantmakers.

Aligned with Target's efforts to physically scale up its retail and video surveillance infrastructure, company representatives began assisting at a conceptual and programmatic level with an effort to scale up the model of corporate relationships with policing through the filtering mechanism of the police foundation. In 2010, Target Corp. joined with the Police Executive Research Forum (PERF) and the U.S. Justice Department's Office of Community Oriented Policing Services (COPS) to support an initiative that would help more municipalities across the United States create police foundations. A PERF newsletter described the "PERF/Target project" as an effort focused "on helping police leaders understand more clearly what a foundation is, what the benefits are, and how to get it off the ground"[71] (see Figure 2.3). A COPS newsletter article noted that the project was launched in September 2010 to promote the expansion of police foundations in small, medium, and large cities and towns across the country. With support from the COPS office and Target, the project offered training workshops and technical assistance to sustain community policing efforts at crime reduction and crime prevention by establishing or expanding existing police foundations. The initiative was named the National Police Foundations Project and was headed up by the former director of the New York Police Foundation. The New York Police Foundation was considered a model because it was one of the earliest established and the most financially successful.[72]

There are restrictions on what police departments can do with public funds. At the same time, receiving direct contributions from corporations can make it "appear that the company is buying special treatment from the police department."[73] In contrast, donating money through a police foundation "insulates the department from that kind of appearance of impropriety and appearance of undue influence."[74] The keyword is

SAVE THE DATE!
PERF Annual Meeting
April 28-30, 2011
Seattle, Washington

PERF and Target Announce Project To Promote Police Foundations

WITH SUPPORT FROM TARGET, PERF IS LAUNCHING a project that will promote the expansion of police foundations—nonprofit organizations that help raise money for police programs and equipment.

The project will include the creation of a National Police Foundation Association, which will serve as a source of information and assistance for existing and newly established police foundations, as well as for police chiefs, elected officials, business leaders and others with an interest in police foundations.

Target said its goal is to provide new resources to local communities. "This new initiative demonstrates how Target's extensive public safety partnerships are helping to strengthen neighborhoods across the country," said Brad Brekke, vice president of Assets Protection for Target.

Leading the effort will be Pam Delaney, former President of the New York City Police Foundation, which was the first organization of its kind in the United States, established in 1971. The NYC Police Foundation has become a model program that many other cities have followed. Ms. Delaney served as its top official for most of its existence and is one of the nation's top experts on police foundation leadership.

Subject to Debate interviewed Ms. Delaney about the new PERF/Target project, about her goals in taking on this new effort, and about some of the issues impacting police foundations, beginning with the current economic downturn:

Q: Pam, in the past, police foundations have been seen as a way to provide "something extra" for policing—special programs, new technology—and not as a way of funding routine items like salaries and patrol cars. With so many police agencies undergoing budget cuts, has there been a shift in thinking on this?

Ms. Delaney: Not really, as far as I can see. Most places are still looking at the "extras" rather than salaries or benefits, unless maybe it's personnel for a specially funded project. But the line may be blurring a little bit. For example, in the past, a new type of police radio might not have been considered by a police foundation because it was considered an "essential" item that should be supported by tax dollars. Today, a police foundation might consider funding radios, especially if it's the first wave of something new in the department, and the police foundation might buy them only for a certain district or a special unit. Or maybe all the officers will get the new radios, but when the radios wear out, city tax dollars will be used to replace them. So police foundations still have an interest in funding things that are new or special.

Pam Delaney

Q: Are police foundations seeing a tightening of donations from corporations and individual donors because of the economic downturn? And are donors more likely to be offering things other than cash, such as use of their facilities, equipment, and expertise?

Ms. Delaney: Yes, there has been some pulling back, because charitable dollars are being

>> continued on page 6

TOP PHOTO BY SERGIO BONACHELA/FLICKR

Figure 2.3. *Subject to Debate: A Newsletter of the Police Executive Research Forum* (PERF), December 2010. Reprinted under fair use. The cover article's opening sentence notes: "With the support from Target, PERF is launching a project that will promote the expansion of police foundations—nonprofit organizations that help raise money for police programs and equipment."

"appearance." In 2014, *ProPublica* reported that police foundations were growing in resources and influence, helping to bankroll the procurement of surveillance technologies, software, laptops, license plate readers, and stingray devices.[75] The report noted that the Los Angeles Police Department (LAPD) initially acquired software from Palantir through its police foundation, including a $200,000 grant from Target Corp. While the LAPD had sufficient resources in its budget, purchasing outright "would have meant going through a year-long process requiring public meetings, approval from the City Council, and, in some cases, competitive bidding."[76] By receiving the funds through the police foundation, the LAPD could avoid public scrutiny and acquire the technology with less oversight.

Police foundations did not just channel money—they also served as new vehicles of corporate influence. Representatives from Target, as well as Bank of America, Microsoft, Starbucks, and other companies, were widely represented on the boards of directors of police foundations. While the foundations raise modest funds compared to the size of police budgets, their more significant impact is extending the influence of corporations and wealthy elites on police department agendas.

Police foundations proliferated in the post-9/11 decades, with the biggest spike in new foundations established between 2014 and 2016.[77] It was not just companies but also police leadership that sought to expand this avenue for supplementing police budgets and working around public policy to avoid scrutiny of police programs. The criminologists Kevin Walby, Randy Lippert, and Alex Luscombe examined membership on a police foundation board to chart the corporate interlocks and influence of board members on police department spending.[78] They also noted other organizations involved in police foundation expansion, including the International Association of Chiefs of Police.[79] Their study challenged the rhetoric of transparency used to promote police foundations, finding instead that they operate like "shell corporations" that facilitate financial obfuscation. With the corporate philanthropic model displacing the tax model and the welfare state, companies were increasingly able to direct police resources to address their own needs, defining it as "charitable giving."

After the murder of George Floyd in May 2020 by a police officer in Minneapolis, the city where its headquarters were located, Target faced a new threat that its relationships with the police posed to its brand. An August 2021 feature article in *Bloomberg Businessweek* told the story of how Target was trying to "recalibrate."[80] The company "scrubbed its 'community & store safety' webpage of any mention of the trademarked name it had used to promote its law enforcement initiatives for the past 25 years: Target & Blue."[81] The article began with a list of actions Target took in the wake of the George Floyd murder to support initiatives aimed at helping Black individuals, rather than prosecuting and incarcerating them. These actions included the funding of job training programs, Black-owned businesses, and civil rights groups. But the article then provided an account of Target's extensive programs over the preceding decades to support surveillance and policing in ways that negatively affected Black communities. "For decades," wrote reporter Peter Waldman, "Target fostered partnerships with law enforcement unlike those of any other U.S. corporation."[82]

Repurposing Store Security Systems for Retail Analytics

If video surveillance infrastructures were designed and installed for retail security and loss prevention, there were other possible uses for the construction of the securitized brandscape. One way that these monitoring systems have been repurposed is for analyzing the behaviors of shoppers, also known as *retail analytics*. The dual use of retail video infrastructure for both loss prevention and the analysis of shopping behaviors promised to seamlessly integrate security with sales, interweaving the machinery of private policing with the machinery of market research.

Retail analytics is the collection of data from physical and online sources to analyze customer behavior and, more specifically, to "measure customer loyalty, identify purchasing patterns, predict demand, and optimize store layouts."[83] According to Michael Hickins, content strategist for the computing firm Oracle, retail analytics can be used "to inform and improve decisions about pricing, inventory, marketing, merchandising, and store operations by applying predictive algorithms against data from both internal sources (such as customer purchase histories) and external repositories (such as weather forecasts)."[84] Retail analytics is billed as a more empirical and scientific way of approaching retail strategies, replacing "instincts and hunches" with insights gained by using data science to analyze data from "a plethora of data sources, including point-of-sale (POS) systems, in-store video feeds, and systems that track individual customer purchase and service histories."[85] As Joseph Turow has shown, "an entirely new layer of routine surveillance activities" has been added to the physical spaces of brick-and-mortar stores as part of the banal experience of shopping.[86]

Retail analytics have emerged as one of the "value-added services" being offered by companies such as Axis Communications, which supplies video surveillance equipment. Axis has a large customer base of retail companies and shopping malls, and untold thousands of the cameras mounted on city streets, parking garages, and corporate and industrial buildings and complexes are Axis cameras. In 2019, Axis, a subsidiary of Canon Inc., began marketing new services that would allow users of its equipment to repurpose their video surveillance systems for retail analytics. This move was part of its efforts to reconfigure its business model to one that generates recurring revenue from surveillance systems managed as a subscription-based cloud service. (As discussed in the Chapter 1, not everyone in the video surveillance profession is thrilled about this new business model, instead describing it with terms such as "hostage as a service.")

According to resources at the Axis website in 2022, video analytics applied to retail security video could afford retailers some basic insights. Useful data included the number of people coming into the store and the distributions of visitors over time; the probable gender and age of each individual; the movement of bodies through the space of the store (shown as "heat maps"); and the length of checkout queues, which was information that would help to manage staffing of registers. The way that Axis described its retail analytics offerings suggested that companies could use their in-store video surveillance systems to increase their profits:

> Your in-store cameras can be powerful tools for gathering and processing numeric data. It's a way to understand the behaviors and needs of your specific customers—they can be the key to unlocking the full potential of your business. . . .
>
> Stay ahead of the competition and improve your store performance by analyzing and acting on collected in-store data. Axis helps you respond quickly and proactively to the situation in your stores, giving you the tools to create a better retail experience with shorter lines, suitable background

music and more. Our technology operates on open standards, so you can combine it with third-party hardware and software to take your customer analysis even further. The Axis partner network provides a huge selection of leading edge solutions for making profitable use of the data gathered from your surveillance network."[87]

"Customer behavior data is all around you," the company's website noted. "With Axis you can turn it into profit."[88]

In addition to the big surveillance equipment suppliers like Axis, a host of startup companies entered the business of leveraging retail surveillance systems for analyzing shopping behavior. A 2014 publication dedicated to multilocation marketing described "five tools that retailers large and small can use to make more strategic operational decisions based on the data they gather from video surveillance cameras."[89] With "camera infrastructures they already have in place," businesses could use the Prism Skylabs platform "to turn customer interactions and movements into real-time data." Brickstream was another "behavior intelligence platform" that allowed businesses to analyze people's movements and activities in stores, using surveillance video feeds from store security cameras. Brickstream also sold special "stereoscopic" cameras designed for more nuanced visual analysis, including the ability "to separate adults from children . . . a key feature that differentiates the company from others in the industry." Brickstream's clients included retailers as well as banks, casinos, and airports. A company called ShopperTrak used information gleaned from store security footage to generate daily reports for its clients on "how many customers entered and exited their businesses, and how their sales conversions compare to others in the market." Cara, a platform developed by a company called IMRSV, turned store cameras into "intelligent sensors" that could extract customer information from images, working best "when cameras have a 'clear frontal view' of the audience's faces."

In-store surveillance systems have always been used for monitoring *workers* as much as surveilling customers. This new slate of technologies promised more effective ways of integrating labor management into retail analytics. A company called RetailNext, with clients that included American Apparel, Caché, and Ulta, designed its platform to integrate existing store video infrastructure with point-of-sale and staffing systems, which is "useful in determining new store layouts or potential staffing changes." Axis has also promoted uses for labor management: "By combining our hardware with video analytics, you'll find ways to reduce queuing times, perfect your store layout, allocate staff efficiently, and, ultimately, increase profits."[90]

Another application on the horizon for video AI was cashier-less shopping—automating the retail environment in a way that reduced labor costs and merged security and marketing in a seamless whole. Fusing together market research and store security was the aim of Amazon's experimentation with logistics and retail technologies along with its movement into brick-and-mortar stores. The company designed prototype stores complete with surveillance systems that would automatically identify people and charge their accounts for the goods they placed in their baskets, allowing them to skip the checkout lines and just walk out. Amazon branded this auto-charge system "Just Walk Out," which it was also planning to sell as a platform service to other businesses. Amazon envisioned stores outfitted with their auto-charge system as frictionless shopping experiences, with the added benefit of eliminating the possibility of shoplifting. Just Walk Out integrated inventory management, labor control, retail analytics, store design, and loss prevention. It represented the complete convergence of marketing and security.[91]

Other Big Tech companies have made their brick-and-mortar stores into securitized brandscapes using their video surveillance infrastructure, combined with their access to data about people's activities collected from both online and offline sources. At a visit to an Apple Store in San Diego in August 2021, I noticed a sign displayed on a table: "We collect your image while you are in the store for security and fraud prevention," along with a an image of a surveillance camera (see Figure 2.4). Given how accustomed we are to retail surveillance, it would be strange to object to Apple's "security and fraud prevention" efforts in their stores. But the sign indicated that Apple store security went beyond conventional video monitoring for theft prevention.

Again, the full extent of what Apple collects is unknown; the tech companies operate in complete secrecy in this regard. The Apple sign included small print with a mailing address and email contact "for more information." I sent an email request for more information and received an immediate auto-response promising that someone would get back to me soon. Months later, I received an email from Apple Privacy explaining

Figure 2.4. Inside an Apple Store in San Diego, California, August 2021. The sign suggests that people's images are being collected for the vague purpose of "security and fraud prevention," implying that the company uses the images to prevent shoplifting and to catch people trying to use false identities. Photo credit: Kelly Gates.

that "Apple retains footage for only a limited duration in line with data protection law and so it may be erased." The email also promised that "Apple does not use facial recognition technology in conjunction with our CCTV footage."[92] However, if we were to read their "privacy policies," we would learn that the companies take great liberties to collect and use our data, which we consent to by purchasing their devices and entering their retail spaces. Tech companies, of course, are also adept at normalizing increasingly invasive surveillance and data collection techniques by making incremental changes to their platforms and devices. The spaces where humans go to acquire food and other goods are also private properties, owned by companies that claim the right to do what they want with information gathered in those spaces. These companies claim expansive privacy rights for themselves, shielding them from having to disclose anything that they do with information they collect about people's identities and behavior.[93] It is impossible for the public, or even regular customers, to know what companies like Apple or Target do with the video generated by their surveillance systems. We are subtly encouraged to accept this extensive corporate surveillance of our lives as completely mundane, in our own best interests, even benevolent. Apple's simple signage functions as informed consent about what the company is doing; we are meant to read it and move on to play with the latest gadgets. But the sign is a black box that, when opened, might reveal uses of our data that some of us would not consent to. The point is that while we are perpetually open to their inspection, the tech companies have protected themselves from legal obligations to reveal the full extent of their uses of our data.

The analysis of behavior captured in retail security camera footage has become a domain of experimentation for training machine learning algorithms and building proprietary platforms that offer data analytics for platform subscribers. The aim is to leverage security video to create new value-added services for organizational users, and new sources of revenue and valuation for surveillance and platform companies.

Conclusion

As twenty-first-century corporations have expanded geographically and extended their reach horizontally and vertically, they have built proprietary video surveillance infrastructures that rival, and even far surpass in some cases, the surveillance systems operated by cities and police departments. This is especially true of corporations that have operations in locations distributed across the country and the world. These large-scale private video infrastructures should not be viewed simply as tools for vaguely defined virtues of safety and security. Instead, large-scale private video infrastructures, including those of major retail firms, have been central facets of corporate growth strategies. Such systems can be constantly adapted to the needs of firms to monitor, analyze, and configure spaces, times, movements, and behaviors. Pointing a lens at these infrastructures reveals the central role of the modern corporation in the shifting technological and political-economic landscape of policing and security in the twenty-first century. Video surveillance infrastructures in retail and other sectors are deeply integrated into both private security and public policing, and much of the video used in the criminal legal system comes from private video infrastructures. Video surveillance infrastructures are *logistical media systems* that provide avenues for integrating private security with public policing and merging security and loss prevention with retail analytics. They help to transform the spaces they cover into laboratories for experimentation on the bodies and behaviors of the people engaging in activities in those spaces, protecting and encouraging certain people and activities and preventing and punishing others.

This chapter has focused on the retail giant Target to better understand the role of the modern corporation in producing, managing, and making use of the avalanche of video in policing and security. Starting decades ago, Target built a massive video infrastructure as an integral part of its effort to create its securitized brandscape. This fact may seem unremarkable. Extensive video surveillance has become a form of "ambient television."[94] We barely bother to notice it—instead, accepting it as the normal business of safety and security. But video surveillance infrastructures are sources and sites for the analytic activities of firms and the police, and their continued significant growth suggests that both firms and the police are finding them well worth the effort and expense.

Equally important for understanding the integration of public policing and private security are the various ways that companies make private investments in the logistical systems of public policing. Target has referred to its investment in public policing as corporate "philanthropy." It includes providing seed money for surveillance equipment, consulting the police on video infrastructure development, as well as the formation of public-private partnerships with police departments branded with names like Target & BLUE, SafeZones, and Safe City. Target conceives of these so-called philanthropic initiatives as avenues for transferring security expertise to police departments and for enlisting local police and other actors to create environments that will attract people to Target stores with promises of safe and comfortable shopping experiences. No one wants unsafe or uncomfortable shopping experiences, but safe and comfortable *for whom* is the question that should follow, given that certain people's safety and comfort takes priority over, and comes at the expense of, others. It is important to recognize the self-serving and carcel logics embedded in Target's model of philanthropy-for-policing.

Target's private investment in policing has also included its private crime labs, which were established to conduct investigations of crimes against Target, specializing in video forensics. In the words of Target's vice president for assets protection, Target "created a forensic lab around video forensics, because we realized that virtually nobody out there outside of law enforcement has the ability to manipulate video data effectively."[95] Noting the enormous amount of video generated by Target's 75,000 cameras, this corporate executive was explicitly acknowledging the need for trained experts to make use of the video avalanche: "to get the most out of it, you have to have people who really know how to work with it."[96]

Target has made much noise about the pro bono work that its private crime labs have done for the police, promoting this work as public service and part of the company's philanthropic spirit. But this pro bono forensic work is not about corporate altruism. It would not reflect well on Target's reputation if the company was better equipped with state-of-the-art digital forensics than police departments but hoarded those resources for its own needs, which of course it largely does. Doing minimal pro bono forensic work for the police and promoting that work loudly is a matter of protecting Target's reputation. Sharing its advanced forensic capabilities with police investigators also helps the company foster relationships of reciprocity with police departments, giving it leverage to enlist the police in supporting its efforts to build and maintained the Target securitized brandscape.

Nothing demonstrates the laboratory-like uses of video surveillance systems better than their repurposing to analyze the activities of shoppers, which is a use that is entirely intertwined with uses for the prevention and prosecution of shoplifting. The continuous engineering of the securitized brandscape has spurred initiatives to repurpose video surveillance systems for retail analytics, giving surveillance equipment suppliers like Axis Communications avenues for reconfiguring their business models around video surveillance delivered as a service. Retail analytics, and market research broadly speaking, is not the innocuous affair it is often assumed to be, involving banal matters of identifying target markets, persuading people to visit stores, and nudging them to spend more money. What Shoshana Zuboff calls surveillance capitalism is the market research system of the social and mobile media age, where companies seek to know everything about human behavior and psychology, analyzing behavior in efforts to manipulate it at scale in service to corporate aims. It is characterized by an intensely intrusive efforts to know everything about people's activities, behaviors, and psychological profiles, with the aim of crafting messages and media experiences that tap into unconscious drives. This digital influence machine has also been weaponized for political purposes, including algorithmic tactics that push people toward extremist messaging and manipulating their sense of what is real.[97]

The analytic operations of market research make use of a great deal of data not derived from audiovisual media, including location and behavioral data extracted from cell phone apps, credit card transactions, Internet searches, and uses of social media. By focusing on video, I do not mean to diminish the importance of other forms of data or data analytics. Instead, I want to suggest that video plays a distinctive role in both police analytics and retail analytics, and in fact the interchangeable uses of video surveillance infrastructures are one place where we see the tightly interconnected relationship between the analysis of crime and the analysis of shopping, between public policing and private security, and between policing and profit-making. The next chapter examines another side of the relationship between the modern corporation and modern policing, focusing on the video avalanche and the wave of corporate influence in policing created by police adoption of body-worn cameras.

3

"Storage Costs Set to Skyrocket"

Camera-Mounted Cops and Police Migration to the Cloud

Introduction

A major wave in the video avalanche came along with police adoption of body cameras. As more and more police officers attached cameras to their chests and eyeglasses and pressed the buttons to record their activities, the devices began generating massive volumes of video to be managed in the legal system. Criminal legal systems were already flooded with video before body cameras, from video surveillance systems as well as dashboard cameras and bystander video. But the adoption of body cameras exponentially increased the amount of video that police officers themselves produced, escalating the cost of video storage as well as the related problems of video management, analysis, and the retrieval of relevant content.

Much of the debate about police body-worn cameras has been shaped by a combination of police reform thinking, police-administrative discourse, and the corporate messaging of companies selling body cameras. Public discussion has focused largely on whether the cameras increase police accountability, which is an unlikely outcome if police agencies control access to the video. The reality is that body cameras have had little to do with the legal or public accountability of the police. Instead, they have been sold to and adopted by police agencies as technologies for managing risk and the public perception of policing and, more questionably, as cost- and labor-saving technologies.

Like most media technologies today, police body cameras are not designed as stand-alone gadgets but instead as devices integrated into backend information technology (IT) networks. For many police officers, body cameras are now a part of their professional identities, just like the uniforms, badges, guns, tasers, handcuffs, and radios that they carry with them. But the wearable camera is not an isolated gadget or fashion accessory. Body cameras are "logistical media," adding new dimensions and form to the way policing activities are managed using media technologies. A police body camera is a node in a distributed network of other cameras, weapons, and bodies. On the backend, they require technology standards, protocols, and operating procedures. They are designed to be plugged into docking stations in police departments where their batteries get recharged and the video gets uploaded to video management software, where it can be manually tagged with information and cross-referenced with other records. As police agencies have adopted the cameras, the devices have embedded the cops who wear them into proprietary infrastructures developed by private companies.

To understand the significance of police body-worn cameras, it is necessary to examine their role in multifaceted dimensions of media-technological change, rather than narrowly focusing on police-administrative concerns or public accountability claims. This requires asking a key question underpinning the historical analysis of media technologies: *Why these technologies, and why now?* It is a question about both the specific forms technologies take and the conjuncture of historical forces that define and drive their institutionalization. To answer this question adequately, it is necessary to examine the role of companies, marketing campaigns, and business models in police body camera adoption.

Diverging from most existing studies of police body cameras, this chapter critically examines the role of corporate imaginaries and revenue models in the way body-camera systems are being envisioned and designed as technologies of policing. With a few exceptions, this is an understudied area in the research on body cameras and on police technologies broadly speaking. Many studies of policing note the increasing scale of *outsourcing* as an important development, but most assume that new police technologies are designed to serve preexisting law enforcement needs. Starting from this assumption fails to fully account for the more entangled relationships that are taking shape between tech companies and the police as police departments adopt new technologies. If the Big Tech companies have built their monopoly empires off the behavioral surplus of people's lives, as Shoshana Zuboff argues, then what happens when tech companies target the domain of law enforcement as a site for data and market capture?[1] A more developed answer to this question is needed to fully understand the expanding role of the modern corporation in twenty-first-century policing and police technoscience.

In 2015, *Computerworld* ran an article asserting that as police adopt body cameras, video storage costs were "set to skyrocket".[2] The article pointed to what I argue was a major pivot point in the evolution of police media infrastructures created by the avalanche of bodycam video. If body-worn camera systems became institutionalized in law enforcement, the result would mean that police departments would be producing massive volumes of video data. And if bodycam video was going to be integrated into police reporting rather than put in separate siloed systems, police adoption of body cameras was going to be a major impetus pushing entire police IT systems onto cloud-based platforms. It was an avenue for IT companies to capture the criminal legal bureaucracy and all the data representing its activities. In short, the *Computerworld* article was an early indicator that police body cameras portended a significant shift in the political economy of policing.

A 2016 U.S. Bureau of Justice Assistance (BJA) document was equally suggestive of this significant shift, offering police agencies "guidance for considering contracts with cloud vendors."[3] The BJA insisted that the cloud services were cost-effective, but in other instances, it made statements about costs that were less decisive. Noting that adoption of cloud services "can change agency funding models from capital expense outlays to operation annuals," the BJA qualified the cost savings claim: "While the cloud may not always result in large upfront savings, it can result in more cumulative cost efficiency over time."[4] Notice the word "can" rather than "will." Precisely how the BJA determined that there might be cumulative cost efficiency over time was not specified, and given that no such time had passed, any estimations would be purely speculative.

Studies of body cameras have repeated these same claims about the decreasing costs of cloud storage, which are essentially IT industry marketing claims. For example, in her discussion of data storage and retention issues associated with body cameras, Mary Fan first notes that video storage is one of the greatest expenses, "far exceeding the cost of the cameras themselves."[5] Then, after outlining some of the storage costs, she insists that these costs are likely to decrease drastically, citing her interviews with technology industry leaders. Any government agency, city, or municipality hoping not to hemorrhage money to IT companies would have been wise to exercise more caution regarding these industry-centric declarations about decreasing costs for data storage and other cloud services. Storage costs were set to skyrocket.

In this chapter, I argue that police adoption of body cameras created an avalanche of video that has done far more to entangle companies into the logistical systems of policing than it has to make police more publicly accountable. If body cameras promised to help police actors manage public perceptions of policing, as Bryce Newell has argued,[6] adopting the cameras dramatically intensified the extent to which *metaphorical* image management (managing public perceptions) required *literal* media management (the technical and perceptual work of processing images as well as audio recordings). For companies in the business of supplying police with video equipment and software, backend media management systems were much more promising avenues for realizing recurring revenues and financial growth models than body-worn cameras alone.

To make this argument, I first provide an abbreviated history of *police logistical mediatization*, by which I mean the design, deployment, and use of media technologies as instruments in the organizational activities and perceptual systems of law enforcement. Body cameras are not the first form of logistical media used in police operations, but they do add different dimensions to the *logistics of police perception*. I then discuss police interest in body cameras as image- and risk-management technologies, where "image" has both literal and metaphorical senses. An intensified "image management" crisis arose in policing as a result of the spread of cell phone cameras and video-sharing platforms. As police began to feel under siege by citizens with cell phones, a host of companies saw the situation as a business opportunity, promising police customers that body cameras would provide them with a means of gaining control over their "new visibility."[7]

The remainder of the chapter focuses on one of those companies, Taser International, a maker of stun guns, considering both its branding strategies and its business model. Building on its existing customer base of police departments using its branded version of conducted electrical weapons (CEWs), called tasers, Taser became a leading supplier of police body cameras in the United States. In 2017, Taser was remade as Axon

Enterprise, adopting the brand name of the company's body-worn cameras. To make this transition, the company engaged in a major campaign to remake its corporate identity, promoting Axon-branded cultural imaginaries about the future of policing. While corporate promotional messaging tends to be disregarded as unreliable and irrelevant to understanding how technologies work in practice, I argue that corporate imaginaries play an important role in bringing technological projects into being.[8] I then turn to the company's plans for revenue recognition, as described in its investor communications and other documents. Here we see that executives did not envision the company solely as a supplier of police body cameras. More importantly, they aspired to become a police *platform company*, establishing an essential intermediary role in police evidence and records management systems with a branded proprietary platform called the "Axon Network." While the company posits the Axon Network as a "technology solution" to the image management problems of policing, it is first and foremost a mechanism for its own revenue recognition. Axon, like other tech companies, aims to achieve market dominance as a police technology and service provider by building a durable infrastructure for recurring revenue—extracted from police budgets—and acquiring the data of police operations. Private companies like Axon are at the center of a reconfiguration of police media infrastructures; they are no longer simply selling weapons or other equipment to police but building the bureaucratic and logistical infrastructure of policing as proprietary systems. They are making a power grab for the entirety of police communications, recordkeeping, and evidentiary systems and envisioning ways to put police data to further profitable use. Before concluding, I discuss some of the obstacles to the police platform business model—obstacles that represent opportunities for intervention and resistance to the financialized inflation of policing and security.

Police Logistical Mediatization

An extensive history of policing's logistical use of mobile cameras has yet to be written. In *War and Cinema*, Paul Virilio examined how motion pictures intersected with twentieth-century warfighting to create a "logistics of military perception."[9] The logistics of *police* perception are related yet distinct, evolving in separate if overlapping domains, with different perceptual and technological trajectories. Attaching video devices to cops' bodies integrates their movements and activities into logistical systems in new ways, creating new human-technology configurations and divisions of labor. But the history of police experimentation with mobile cameras begins well before body cameras.

Police have a long history of using handheld still cameras as instruments of law enforcement—namely, for crime-scene photography and criminal identification.[10] Police have also made regular use of motion picture cameras, including film and then video cameras and camcorders, from the earliest introduction of these devices.[11] The New York Police Department (NYPD), for example, produced a trove of black-and-white, 16-millimeter silent films throughout the twentieth century as part of overt and covert surveillance operations.[12] In 2019, some of these short NYPD films produced between 1960 and 1980 were digitized and made accessible at the website of the New York City Municipal Archives, but this type of police-produced motion picture content had limited distribution at the time the films were produced.

Mobile video cameras were also integrated into policing by mounting devices inside police cars on their dashboards, facing forward to record what took place in front of the car. According to a 2004 report from the International Association of Chiefs of Police, dashcams were installed in police cars largely to document drunk driving incidents and roadside sobriety tests in response to the campaigns launched in 1980 by Mothers Against Drunk Driving (MADD), and "these records came to be viewed as the most effective method of providing the necessary evidence to support a conviction."[13] Criminalization of the problem of drunk driving persisted despite the distribution of state-licensed drinking establishments along roadways and the paucity of public transportation options in much of the United States. As logistical technologies of policing, dashcams literally mobilized the production of police video, taking it out of the hands of humans and giving sight to vehicles. But while the area directly in front of police cars was the site of a range of activities, including arrests, dashcams have a limited field of view and typically do not record the voices or other sounds of that activity.

The relationship between police logistical mediatization and police mobility begins before dashcams. In his genealogy of police patrol automation, Dean Wilson discusses the integration of wireless radio into police organizations along with new forms of police mobility.[14] In the United States, two-way wireless radios were installed in police cars in the 1930s and then carried by cops starting in the 1940s.[15] As Wilson explains, "the fusion of radio communications with automobility" was part of a broader drive to automate the police patrol function, largely in response to persistent criticisms of poorly managed policing.[16] As cars proliferated and more roads were built, policing started to play a bigger role in regulating people's mobility by licensing drivers and monitoring roadways. James Rule's account of the criminal records system in the United Kingdom around 1970 highlighted this relationship. "The police have a deep interest in vehicle and driver licensing, since much of their work has to do with traffic control and with crimes associated with the use of vehicles," he noted.[17] As roadways were laid across the United States, other scholars have shown, traffic stops became a major site of racial targeting and discriminatory policing.[18] Drawing on Anne Friedberg's work on windows as metaphorical framing devices in visual culture, Christina Aushana has examined the way the police car windshield itself functions as a mobile viewing technology, structuring the way cops screen situations and people on the streets.[19]

An adequate genealogy of police logistical mediatization must include the way camera crews and equipment were embedded with police officers for the production of police-themed reality TV shows, most famously *COPS* (1989–present). The production of these television shows mediatized policing in new ways, building on existing police media relations efforts by making some of the street-level work activities of policing consumable as entertainment media. Unlike most existing police-produced media, this content was recorded and edited by production companies and distributed on cable television networks. One key change that reality television brought about, as noted in a study of officers' perspectives on *COPS* published in the *American Journal of Police* in 1995, was "the increasing prominence of media personnel in previously taboo or 'back regions' of police work."[20] The study focused on "the Nashville episodes," contracted in 1989 and giving "full editorial control of the footage to be aired" to the Nashville chief of police and public relations officer.[21] Individual officers were given the choice to participate, and 31 chose to do so, each having veto power over any segment they did not want to be aired. According to one interviewee from the Nashville Police Department, "Anything we didn't want kept on tape had to be erased—that was the deal—and each officer could have erased whatever he wanted to have erased."[22]

Giving police of all employment levels the power to control their image was a condition embedded in reality television's form of mediatized policing. In turn, police-themed reality television helped to perpetuate the belief that street crime, especially drug-related crime, was a dramatic problem in need of stepped-up policing, prosecution, and incarceration. At the same time, police-themed reality TV suggested that the labor of policing could be leveraged and made into revenues, in this case in the form of advertising dollars from low-cost television production, with cops who are paid by the public purse replacing paid actors. Completely unpaid were the legions of unfortunate people having encounters with the police, who often ended up saddled with fines and legal fees while having their arrests recorded as entertainment for a viewing audience.[23]

Attaching cameras to cops' bodies to extend the logistical mediatization of policing required some minimal technical innovations in camera design. The cameras had to operate more or less "hands free" and have durable mounting devices. Battery life, storage capacity, noise filtering, and lens focal length and aperture were all aspects that influenced the design decisions of various developers. In addition, body cameras are almost by definition "viewfinderless" devices.[24] In this way, body cameras are detached from the wearer's visual perspective, although some of the cameras mount to eyeglass frames, more or less at eye level. But while the design features of body cameras have an important role in shaping what gets recorded, the rise of police body cameras and their integration into the logistics of police perception cannot be adequately understood as an outcome of technical developments in camera design.

Body Cameras and Image-Risk Management

Police have long engaged in battles for strategic control over public perceptions of crime and policing. Police scholars of all stripes have recognized that police legitimacy is tied to the performative and symbolic aspects of policing and managing the police image.[25] Image management, understood as a process of trying to shape public perceptions of policing, is inextricably tied to risk management. In the 1990s, the criminologists Richard Ericson and Kevin Haggerty argued that the entire institution of policing had become a system of risk communication, serving the risk management needs of other institutions, especially the insurance industry.[26] As we saw in Chapter 2, big retail companies like Target were interested in influencing the criminal legal system to address their own loss prevention priorities as well as public perceptions of their stores and store locations. Target developed its own legal-investigative apparatus and even exercised a form of governance through private "philanthropy" and the in-kind transfer of expertise to police departments. But if the police served the risk management needs of other institutions, police agencies also became relentlessly focused on their own risk management needs, which included controlling the police image.

While the combined image and risk management orientation of policing helps explain police interest in body cameras, it does not fully explain the *timing* of their widespread adoption. Given the relatively minor technical innovations required to produce the cameras, why did police departments not adopt body cameras much sooner? One answer is that policing's interwoven problems of image and risk management intensified with the spread of mobile phones equipped with video cameras and social media platforms equipped for sharing the videos.

The widespread use of video-enabled cell phones to record the police dramatically increased the visibility of police violence, suggesting a critical area of social need among those most often having encounters with cops. People were desperate to show perspectives that were different from those that circulated ad nauseam on *COPS* and across the entire police-themed television and crime news genres. Cell phone video combined with video-sharing social media platforms exposed the excessive use of police violence against people of color. At a rapid clip, many more people became cop watchers, video activists, and witnesses to police violence.

In the United States, the first shocking case of a bystander capturing a police killing on cell phone video was the murder of Oscar Grant by the Bay Area Rapid Transit (BART) Police in Oakland, California, on January 1, 2009. Bystander videos of the young man's execution-style shooting were aired on the news, but sharing this type of violent vernacular video on social media was not yet the common practice it would soon become. By the time Ramsey Orta recorded Eric Garner being strangled to death by an NYPD cop for selling loose cigarettes in July 2014, Facebook and Twitter were places where millions of people regularly accessed cell phone video content. The fact that there was no equivalent video of the shooting of Michael Brown in Ferguson, Missouri, a month later stood out in contrast, stepping up calls for more police body cameras, a demand emanating from a range of actors, including people from communities on the receiving end of brutal policing.

These conditions of intensified vernacular videos of police activities, and new avenues for sharing them online, suggested that a more level playing field of surveillance was taking shape. What criminologist Andrew Goldsmith called "policing's new visibility" was challenging the established ways that the police managed public perceptions of policing.[27] But while incidents of police brutality recorded on video got people's attention, the ability of vernacular video practices to level any playing field of power was overstated. The police were becoming proficient at using social media platforms for police media relations and image management.[28] And as Tyler Wall and Travis Linnemann have argued, the police have engaged in a "war on cameras," forcibly preventing people from recording video of police actions in order to control media representations of police activity.[29] In short, law enforcement actors were not going to succumb to their "new visibility" without a fight for control over perceptions of crime and policing.[30]

This type of image control was from the start one of the main selling points that the companies making body cameras promised their potential police customers. From the police perspective, body cameras would be useful only to the extent that the video could help reduce complaints against the police and give them more ammunition in the battle of interpretations about crime and policing. Not surprisingly, the police were less interested in their own accountability to the public than in the possibility of using bodycam video as evidence to support the police perspective, and especially if the video would help counter any charges of misconduct leveled against cops.[31]

Studies of police body cameras and other technologies often note the presence of private companies in the mix of relevant actors playing a role in police adoption of new technologies, but they rarely dig deeper to elucidate that role.[32] Rather than assuming that the role of companies supplying police technology is of only marginal or secondary importance, I want to turn the lens in their direction. Companies are endeavoring to embed their proprietary technologies and models for revenue recognition into the bureaucratic and logistical infrastructures of policing. To an extent that seems unprecedented, companies are deeply involved in new forms of police logistical mediatization, and this involvement has significant implications for the political economy of policing, not least of which is a more aggressive, designed-in orientation toward growth.

From Tasers to Body Cameras to Evidence.com

By the 2010s, the companies marketing body cameras to the police included COBAN, Mobile-Vision, WatchGuard, Wolfcom, Digital Ally, VieVu, and Taser. Some of these companies previously sold dashboard cameras. Mounting cameras to the bodies of cops would mobilize the perspective offered by dashcams and open up the possibility of including microphones and sound-recording capabilities that dashcams lacked based on their position inside police cars. If police decision-makers could be convinced of their cost-benefits, body cameras would expand companies' product offerings and sources of revenue.

The trajectory of Taser was unique relative to other companies because it had developed significant expertise in risk management, owing to the nature of its original product. Taser weapons had always been risky. These CEW devices were involved in countless complaints against both cops and the company, and their use had been blamed for an uncounted number of deaths. Disputes about the safety of CEWs prompted the company to invest considerable effort into risk management strategy. Taser challenged every claim that pointed to a Taser device or tasing as a cause of death. It also funded studies to support the safety of the devices and subjected some of its own employees, including executives, to painful taser shocks to prove that the product was safe. But the riskiness of the product from a legal perspective (in addition to its limited capacity for growing revenue) was probably among the reasons the company began exploring other types of products. It was clear from its filings with the Securities and Exchange Commission (SEC) that the company saw litigation and bad publicity from Taser devices as risk factors that could affect the company's earnings in sizable ways, as well as its stock price.

Taser began developing body cameras after first experimenting with attaching miniature cameras to its stun guns. These taser-mounted mini-cameras were designed to record the actual incidents when cops tased people. The idea was that video from the perspective of the taser weapon would resolve disputes about what happened (according to Taser's messaging, by absolving cops of wrongdoing). But Taser-mounted mini-cameras did not prove particularly effective; video generated from the mobile point of view of the weapon was unable to settle disputes. Nor was a Taser-mounted minicam as broadly useful for recording the activities of policing as body cameras promised to be. So, in 2009, Taser began beta-testing a product that it called the Axon body camera.[33]

One way that Taser conveyed the benefits of body cameras to police customers was by hosting events called "Taser Technology Summits." (After Taser became Axon, the events were rebranded "Axon Accelerate." I attended three of these events between 2014 and 2017, two at the company's headquarters in Scottsdale, Arizona, and one in Arlington, Virginia.) Speakers at these events included company executives as well as police chiefs from agencies that had adopted Axon body cameras. At the events and across their marketing materials, the company promoted the body cameras as having multiple benefits for the police. Among them was the message that police were under siege by people with cell phone cameras, and that body cameras would allow law enforcement agencies to regain control of the narratives about policing. A second, related theme was the cameras' capacity to function as risk management technologies by reducing use-of-force incidents and decreasing complaints against the police, thereby lowering costs from legal settlements. A third claim centered on the so-called labor-saving benefits of body cameras. Here, the initial idea was that bodycam video would replace the police report and relieve cops of their significant bureaucratic burdens.

Axon made many more claims about the benefits of body cameras. Most of these claimed benefits required another "technology solution" to help the police manage all the video produced by those cameras. In other words, body cameras would produce output, volumes of it, that would need to be managed, stored, labeled, and made available for future use. The solution that Taser/Axon offered for managing the bodycam video avalanche was *Evidence.com*, the brand name and landing page website for the company's proprietary web-based backend evidence management software. The general domain name underscored the system's source-agnosticism; the company envisioned Evidence.com not as a separate siloed system but a clearinghouse that would subsume all forms of evidence, across police agencies of all levels and jurisdictions.

It was also clear that the company saw Evidence.com as the main avenue for growing its business and expanding its role in policing. According to the company's messaging, Evidence.com would not only help police agencies manage volumes of video, it would also save them on computing infrastructure costs, including the costs of in-house data storage, cybersecurity, and personnel. Taser, more so than other companies selling body cameras, seemed quick to foresee backend evidence and records management as a lucrative avenue for growth.

Branding the Future of Policing

If *police* actors have focused on image management to influence public perceptions of policing, those efforts pale in comparison to the amount of investment corporations put into their own image management. Corporate branding and marketing have been major sites for the production of imaginaries about technology, and this form of cultural production is both underestimated and understudied. Since their emergence in the nineteenth century, modern corporations have poured immense resources and effort into branding campaigns that collectively reproduce the message of "technological solutionism."[34] And while these campaigns tend to be dismissed as unreliable evidence in social research, this vast terrain of cultural production has profoundly shaped modern thought and reality.

From its beginnings as a company selling less lethal weapons, Taser International invested considerable effort into building a unique and recognizable brand identity, far more so than any of its competitors. From my first introduction to the company, I was struck by its obsession with all things futuristic. Its over-the-top efforts to catapult itself forward in time seemed to go beyond branding. The company's brand of corporate police futurism was embraced as a kind of mission or philosophy. Everything about the company seemed oriented toward this aestheticized vision of the future of policing.

This futuristic corporate identity was even architecturally designed into the company headquarters in Scottsdale. Walking into Taser's headquarters was like entering a Universal Studios theme-park version of the set for Steven Spielberg's science-fiction noir film *Minority Report*.[35] Open stairways and catwalks crisscrossed the central space of the building, surrounded by three stories of cubicle office space visible on either side of the open floor plan. Sunlight filtered in through a wall of glass windows on the front of the building, covered with screens displaying giant, translucent images of uniformed police officers fully equipped with Taser devices. The giant figures were also visible from the outside, covering the façade (see Figure 3.1). A tour of the building during a "Taser Technology Summit" revealed that the space was also designed to house a wide variety of work activities, from product design to device assembly, software engineering, strategic planning, legal management

Figure 3.1. Axon Enterprise headquarters in Scottsdale, Arizona, June 2017. Photo credit: Kelly Gates.

of intellectual property and patents, and marketing and public relations. Rooms off the side of the open floor plan were secured with biometric eye-scanning devices, also part of the *Minority Report* mise-en-scène. Most of the doors were propped open during the event, making the biometric devices seem more theatrical than functional. A circular dark glass enclosure visible on the top floor of the building was Taser's secret design space, we were told by our tour guide; it was accessible only to the engineers and off-limits to both visitors and other Taser employees. The room hovered above the wide-open office spaces, obscured with one-way glass so that its occupants could see out but no one could see in. The space was referred to in-house as "the black box," suggesting that for everyone but the engineers, only the room's input and output mattered. The building was designed to make an impression.

The company's futuristic vision was fully on view in early 2017, when Taser launched a major promotional campaign to redefine the company under its new name, Axon Enterprise (see Figure 3.2). Axon was the brand name Taser had earlier given to its body-worn cameras, and Taser's reinvention as Axon Enterprise would mean downplaying its association with CEWs and creating a new corporate identity that was more aligned with the business models and tech-oriented mythos of Silicon Valley. The company was promising police customers an entire distributed infrastructure of networked cameras, bodies, weapons, vehicles, and backend data management and logistics—what it called the "Axon Network."

At the launch of the campaign, the company posted a promotional video on the main page of its website presenting its vision for the Axon Network and the role that this branded ecosystem of interconnected devices and software would play in the future of policing. It provided a snapshot *infrastructural view* of the network in action, so it is worth describing at some length. The video had the realist aesthetics of a television crime drama, with high production values, visual effects, and actors playing dramatic parts. The staged scenario used as proof-of-concept was a domestic violence call, with two cops responding to a violent scene playing out in front of a suburban house. As the officers get out of the police car and draw their weapons, their body cameras automatically begin recording. The bodycam video appears hovering around the officers' heads, simulating its live capture. We also see the

Figure 3.2. Inside Axon headquarters in Scottsdale, Arizona, June 2017. The company had just changed its name from Taser to Axon. Photo credit: Kelly Gates.

word "recording" displayed in red. The same footage appears in another location as the crime drama cuts to a command center, where a third man, seated at a desk, monitors the unfolding incident live on computer screens. These shots visualize the real-time operative use of bodycam video in the logistical management of the incident as it unfolds.

The officers intervene and arrest the violent offender, and afterward we see one of them interacting with the victim. He holds her ID in front of his eyes, where a minicamera affixed to his glasses is visually highlighted. We then see a simulation of her information automatically being scraped from her ID document. As she speaks, her spoken words are automatically transcribed below the video from the officer's body camera, which shows the woman from the officer's perspective. Then, we see the officer's bodycam video circulate through the legal system, appearing in different contexts, first at the desk of a "public information officer" who prepares segments for release to the press. She does some quick editing work at her computer, then sends the finished product off to the news media where we see the headline change from "More Police Brutality" to "Officers Rescue Family." Here, the police perspective afforded by the bodycam video is extended into the news media, correcting the record. Afterward, we observe a meeting with a public defender who presents the video evidence to the accused, who hangs his head in resignation. The implication is that the bodycam video enables the expeditious conviction of the guilty party, who presumably pleads out.

The promotional video cuts back to the two officers, now fixing someone's flat tire on the side of a road. A vertical drone shot shows their police car emitting "Axon signals" to the "Axon Network." The video then zooms all the way out to a satellite view, revealing a map of a city, with little yellow Axon logos scattered throughout the map, marking dispersed locations of police activity with the Axon brand. The map view zooms out even further to reveal the Northern hemisphere, with Axon logos visible across North America. The video ends with this visualization of a branded police media infrastructure that extends across the planet.

This imaginary projection of a police-media infrastructure is an example of what Bruno Latour calls a *panorama*: a place where the totality, or the "big picture" is staged in bird's-eye view.[36] Latour cautions that panoramas "shouldn't be taken too seriously," but "they also have to be studied very carefully because they provide the only occasion to see the 'whole story' as a whole."[37] The Axon video makes visible a scalar perspective of police-media infrastructure, an idealized "infrastructural view" that gives viewers a combined sense of both the "signal traffic" and "how [media] content moves through the world."[38] The editing and visual effects depict a smoothly functioning assemblage of humans and technologies. Visual effects are used to illustrate the signals emitting from police devices and vehicles, and the spatial distribution of networked police activity is represented by little yellow Axon logos. The distributed activities of the police merge with the Axon brand.

Practical problems for the police are cleverly embedded in the storyline of this panoramic projection. The domestic violence scenario was an intentional choice, as a special source of police frustration and prosecutorial difficulty.[39] Axon's storyline offered a gendered narrative of feminine victimization and masculine police heroics. In Axon's video production, careful diversity casting suggested a racially equitable distribution of heroes and villains. (A police officer and the public information officer are played by Black actors; the violent perpetrator and the victim are white.) This type of incident was often used to demonstrate the labor-saving benefits of body cameras, where video was touted as better suited to capturing the emotion of these incidents than officers' written descriptions. But it was the prosecutorial challenges of domestic violence that made it low-hanging fruit for positing the benefits of body cameras. Given the reluctance of victims to testify against their abusers, bodycam video promised to offer evidence that would successfully secure convictions and justify any use of force that may have occurred.

The more practical claim being made to Axon's primary audience of police customers centered on the labor-saving aspects of body cameras, bodycam video, and multiple forms of automation: optical character recognition, speech-to-text, and automated redaction. In combination, these technologies are shown to solve the enormous problems, for the police, of image management: both managing perceptions of policing as well as managing the video generated by all the cameras attached to the bodies of cops. The promotional video's domestic violence narrative is woven together with a promise that "AI technology" would allow officers to "focus on people not paperwork." As the officer stands face-to-face with the victim, Axon's technologies perform the reporting work automatically, so the officer's attention is freed up to perform care work for the victim. The message is that AI technology will make policing more bureaucratically efficient and, at the same time, more humane—ironically, more people-focused.

As their police customers would know intuitively, Axon's video provided an unreliable account of how these technologies would work in practice. Omitted from the text, for example, were all the new bureaucratic burdens and new forms of media work that body cameras and their backend systems introduced into policing. But imaginary visions like this one nonetheless do important, performative work in bringing technological projects into being. If this type of messaging tends to be dismissed as meaningless hype, the text reveals the way this company was staking claim to the future of policing, inserting its brands into panoramic visions of its own creation. In the modern fantasies projected by corporate marketing campaigns, technology creates efficiencies and saves labor, while providing widespread benefits to humanity. Omitted from these imaginaries is the main purpose of any technology that a firm puts to market—that is, to increase the firm's value. The claim that technology has the inherent capacity to save labor and provide other benefits for customers obfuscates the ways this platform would enable the company to extract value from police labor and from paying customers: cities and municipalities.

Corporations spend enormous sums on marketing and branding to define their corporate image and attach brand identities to their products and services—sums that would be hard to justify if this branding arsenal were ineffective or insignificant in achieving its purpose. Branding and marketing are material-semiotic practices that combine the physical and the symbolic to establish corporations and their brands in spatial arrangements, embodied activities, individual and collective consciousness.[40]

In addition to its promotional videos, Axon has employed branding tactics that physically integrate its brand into police work. When police departments adopt Axon body cameras, for example, the Axon brand is physically inserted into police activities. The Axon logo is molded into the black plastic design of the cameras and imprinted on the button in the middle that the user presses to begin recording. Embedding the triangle logo onto the cameras also attaches the Axon brand to the bodies of cops. In this way, Axon's body cameras are designed to blend into the fashion style of the police uniform and into the new media production practices of police work. Physically pressing the logo button activates the camera and, by extension, the connection to the Axon Network. In Axon's promotional video, the body cameras begin recording automatically, but that form of automation was not the default mode at the time (nor is it now). The police body camera is typically designed to delegate button-pressing to the person wearing it, again giving cops the designed-in capacity to determine what gets recorded and what does not.

A more significant material-semiotic maneuver in Axon's police branding efforts began with the 2017 camera models, when the camera software was modified to imprint the company's yellow triangle logo in the upper right corner of every frame along with the time-date stamp and camera ID number (see Figure 3.3). From then on, every video produced on an Axon camera was branded with the Axon logo. The logos imprinted on volumes of branded bodycam video align with the logos on Axon's imaginary map in its promotional video, marking dispersed locations of police activity scattered across the planet. The automatic imprinting of the logo onto the video could be interpreted as a proprietary claim on the video content. The imprinted logo declared the bodycam videos were the company's intellectual property. Yet it would be hard to imagine the company seeking payments from police, prosecutors, or defendants for using specific videos in legal cases. It is more conceivable that they might seek royalties from news organizations or documentary filmmakers. But the significance of imprinting the logo on police bodycam video is not limited to literal claims of ownership or the possibility that Axon will seek payments for subsequent uses of bodycam video content. Instead, the imprinted logo effectively embeds Axon's brand identity into all future uses of the video and all the activities that video content depicts.

The contemporary media ecology of policing now carries large volumes of video imprinted with the Axon brand. The company logo appears on bodycam video showing the killing of George Floyd as well as Tyre Nichols and many others. It is imprinted on the video of a man smashing the head of House Speaker Nancy Pelosi's husband with a

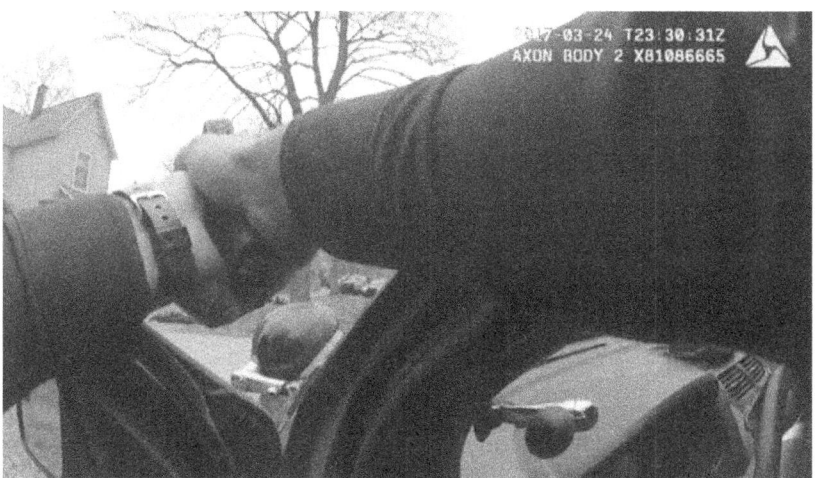

Figure 3.3. Screenshot of a police bodycam video, taken on March 24, 2017, displaying the Axon logo in the upper right corner and the common visual trope of a subjective shot, with a gun in the hand of outstretched arms. Photo credit: MLive on YouTube.[41] Reprinted under fair use.

hammer after breaking into their home, and on the voluminous bodycam videos of the U.S. Capitol riot on January 6, 2021, including video displayed on a giant screen inside the Capitol building during the televised congressional committee hearings. And it appears on videos of countless scenes of domestic violence—scenes that diverge radically from the idealized vision depicted in the company's promotional video.

Although Axon's pervasive logo-memes are barely noticed and never commented on when these branded videos are reused in a variety of forums, inserting brands into barely conscious awareness is one of the ways that capital abducts memory, as Goodman and Parisi have argued.[42] "Contemporary branding culture . . . sets out to distribute memory implants across technical media platforms" creating "a repetition of a memory that you haven't had," they write.[43] What is being capitalized through branding, they argue, "is the gap between short-term and long-term memory, between moments of attention" in media-saturated environments.[44] Imprinting the logo on bodycam video fuses the Axon brand with the logistics of police perception. The effectiveness of this fusion stems from the fact that we barely notice it.

A Police Platform Revenue Model

Of all the claims made about police body cameras, the labor-saving claims were the most suspect. The adoption of body cameras significantly increased the amount of video that cops produced in their daily work activities, and all this video would have to be labeled and otherwise managed in some way. In this sense, body cameras are much like other digital technologies and their persistent upgrades, which almost always come with more work and more expense, not less.[45] While the work activities and divisions of labor change, there is rarely if ever less work in an absolute sense. There is often much more work to do, including learning to use perpetually "upgraded" technologies. Obviously, certain human tasks do get automated, but the intention behind the design of automation technologies is to extract more value from labor rather than liberate workers from drudgery. "Firms and technological systems often redefine," rather than automate, "the human tasks they claim to replace."[46] From the IT industry perspective, any additional bureaucratic burdens that new technologies create are more opportunities for companies to sell new "technological solutions," what they euphemistically refer to as "value-added services."

For Taser/Axon, the value proposition of body cameras and their backend video management systems differed from the labor- and cost-saving promises made to police customers. Instead, from the supply side, the body cameras were something like what economic sociologists call *market devices*. What these scholars have in mind are not electronic gadgets but instead a range of physical and conceptual forms, "from analytical techniques to pricing models, from purchase settings to merchandising tools, from trading protocols to aggregate indicators."[47] But artifacts like cameras can also function as market devices, especially when sold not as stand-alone products but as component parts of subscription services, where purchasing and using them comes with a contract. Donald MacKenzie has argued that a financial model is an engine not a camera.[48] But cameras are themselves engines, mechanisms for producing models that drive reality as much as reflect it. And the engine-like agency of cameras has long been deeply entangled with markets. This market entanglement includes patents as well as selling the cameras as commodities and, of course, all the ways camera output gets commodified and rendered as intellectual property. It also includes the integration of cameras into more complex business models, like those pioneered by Eastman Kodak starting in the late nineteenth century.[49]

In Axon's vision, the body camera was, from the start, a market device, and camera sales alone would not be the source of the most significant revenues. This was apparent in early 2017, when Axon staged a promotional giveaway: a free camera for every police officer in the United States for a one-year free trial, "to commemorate" the company's name change. The camera giveaway was something like an experiment in using a product as loss leader, a common pricing strategy where the product is sold below cost to stimulate sales of more profitable goods and services. Some classic examples are Gillette razors and desktop printers. But the strategy is different when the aim is to enroll customers into contractual, subscription-based services that include software licenses and data storage.

A bar graph appearing in an Axon press release about quarterly earnings in August 2018 articulated the way the Axon body camera was being positioned as a market device.[50] As a two-dimensional representation of model for recurring revenue, the graph was also a market device, although a different sort than the body camera. It was titled "Officer Safety Plan," referring to a package deal of equipment and subscription software that the company had developed to sell to police customers. Officer safety was another selling point aimed to appeal to police customers, but the subheading was more clarifying of the company's intent. It read: "Revenue Recognition and Cash Flow per Officer." Axon's press release described the chart in these terms:

> The following chart illustrates the expected revenue recognition and cash flow per officer on a regularly priced standard Officer Safety Plan, which is our $109 per month plan that includes a TASER weapon, cartridges, an Axon body camera, camera hardware refreshes, and an Evidence.com seat license with data storage.[51]

The bar graph (see Figure 3.4) represented projected revenues that Axon hoped to derive from this "Officer Safety Plan," showing a cash flow model from a hypothetical rather than an actual customer over five sequential years. Each bar represented one year of cash flow (labeled

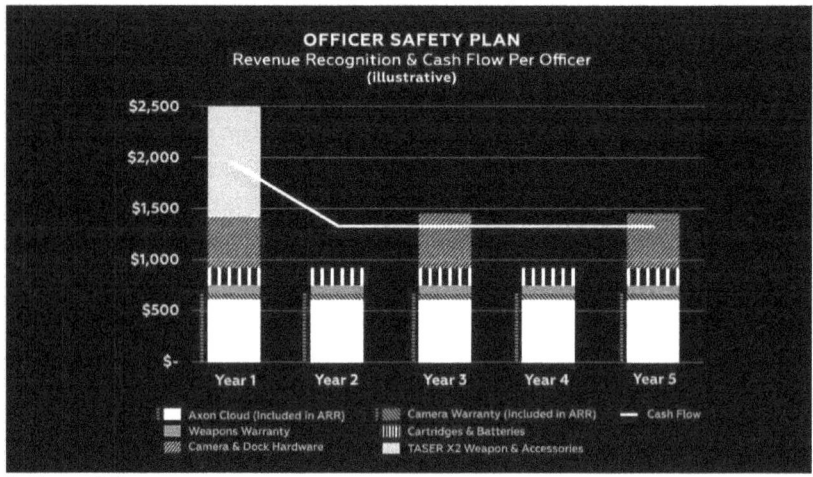

Figure 3.4. A bar graph from a press release, "Axon Reports Second Quarter Results," August 7, 2018. Source: Axon Enterprise (https://investor.axon.com). Reprinted under fair use.

year 1, year 2, and so on), with dollar increments from $0 to $2,500 per officer. Each bar was divided graphically by different sources of cash flow, too: Axon Cloud, Weapons Warranty, Camera and Dock Hardware, Camera Warranty, Cartridges and Batteries, and TASER X2 Weapon and Accessories. Year 1 had the tallest bar, with the bulk of its margin representing TASER X2 Weapon and Accessories, which would generate revenue the first year only. Camera and Dock Hardware would generate revenue in years 1, 3, and 5, with the margins in years 3 and 5 projected to come from "camera hardware refreshes." The solid portion at the base of each bar, representing Axon Cloud, stood out visually to emphasize the most consistent chunk of recurring revenue.

The body cameras were like iPhones—not profitable, stand-alone products but engines for driving revenues from their use as data-generating "edge devices." Their market capacity derived not from direct sale of cameras but from their integration into a package-deal of gadgets, software licenses, data storage, and access to that data in the cloud. It was the subscription package—and especially control of access to the data—that promised to provide the company with the projected "revenue recognition and cash flow per officer."

The point is not that the body cameras were unimportant or inert gadgets, but rather that, in Axon's actual business plans, they were not tools for police accountability, officer safety, or saving labor. The body cameras were data-collection sensor devices in a business model for building a *platform*, here referred to as Axon Cloud. As Nick Srnicek has succinctly defined them, platforms are digital infrastructures positioned as intermediaries between different user groups, becoming "the ground upon which their activities occur," thereby giving platform companies access to those activities and the ability to record and analyze them.[52] A second essential characteristic of digital platforms is that they "produce and are reliant on 'network effects': the more numerous the users who use a platform, the more valuable that platform becomes for everyone else."[53] Third, platforms have "a designed core architecture that governs the interaction possibilities."[54] Companies present their platforms as "empty spaces for others to interact on," but this elides the way "the rules of product and service development, as well as marketplace interactions, are set by the platform owner."[55]

What the Axon Cloud encompassed was apparent in the company's descriptions of four "strategic growth areas" in its 2017 SEC filing. These strategic growth areas included two that were most clarifying of its platform business model: "expand Axon body cameras and Evidence.com market share and increase revenue per user," and "expand into police agency records management systems and computer-aided dispatch software." Axon was expanding its platform by moving into police records management systems (RMS). The brand name Axon gave its proprietary RMS was Axon Records. The company also changed the brand name of Evidence.com to Axon Evidence, consistently branding the components of its platform.

Police RMS are complex bureaucratic systems that extend to a broader range of information about law enforcement activity than evidence management alone. "An RMS serves as a repository for linking many different data types, including crime and arrest records and information from computer-aided dispatch," according to criminologists James Willis, Christopher Kopper, and Cynthia Lum. "As such, it is the 'information heart' of any police agency's operations and essential to many of its work tasks."[56] Recordkeeping systems have long been the foundation of law enforcement's logistical operations.[57] In fact, modern law enforcement and modern recordkeeping systems have co-evolved, mutually facilitating one another's functioning and development over time. As Ericson and Haggerty found in their study of the administrative work of policing in the 1990s, much of the crime-related knowledge that the police produced was disseminated to other institutions, including "health, insurance, welfare, and educational agencies."[58] This dissemination occurred through the bureaucratic systems of these institutions.

If records management systems are the "information heart" of police agencies' operations, then it may be more accurate to define the work the police do as administrative knowledge work than street-level crime fighting. However, it is in the interests of companies like Axon to amplify the idea that the administrative work of policing is a burdensome distraction from the "real" work that police *should* be doing. Of course, police do in fact perceive this bureaucratic work as burdensome, especially given its tendency to expand continuously with the introduction of new technologies. As Ericson and Haggerty also observed, the introduction of new technologies into policing for the purposes of increasing efficiency would, in turn, produce "more data, which fuel demands for more experts, communication formats, and technologies to manage such data."[59] As studies like the one conducted by Willis, Koper, and Lum have shown, officers were spending *more* time on bureaucratic work after the transition from paper to software.[60] Their study of police RMS also showed that computerization pushed police reporting work into standardized formats that did not always fit the circumstances of the incidents being reported. Time-consuming data entry work left rank-and-file police workers with less time to write descriptive narratives, leading to shorter amounts of written text in the reports (frustrating detectives, who had come to rely on the lengthier descriptive prose).

In short, policing's "paper burden" has become more burdensome, not less, as it has morphed into a heavy workload of digital labor, which now includes the added work of managing the video avalanche from body-worn cameras. As Axon's competitor, Motorola Solutions, declared, "The definition of a police record is changing" to include "video, images, sensor data, audio recordings and more."[61] New technologies have created a "new reality" for police agencies that requires a "next-generation records management system."[62]

Axon, Motorola, and other companies are vying to capture the next-generation police RMS as a single, all-encompassing proprietary platform. Competition in this industry creates siloed systems with different police departments using different proprietary software products. The "network effects" of a single digital platform would mitigate the problem of information siloes and make police IT systems more interoperable across agencies. Migrating police IT systems to a digital platform also promises to defray the complex technical demands associated with managing IT systems, including cybersecurity, which only intensifies as IT systems grow in scale and number of users. The migration to the cloud created the possibility of greater integration of police records across jurisdictions. The profits could be enormous for any company able to achieve market dominance, as would the amount of influence it would have to shape the "information heart" of law enforcement logistics to its own strategic and logistical advantage.

If the police departments could avoid some operating costs by delegating IT expertise to a platform provider, those benefits would not come for free. The only "free labor" was the labor that police officers would be doing by producing the video and other data that would populate the platform. The cops who wear the cameras and produce the video would also be tasked with the time-consuming work of watching and labeling it. The work of producing and labeling the video was essential to Axon's development of "value-added services," the bread and butter for growing its "recurring cash flows." Of course, this digital labor would in fact be compensated—not by the company seeking to realize the revenues, but by cities and municipalities employing the police workers (i.e., from tax revenues). In fact, it is hard to see how any of Axon's so-called value-added services would avoid *increasing* labor and costs to police customers, given the company's always present strategic aim to "increase revenue per user." And when it comes to paying customers for police records management, there is no apparent source of revenue other than those extracted from police budgets (along with the sale of these systems to foreign governments). Like the lease revenue bonds that Ruth Wilson Gilmore identified as an important source for funding the devastating California prison-building boom, for public policing's IT systems, there is unlikely to be any "potential or actual nontax revenue at all."[63]

In short, body-worn cameras created more work for cops and more expense for police departments.[64] That led Axon to turn its attention to the next wave of labor- and cost-saving measures involving the use of AI technology, which Axon claimed would allow cops to "focus on people not paperwork" while giving law enforcement "complete analytics of their data."

Axon's Obstacles to Growth

Embedding a proprietary platform into police departments or the criminal legal system, broadly speaking, is no simple undertaking, and while imaginaries and business strategies are essential, the platformization of policing nonetheless hits up against many obstacles. Three obstacles I will discuss briefly are (1) competition from other companies and relatedly, antitrust actions; (2) downward pressure on public police budgets; and (3) the ability to recruit highly trained data scientists and engineers needed to develop the platform. These challenges to the success of aspiring police platform companies are also each in their own way avenues for pushing back against the overdevelopment of policing and the prosecutorial system that the growth models of platforms depend on.

The first obstacle is *other companies*, meaning all the competitors vying to build their own platforms and carve out their own domain of control and revenue recognition. A related problem, but one that has only minimal teeth in the U.S. regulatory context, is *antitrust law*, which aims to prevent anticompetitive practices that allow companies to achieve their aims of market dominance.

Without question, any company endeavoring to build a police platform would need to secure contracts with a majority of agencies, and certainly with the *largest* police departments. The three largest law enforcement agencies in the United States are the Chicago, Los Angeles, and New York Police Departments. The LAPD contracted with Axon to use its body cameras relatively early in the product life cycle, when Axon was still Taser. The Chicago Police rolled out Axon body cameras to over 7,000 officers in 2016.[65] However, the NYPD, with over 30,000 officers, was a different story. In 2016, one of Axon's competitors, a company called VieVu, won the NYPD contract for body cameras. VieVu's success in securing a contract with the NYPD was a big problem for Axon (still Taser at the time). Not only did Taser/Axon's share price take a hit, but so did its aspirations to become a platform company, one that by definition would need to dominate the market.

Given the playbook for platform building that the company adopted, it was perhaps not surprising when Axon announced in the spring of 2017 that it was acquiring VieVu from the Safariland Group (a police equipment supplier made up of more than 20 companies selling products like body armor, holsters, radios, and forensic testing products). By purchasing VieVu, Axon acquired the NYPD body-camera contract as well as VieVu's other customers, "hundreds of law enforcement agencies," including "the Miami-Dade Police Department, the Phoenix Police Department, the Oakland Police Department and the Aurora, CO Police Department."[66]

Axon's acquisition of VieVu caught the attention of the U.S. Federal Trade Commission (FTC). In January 2020, the FTC filed an administrative complaint against Axon, moving to block the merger of the two companies in an antitrust action.[67] Ironically, the likely reason that the deal triggered FTC intervention was because Axon was a not diversified enough company, making its acquisition of a competitor too obvious a move to monopolize a market. Motorola Solutions had acquired the body-camera company WatchGuard and the surveillance equipment company Avigilon without any FTC action. The way Axon had moved to acquire VieVu, right on the heels of the latter's successful bid for the NYPD contract, seemed like a clear and winnable case for an antitrust action. Axon responded by filing suit against the FTC, arguing that the FTC was a biased agency and that its suit against Axon was unconstitutional. In April 2023, the Supreme Court ruled in favor of Axon's standing to bring constitutional challenges against the FTC, in a ruling that has far-reaching implications for the status of the FTC's regulatory powers.[68] In October 2023, the FTC dismissed its action against Axon over the acquisition of VieVu, stating that Axon's constitutional challenges "will likely result in years of additional litigation."[69] Axon ultimately won this legal battle, in the process, possibly kneecapping the anti-trust regulatory capabilities of the FTC. The acquisition of VieVu was permitted, removing an obstacle to Axon's aim to build a police platform.

These kinds of business deals and legal battles receive little or no attention in studies of police body cameras and other technology adoption. The activities and business strategies of the companies developing these technologies and their backend data management platforms are seen to have little relevance to answering significant questions about policing. This omission implies that companies' own interests to be profitable, to grow and achieve market dominance, function in a way that directly serves the needs of their police customers. But the reality is that if platforms become established as intermediaries within the legal system, companies can use that embedded position to create pressures and incentives to push the budgets and material infrastructures of policing toward corporate growth strategies.

A second threat to corporate efforts at building proprietary, revenue-generating police platforms is *downward pressure on police budgets*. This pressure can come from many sources: a decrease in the fear of crime among those whose opinions on the issue matter; a sense among these enfranchised political constituencies that there are more important priorities; and a belief that there are better ways to address social problems associated with crime than policing, prosecution, and incarceration. Social problems like poverty, homelessness, addiction, mental illness, joblessness, and income inequality are all intertwined with legal categories of crime. A prosecutorial and carceral approach may in fact worsen these problems, not alleviate them.[70]

Companies that generate their revenues from police agencies need a persistent and expansive domain of crime and criminality in order to fulfill their growth imperatives. Like the police themselves, they have a vested interest in constructing the problem of crime in such a way that the answer is always more investment in policing. Paradoxically, even as new technologies and strategies of policing are proposed as solutions to the crime problem, crime as a field of activity must continue to grow in order to justify police budgets and expanded markets in police technologies. Calls to defund the police—to reduce police budgets and reinvest those resources into things like social programs, affordable housing and healthcare, and public education—are threats to the police platform business model.

For Axon, any potential avenues for the reduction of police department budgets would undermine the company's plans to "increase revenue per user"—in other words, their strategy to increase the price paid by police customers on a per-officer basis. In describing the "risk factors" to its business plan, Axon has pointed to "budgetary and political constraints that may delay or prevent sales," "political pressure that may dictate the manner in which they spend money," and "economic and budgetary issues" that could "worsen and adversely impact sales of our products."[71] Axon's list of risk factors has included any change in civil forfeiture laws, which "may affect our customers' ability to purchase our products."[72] Civil forfeiture is a long-standing practice where police seize property that they deem to be associated with criminal activity and keep the money or property, even in cases where the suspects are never charged with a crime. Nearly every time investigative journalists or legal researchers take a closer look at civil forfeiture, they find practices that are parasitic on vulnerable people and rife with abuse.[73] In response, policymakers have moved to impose limits on civil forfeiture, and those limits pose a threat to companies seeking to realize their growth models by extracting ever more revenue from police departments. For Axon as well as its competitors, it would be important that budgetary and political constraints, political pressure, and civil forfeiture laws *not* be successful at curbing the growth of police budgets.

A third obstacle to realizing the police platform business model concerns the *competition for the highly educated data scientists and engineers* needed to develop digital platforms. This obstacle is another form of competition with other companies. Shoshana Zuboff calls it "an arms race among tech companies for the 10,000 or so professionals on the planet who know how to wield the technologies of machine intelligence to coax knowledge from an otherwise cacophonous data continent."[74] I call this group of professionals "the AI vanguard," to capture the sense in which they seem to stand at the precipice of the future, armed with highly valued technical knowledge in data science and adjacent fields. They are indeed highly sought after, and their expertise in data science has proven highly commensurate with financialization and the growth imperatives of capitalism.

Axon seems keenly attuned to the question of what motivates tech workers to work. The company name change was an effort to transform its corporate identity, dissociating it from stun guns and aligning it with a much cooler breed of IT company. A corner of Axon's public-facing

Internet presence is devoted to the recruitment of tech workers. One of the recruitment landing pages reads "We're on a Mission to Protect Life" and shows a photo of four smiling young adults wearing Axon t-shirts and employee badges. The impression is one of a young, hip workforce, enjoying their jobs and having a sense of doing good work for the world. Another reads "The Future of Public Safety Needs Your Brain Power." It would be more accurate, if less effective, to replace the euphemistic term "public safety" with the company's name. Axon needs the "brain power" of well-trained experts in data science to build its platform capacities—that is, to "leverage the data [it] hosts" on its platform.

Conclusion

Economists have argued that a company's value comes from technological innovations that it introduces to the market.[75] Technology is viewed as having almost magical revenue-generating capacities, creating value in the form of benefits to users and profits to companies—a win-win for the twin objectives of solving problems and making money. According to this simplified view, technology itself creates efficiencies and labor-saving benefits while at the same time generating profit for firms and providing widespread benefits to humanity. The role of modern corporations in the production of this view—and their role in the production of cultural imaginaries, broadly speaking—is both underestimated and understudied. Along with economists, modern corporations are largely responsible for the widespread view that technology is both the main avenue for solving social problems and a source of economic value generation.

Despite bold claims about the value-added services that will flow from "leveraging the data" of police evidence and records management systems, the promised growth of Axon or any other company competing in this domain will not come from technology itself—neither the devices nor the cloud-based software. Instead, it will come from police departments, including the labor of police workers who would perform the work of generating data, as well as the cities and municipalities paying for proprietary software and infrastructure. In the platform business model, police departments pay for the privilege of giving away the data that cops generate in the course of doing police work. Platform companies in turn experiment with that data to develop ways of increasing the value of their platform services—not only the value to customers but also the value to companies and their shareholders. Ultimately, the wallets being charged for the privilege of this data giveaway are those of cities, municipalities, and the people who live there. Claims on the future of policing are being built in partnerships between businesses and governments. Yet, to be clear, these claims will be paid by workers and citizens.

4

"Our Machines Watch So You Don't Have To"

Video AI for Policing and Profit

Introduction

A 2015 *Computerworld* article (referenced in Chapter 3) correctly forecast that data storage costs were "set to skyrocket" along with police adoption of body cameras. Cloud service providers were poised to make significant profits by charging rents for video data storage.[1] However, it was not storage alone that would increase revenue for IT companies and escalate costs for police agencies; it was also the need for *analytic operations* to manage the stored and streaming video data. Analytic models that produced "actionable intelligence" from video and other data would be needed to further expand the functionality and realize the profitability of police video platforms. "If data collection is a key task of platforms," Nick Srnicek explains, "*analysis* is the necessary correlate."[2]

Two shorthand terms that I use interchangeably for the wide range of experiments in the computational treatment of video are *video analytics* and *video AI*. These technologies overlap with computer vision broadly speaking, although the latter term includes other technologies that address depth perception, including "Time of Flight (ToF), Stereo, Structured light and LiDAR."[3] Still, the effort to develop autonomous computer vision has depended to a significant extent on the medium of video as a substrate or terrain of experimentation. In overly anthropomorphic terms, if computers are learning to see, they are learning by watching videos. In this sense, they are not entirely different from humans of the twentieth and twenty-first centuries. But what the philosopher Hubert Dreyfus famously argued in his critique of "good old-fashioned AI" is still true of the latest developments in artificial intelligence: computers do not have the embodied perceptual capacities of humans because computers do not have human bodies.[4] Video AI and other computer vision technologies promise to extend the logistics of perception on a scale far greater than the individual human body, replacing the perceptual capacities of the many human bodies that would otherwise be needed. Here again, it must be noted that while vision is an important form of sensory perception, abstracting it from the other senses tends to degrade its capacities and usefulness. For this reason, as we will see in this chapter, video AI is concerned as much with processing sounds and recorded speech as it is with processing images.

Policing, and specifically police image and risk management, is an early site of experimentation with video AI. Policing is one of video AI's early use-cases, and video AI promises to extend and scale up the logistics of police perception. Critical data studies and anti-racist scholarship on policing have made strong critiques of the inevitable racial bias embedded in AI systems built on the "dirty data" of policing.[5] In this chapter, I contribute to these critiques but take a different direction, building on my argument in Chapter 3 about the expansive logics driving both the video avalanche and the methods being developed to manage it. I do not set out to make an exhaustive argument about the science or the deep design of AI. Nor do I argue that video AI is radical break from previous approaches to surveillance, rapidly transforming the practices of policing and security. Instead, I argue that the differences between AI and what came before are less significant than the new relationships being created between corporations and the police.

For the companies vying to capture police evidence and records management systems as their platform-building business strategy, the development of video AI is vital for multiple reasons. When addressing their police customers, these companies posit video AI as a cost-saving, labor-saving, value-added service of the platform. They promise that their platforms will be designed to create efficiencies and improvements in law enforcement operations, especially for the new workloads created by exploding volumes of video. But the relationship between police labor and automation is more complex and reciprocal. In its policing applications, video AI is *built on* police media work as much as it promises to replace it. At the same time, platform companies need automated video analytics to increase the value of their platforms and their embedded role in policing, especially since there is far too much video to be useful without it. In this sense, video AI is like the body camera—it is as much a market device as it is a technology of police logistics. For this reason, companies developing the *infrastructure* of video AI are also hard at work creating an *imaginary* of video AI, insisting that it has immediate practical uses as well as more expansive future possibilities. Embedded in both objectives are the fused priorities of policing and profit-making.

To unpack the role of video AI in the evolving relationship between tech companies and policing, I begin by discussing the infrastructure and imaginary of AI in general. It is important to recognize that both AI and video AI are technological projects and works of cultural production, with many of their uses considered promissory and speculative. Video AI has wide-ranging possibilities that are always yet to be fully realized. For companies and their investors, the promise of video AI is likewise speculative since the promise lies in its potential future profitability, a speculative future that is traded on in the present as shareholder value. Like the mechanism of the shareholder corporation, its function is to generate value in the present by extracting it from the future.[6] I then discuss the video AI initiatives of two of the Big Tech platform companies, Google and Amazon. These companies have made video analytics a major focus of their infrastructural, scale-building missions. The tech giants made advances in image search through their internal research and development as well as by funding academic research (influencing the kind of work that gets done at universities) and acquiring other companies and patents, expanding their portfolios and neutralizing any external threats that might come from "disruptive innovation." In turn, the strategy is to make video AI available as application programming interfaces (APIs) to platform users. One obvious application of video AI is automated facial recognition. This technology has extremely problematic uses and implications, but the tech industry nonetheless has been incrementally experimenting with it and making it available on larger scales. Our biometric future is being gradually realized, thanks to the relentless pursuit of computational advancements, securitization, and financial growth, no matter what the social cost.

If the Big Tech companies have played the dominant role in ushering in the current "AI era," there are other actors playing their parts. After discussing Google and Amazon, I recount the story of a small computer vision startup company called Dextro, which is revealing for multiple reasons. First, it shows how machine learning experts aiming to build general-purpose computer vision immediately turned to the potentially lucrative use-case of policing and security. In addition, Dextro was acquired by Axon Enterprise in 2017 to form "Axon AI," an in-house team of computer vision experts that Axon needed to develop video analytics. Only by pursuing video analytics would Axon be able to realize its platform aspirations, and only by joining a company like Axon would the Dextro team be able to make more significant advances in computer vision technology. I then examine in more depth what video AI promises to do for law enforcement—namely, to analyze video *in its totality*, fulfilling the promises that previous technologies failed to deliver and solving the problems that the video avalanche has created. But I argue that we should be skeptical of claims about the totalizing analytical capacities of machine learning algorithms. Before concluding, I briefly discuss generative video AI and the threat of "deepfakes" to bring on another wave of misinformation and epistemic chaos, courtesy of the tech industry, all in the name of "user engagement."

AI as Infrastructure and Imaginary

Like other large-scale technological projects, AI and video AI are simultaneously infrastructures and imaginaries. Video AI requires the physical construction of interconnected devices and technical systems, along with material processes of datafication. But it also requires more symbolic panoramas—imaginary projections that simplify its complexities and carry mythological promise. On the infrastructure side, there are "material resources, human labor, and data" that can be anatomically mapped.[7] On the imaginary side, there are all the beliefs about what it can achieve, including the uber-myth that AI is a singular, superior lifeform coming into existence.

AI imaginaries are constructed in corporate marketing and branding discourse as well as in popular media and press coverage. In one noteworthy example, a 2016 article in the *New York Times Magazine* recounted the Google Brain team's yearlong effort to improve Google Translate using machine learning, referring to it as "the great AI awakening."[8] The story of Google Translate resonated and radiated beyond the rarefied world of Google headquarters, breathing new life into the imagined possibilities of AI, including its wild profit-making potential.

AI emerged as the new Internet, the new social media, the new Big Data, the new game-changing technology that has no historical precedents, even the so-called last technology humans will ever invent.[9]

The entangled imaginary-infrastructural ontology of AI was crystalized in a pithy statement made in 2017 by Andrew Ng, cofounder of Google Brain and former vice president and chief scientist at Baidu. Speaking to CEOs assembled at the annual EmTech event hosted by *MIT Technology Review*, Ng scribbled the words on a whiteboard then proclaimed: "AI is the new electricity." This declaration brought to mind what the media theorist Marshall McLuhan said about electricity—namely, it is a medium without content, and for that reason has gone unnoticed in its pervasive, profound effects on the pace, scale, and pattern of human affairs.[10] McLuhan used the example of electricity to argue that "the medium is the message," meaning that by focusing on media content, media effects research was missing the more consequential impact of media technologies. Far more revolutionary than the content of any specific printed book or pamphlet, for example, was the massive output of printed material that flowed from the technology of the printing press. As McLuhan argued, among the direct effects of the printing press was mass literacy and the rise of nation-states. He saw electric light as having equally immense and direct consequences on the scale and form of human association and action.

Although Ng did not elaborate much on his comparison between AI and electricity, in some ways it made sense. Like algorithms and computation, electricity operates largely at a subvisual level.[11] And like computational infrastructures, electrical grids are controlled by large corporations in the United States and many other countries. But the analogy was also obfuscating and smacked of inevitablism,[12] suggesting as a foregone conclusion the diffusion of technology designed by and in the interests of the tech industry. For one thing, electrical companies typically operate under more government regulation than do the Big Tech companies, which instead have turned the law to their extreme advantage, as the legal scholar Julie Cohen has shown.[13] If AI is the new electricity, it is also a buzzword for the brute-force computing power that Big Tech companies built to amass their monopolies and lay claim to the world's information and knowledge-production infrastructure. And while, like electricity, AI may have wide-ranging applications, it is a powerful misconception to believe that AI is a medium without content. The content of AI is data, and much of the content of that data is human activity.

According to Michael I. Jordan, professor of electrical engineering and computer sciences at Berkeley, AI "is the mantra of the current era."[14] It has become a catchall acronym for a long list of research and systems-building areas, including, to borrow Jordan's list, "document retrieval, text classification, fraud detection, recommendation systems, personalized search, social network analysis, planning, diagnostics and A/B testing."[15] As Jordan and others insist, what people began referring to as "AI" in the 2010s was actually the branch of computer science known as machine learning (ML). This explanation of AI as ML has become obligatory, as if it clears up any confusion about what AI is. There is also the specific branch of machine learning called "deep learning," which uses computationally demanding "convolutional neural networks" to "provide a more scalable approach to image classification and object recognition tasks."[16] A computer scientist friend of mine explained that a key moment in the development of AI came when "they figured out how to make backpropagation work in deep learning networks." I understood what he meant, but not *deeply*.

It is easy to get the impression and to begin to believe that what is being referred to as AI is the achievement of "the quest" to create artificial intelligence and that we have seen the beginnings of computer systems performing mental operations. Maybe so. But it is probably more accurate to understand AI today as brute-force computing power. It is what massive amounts of data and computing infrastructure and much faster processors have made possible in the form of trial-and-error automated connection-making, along with some theoretical insights and developments in the machine learning branch of computer science. It is also more accurate to understand AI as a technology that promises to scale up the analysis and control of human behavior—a way of reaching back to past activity in the effort to predict, influence, or forcibly control the way people perceive and act in the present. If a great AI awakening was taking place in 2016, what this meant was that, as Katherine Hayles put it, "the pockets within which technical systems operate autonomously" were "growing larger and more numerous."[17] New forms of computational automation were being integrated into "virtually all complex technical systems."[18] How and why this was happening is made more opaque by references to cosmic "big bangs" and techno-spiritual "awakenings."[19]

The term "video AI" comes from Google. In the early 2000s, the Big Tech companies made image search capabilities part of their platform business strategies, starting with billions of still images that flooded photo services like Flickr. Notably, Google's acquisition of YouTube in 2006 moved it decisively into the business of video asset management. It took another decade for Google to launch its video intelligence API in 2017, which was described as "a new machine learning API for automatically recognizing objects in videos and making them searchable."[20] Product descriptions on the Google Cloud Platform boasted that "you can now search every moment of every video file in your catalog and find every occurrence as well as its significance."[21] The "you" did not refer to everyone; rather, it referred to users of Google Cloud Platform services, and "your [video] catalogs" would have to be housed in Google Cloud Storage to be searchable.

Like Google, Amazon and other tech companies moved everyone onto their expanding, proprietary computer infrastructures ("the cloud"). In the process, they gained access to unfathomable quantities of data and needed to develop the capacity to manage it for their own platform development. These companies pursued experiments in machine learning to address their own data management needs (like search for Google and logistics for Amazon). Then, once their ML systems worked sufficiently well, they made them available as APIs to other companies and developers. (APIs are software components that serve as "reusable building blocks that allow modular pieces of functionality to be incorporated into end-user applications."[22]) Google's chief scientist of AI and machine learning at Google Cloud, Fei-Fei Li, noted that the company's "Vision API is another example of this."[23] Li explained who and what the Google Vision API was designed for:

> This API is *for large media organizations and consumer technology companies* who want to build their media catalogs or find easy ways to manage crowd-sourced content, and for partners like Cantemo to build it into their own video management software. . . . These APIs let customers build the next generation of applications that can see, hear and understand unstructured data—greatly expanding the use cases for machine learning

for everything from next-product recommendations, to medical-image analysis, to fraud detection and beyond.[24]

Google Vision API would allow "large media organizations and consumer technology companies," as well as video management software companies, to build more automation into processing the video avalanche. Built with Google "Cloud Video Intelligence," those applications would ostensibly see, hear, and understand unstructured video data, thereby expanding the use-cases for its Vision API.

In her explanation of Google Vision API, Fei-Fei Li specified several carefully selected applications: next-product recommendations, medical-image analysis, fraud detection, and "beyond." Medical-image analysis was a common example used to promote the benefits of computer vision. The promise was that AI would be better at visual diagnostics than radiologists and other trained medical professionals, and much has been made of a selection of studies that have produced these results. Regarding the far less mission-critical application of "next-product recommendations," Li did not specify exactly how Google Vision API would be useful. We can speculate that both this application and those in the "beyond" category pointed to the potential for analyzing video datasets to find content relevant to user interests and to gain insights about and predict human behavior. The mass quantities of live and recorded video flowing onto the cloud carried with them a vast "behavioral surplus," which is Shoshana Zuboff's term for voluminous traces of behavior in the data trails that humans leave in the wake of their life activities.[25] In Zuboff's analysis, behavioral surplus is the main source of value for surveillance capitalism. Excavating behavioral surplus from live and recorded video is a kind of holy grail for companies in the surveillance business, and it will only be made possible with the development of video AI.

Among the specific applications that Li mentioned, the one most obviously associated with policing and security was *fraud detection*. Presumably, video AI for fraud detection would mean extracting faces and other identifying features from people captured on video and matching that information against data from other sources to determine people's identities and prior activities. In other words, the application of Google's Vision API for fraud detection would likely mean applying it for automated facial recognition. So much for the company's earlier decision "not to offer general-purpose facial recognition APIs before working through important technology and policy questions."[26]

Facial Recognition Technology (Will Never Go Away)

The potential use of Google Vision API for fraud detection had far more practical appeal than the lofty imaginaries of AI as "the new electricity." Yet these appeals to practical uses of machine learning technology also shape our perceptions of it, defining it as necessary and reassuring. For most of us, *fraud* seems far more threatening than fraud *detection*. Fraud is threatening in a very democratic way—*everyone* is a potential victim of fraud, especially given the major data breaches that occur regularly. Fraud is also a problem for all kinds of enterprises, from small businesses to major corporations. But terms like "fraud detection" are simplifying abstractions as much as they are practical use-cases. They are terms that stand in for the significant complexity and secretive data-analytic operations of tech companies. Recall the signage that I mentioned in Chapter 2 from the Apple Store: "We collect your image while you are in the store for security and fraud prevention" (see Figure 2.4). As I have argued, security and retail analytics have become two parts of the same project, as retail firms and video surveillance companies envision new uses for video infrastructures. Surveillance companies are promoting interchangeable uses of the same video infrastructures for both security and market research, striving for ever-more automatic, pervasive, and intensive analysis of behaviors in stores and other spaces.

Simplifying abstractions like fraud detection belie these more encompassing and interchangeable uses of surveillance systems. They also belie what Simone Browne calls the "prototypical whiteness" embedded in the research and development of facial recognition technology.[27] Browne has examined the close alignment between the history of biometrics and the commodification of Blackness. Surveillance capitalism promotes itself as racially neutral, even at times anti-racist, but surveillance has long been deeply racialized. Nicholas Mirzoeff argues that "racial surveillance capitalism" begins with settler colonialism and continues today, and it now relies on automated machine vision, where racialized "intelligence" "is formulated into facial recognition."[28] Appeals to practical needs like fraud detection conveniently elide the alarms raised by facial recognition technology and the inescapable ways that automated surveillance encodes and proliferates racialized forms of sorting out people.

In my earlier book, *Our Biometric Future*, I argued that claims about the inevitability of facial recognition technology and its ever-increasing accuracy were essential to pushing its development, which was far from inevitable. And while there were efforts to *invent the accuracy* of the technology by testing it in constrained experiments, developers knew that the path to improving the technology would require using real-life settings as laboratories.[29] I recounted an early experiment at integrating facial recognition technology with a closed-circuit television system in the historic neighborhood of Ybor City in Tampa, Florida. The project, a collaboration between the Tampa Police Department and a company called Visionics, got started in June 2001, with the aim of identifying criminal suspects on the streets of Ybor City and creating a safer public image for the struggling tourist destination. Visionics made the technology available for free to the police, acknowledging its experimental stage of development. The project was quietly shut down two years after it began, without having successfully identified anyone, but there were plenty of lessons learned from the failed experiment. For one, people needed to be habituated to performing tasks that would help build the datasets, algorithms, and software programs, including the essential digital labor of tagging faces in images.

This was also before the heady days of digital platforms, cloud computing, and AI. Since I wrote *Our Biometric Future*, the expansive data infrastructure projects of Big Tech companies have fueled advances in automated facial recognition—again, for both their own analytic needs and, in turn, the development of products (APIs) that they offer to other businesses and institutional users of their platforms. As the world migrated onto their cloud computing infrastructure, these companies had access to massively growing volumes of data from both the online and physical worlds, including enormous video datasets on which to conduct machine learning experiments. Despite widespread concern about the implications of ubiquitous automated identification, Big Tech went ahead with integrating "vision APIs" with facial recognition capability into their platforms, significantly scaling up its uses and enabling its diffusion across their expansive online infrastructures, which were increasingly integrated into every domain of social life.

Most brazenly, in November 2016, Amazon launched a cloud-based image and video analysis service through the Amazon Web Services (AWS) platform, with the not very clever brand name "Rekognition." AWS billed Rekognition as having broad applications, including in marketing and manufacturing. The company also promoted Rekognition to police agencies, touting its facial recognition capabilities. One of the "Featured Rekognition Customers" at the AWS Rekognition website was the City of Orlando, which declared itself

> excited to work with Amazon to pilot the latest in public safety software through a unique, first-of-its-kind public-private partnership. Through the pilot, Orlando will utilize Amazon's Rekognition Video and Amazon Kinesis Video Streams technology in a way that will use existing City resources to provide real-time detection and notification of persons-of-interest, further increasing public safety, and operational efficiency opportunities for the City of Orlando and other cities across the nation.[30]

While it seems only slightly strange to find the City of Orlando looking to Amazon for "operational efficiency opportunities," what was more shocking was how easy it was for Amazon to make a large-scale facial recognition system with enormous capabilities available to the police. The launch of Rekognition and its use by law enforcement rightfully generated outcry among the privacy policy community and other actors concerned about the power that Amazon could bestow on the police. The American Civil Liberties Union (ACLU), along with a cadre of other opponents, including a group of Amazon tech workers, sent letters to Jeff Bezos demanding that Amazon not make Rekognition available to the police or governments.

Notable again is the assumption that the decision-making authority over police uses of surveillance technology lies with a corporation. Like its weaker retail competitor Target Corp., Amazon can exercise a form of governance over policing, in this case through its control over the design and uses of the features of its cloud platform. The ACLU requested information from the City of Orlando and Washington County in Oregon, where the sheriff's office had also begun using Rekognition. The

ACLU wanted to see evidence of whether "their communities had been provided an opportunity to discuss the service before its acquisition."[31] They also requested information about the "rules governing how the powerful surveillance system could be used and ensuring rights would be protected."[32] Neither locality had anything to provide.

The call for Amazon to restrict police and government uses of Rekognition also failed to acknowledge the indistinct boundary between companies and government agencies. Tech companies have become tightly entangled with both police departments and federal security agencies, making it virtually impossible to parse the technology's users along these lines. The demand that Amazon make Rekognition available only to other companies also suggested that those companies were somehow more trustworthy users and that they should be free to use facial recognition technology according to their needs. Given the extent to which corporations have built private security capacities and established close ties with the police, as we saw in Chapter 2, allowing companies to use Rekognition while preventing its use by police departments was neither meaningful nor effective as a way of limiting the use of facial recognition technology. As long as the tech industry operates with legal carte blanche, facial recognition technology will never go away, nor will there be any way to prevent its use as a technology of discrimination.

Since the development of video AI requires large-scale video datasets, it is tempting to focus solely on Big Tech efforts to create and implement marketable applications for the technology. However, concentrating on Big Tech alone misses other slices of the story relevant to understanding video AI and the important role that the use-case of policing plays in its development.

A Computer Vision Startup

The story of Dextro, a computer vision startup, is one place where we see the central role that the logistical mediatization of policing and security plays in the development of video analytics. This is a story about how a group of young, well-trained entrepreneurial machine learning experts envisioned the usefulness of video AI and how their broad vision for the technology depended on the avalanche of video produced in the domain of policing and security. According to a 2015 article in *Wired*,

Dextro cofounder David Luan came up with the idea for the company after landing a coveted Thiel Fellowship and leaving Yale.[33] (Recipients of the Thiel Fellowship are encouraged to drop out of college to start new companies. Luan later returned to Yale and finished his degree.) With $1.56 million in seed funding from a group of early investors (including Yale, Two Sigma Ventures, and KBS+), Luan and his partner Sanchit Arora launched Dextro in 2013, setting up shop in New York City and building a team of people with training in computer vision, AI, robotics, and economics. Members of the team had degrees from prestigious universities like MIT, Columbia, Penn, and Dartmouth and professional experience with other startups as well as Big Tech companies like Google, Microsoft, and IBM.

Dextro sought to distinguish its video asset management software by training machine learning algorithms on videos in their full chaotic complexity. This approach differed from prevailing methods of object recognition based on single-subject images or methods that chopped video into frames.[34] Dextro was building its software with *deep learning*, a branch of machine learning that uses multilayered artificial neural networks.[35] Other computer vision startups at the time, such as Curalate and Clarifai, were reportedly using deep learning in more constrained ways to train algorithms "to recognize objects photographed in front of a nice plain background."[36] Dextro was training its algorithms on video as it appeared "in the wild." "Our machines watch so you don't have to," Dextro's website proclaimed.

In May 2015, Dextro launched a product called Stream that used deep learning to sort livestreaming videos into thematic categories. Stream analyzed the audiovisual content of video (the "essence") instead of only searching tags or other metadata attached to video. Stream promised to sort large quantities of livestreaming content so that users could better find material relevant to their needs. The amount of live video streaming online was exploding at the time, thanks to the launch of the Periscope app in 2015 (acquired by Twitter) and Facebook Live in 2016.

A few months after launching Stream, Dextro started promoting a new product that it called "a powerful system that rapidly understands the totality of your video."[37] The company's description of the product explained some of the challenges of algorithmically analyzing video, given that video is, by definition, not solely a visual medium: "Dextro's

Sight Sound and Motion (SSM) platform uses deep learning systems to analyze and categorize video based on its fundamental sensory components: what's visually present (sight), what's heard (sound), and what's happening across time (motion)."[38]

The use of video as a container technology for sound and motion, in addition to sight and images, makes it an extremely challenging and data-intensive medium for computational analysis. The newer version of Dextro's deep learning video analytics system processed sound as well as images as a means of sorting video content, with an eye toward building machine learning algorithms that would be more attuned to all of video's affordances as a medium. The audio component targeted not just words but "major audio topics" and nonverbal auditory cues that would help make better sense of the content. And rather than analyzing videos as a series of still frames, Dextro was also training its algorithms to analyze movement, tracking changes in multiple frames in sequence.

The big promise that Dextro made to potential customers was that its new SSM platform "parses through junk to establish a subset of the best video available."[39] SSM would sort content and identify the material of most relevance to users, "blocking out noise" and "scaling the capacity of editorial and curation teams." It would not just search for objects or faces in rote fashion; instead, it would analyze holistically, understand what users were looking for, and identify what was meaningful and relevant. To be clear, Dextro was not describing what the technology was fully capable of, only what Dextro's team promised. At the very least, the technology would require more development, on more video datasets, before it could deliver.

Importantly, Dextro sought to avoid "focusing on a narrow set of technologies or use cases," instead envisioning and aiming to design a more general-purpose platform for video analytics.[40] Luan was convinced that machine learning video analytics would "ultimately be a winner-take-all space," so the company that captured the most content would end up having the best models.[41] Luan wanted Dextro to be that company: "We want to power all the cameras and visual datasets out there," he said.[42]

But if Luan and the team at Dextro envisioned their system as a general-purpose computer vision platform, they clearly saw the need to put forward specific use-cases as proof-of-concept. Those use-cases represented the needs of potential paying customers—namely, organizations with large-scale video management needs. That included companies with an interest in analyzing and influencing human behaviors (e.g., marketing users) as well as companies and government agencies in the business of policing and security.

One of the companies in the latter category was of course Axon. In its efforts to transform itself into a police platform company, Axon needed both the technology and talent to be able to offer more effective ways of managing large volumes of video data. As discussed in Chapter 3, at the time of the company's redefinition as Axon, it acquired two startup companies in the machine learning space. One was a company called Misfit that specialized in analyzing data from wearable activity trackers. The other was Dextro, which Axon described as forming "the technology backbone of the new Axon AI platform." In his remarks at the opening session of Axon Accelerate 2017, Luan announced the Dextro team's new vision. It was no longer creating a computer vision platform for a wide range of uses but something more specific: using AI to "eliminate police paperwork" and "give LE [law enforcement] complete analytics of their data."[43]

The team at Dextro and other computer vision experts have eyed video from police body cameras as a valuable dataset for training machine learning algorithms precisely because it represents a large-scale, domain-specific use-case and massive video dataset of labeled data. Paradoxically, domain-specific labeled data is seen as a promising basis for building more encompassing general-use machine learning models. In a blog post on *Medium*, Dextro's cofounders proclaimed themselves "Excited to Join Axon" because it meant gaining access to the video Axon "hosts" through Evidence.com, its software-as-a-service platform:

> Law enforcement departments are generating a massive unique dataset of first-person video from body worn camera programs, and the vast majority of the data—5.4 petabytes of it—is stored within the Axon ecosystem. Not many research teams gain access to this kind of data, let alone high-quality data specific to the depth of a particular domain.[44]

As this comment suggests, part of what made the police bodycam video data "high quality" for training machine learning systems was its domain specificity.

Given that the domain represented police activity, it begged the question of how this type of data would affect the perceptual schema of video AI. If machine learning algorithms are trained on police bodycam video datasets, what do those algorithms learn to perceive? Developers of video AI have a more expansive vision for the technology, training ML systems using other large-scale video datasets as well. But while a big claim about video AI is domain-agnosticism and technically neutral machine perception, *selective perception* is the main and perhaps only practical path to its development. And since the police are both a source of video datasets as well as one of the early users of video AI, the ML algorithms reflect and reproduce the "professional vision" of policing.[45] The basis for the development of video AI is the presence of large-scale video infrastructure and the avalanche of audiovisual data produced. It so happens that policing and security are among the domains that have delivered the data.

Giving the Police "Complete Analytics of Their Data"

The idea that AI would not only eliminate the paper burden of policing but also give the police "complete analytics of their data" was a big promise. The power to completely analyze vast amounts of data in totality—in the case of video, examining everything there is to see and hear in a single video or a collection of recordings, no matter how large—is one of the big claims that the tech industry has made about video AI. In the case of police bodycam video, an inconvenient fact was that no one was ever watching the vast majority of the video being produced by this so-called labor-saving police accountability technology. At Axon Accelerate 2017, one speaker noted the small fraction of bodycam video being reviewed, adding that there was "a whole host of information that never gets taken advantage of."[46] The implication was that machine learning would offer a means of making this surplus audiovisual data useful. In other words, once police agencies deployed body cameras, they needed video AI to process and make adequate use of the video that these cameras produced. Video AI would process more of the video—in fact, it would watch and listen to *all* of it—rather than only the small fraction that paid police workers would have time to review. Put another way, if the problem was that most of the video from expensive body-worn camera systems would never be viewed, making it essentially useless, then yet another new technology was needed to "fix" the problem.

Was this a realistic claim? Could AI analyze *all* the video produced by police body-worn cameras, seeing and listening to the entirety of the content, parsing through the irrelevant material and locating the most relevant segments? What was the "whole host of information" in police video that was not being "taken advantage of" that AI would analyze and make available for advantageous use? While the uses of video AI in policing and security might seem self-evident, it is necessary to consider more closely, and with a bit of healthy skepticism, what the tech industry was promising.

In a 2017 post at the Axon website, CEO Rick Smith claimed that there were immediate, concrete benefits that AI would provide to police customers. Smith explained that the company was "establishing a clean break with previous speculation around AI and focusing on the new roadmap put in place by the Dextro and Misfit teams."[47] The comment suggested that there were prior claims about AI that were perhaps too vague or lofty, promises that did not turn out to be realistic deliverables. Axon's new plan involved two seemingly more tangible applications for police customers: "eliminating paperwork and automating tedious back-office workflows such as redaction."[48] Smith suggested that AI would offer three specific forms of automation: automated redaction, automated transcription, and automated reporting.

Notably, each of these more practical applications focused on police reporting work associated with video, and none of them was particularly analytic except in the sense that all computational processes are mathematical calculations. The first, *automated redaction*, was ironically an application for *occluding* vision. The most obvious form of video redaction, and the one the company showed in its demos, used face detection to blur out faces in video footage. This type of redaction was developed largely in response to what Bryce Newell has referred to as the "collateral visibility" of people in police-produced videos—namely, the visibility of victims, minors, and bystanders caught up in police recording scenarios.[49] Redacting faces manually, frame by frame, was indeed a tedious and time-consuming process that would take an amount of labor and time that in many cases would not be feasible. According to Axon's CEO, automated redaction would "speed up the process of sharing footage with the public while protecting the privacy of citizens captured in video."⁵⁰ This way of defining and operationalizing privacy, it should be noted, was the one-sided paternalistic conception that platform companies often trumpeted. It provided certain people some anonymity from public view but not from platform companies, nor from police users of the platform.

The second AI application that Smith noted, *automated transcription*, targeted audio recordings rather than visual images. Voice-to-text transcription as a baseline AI application suggests that speech and sound were important information to be taken advantage of in video. Automated transcription would presumably allow records to be populated with words directly, either live or from video recordings. This kind of auto-fill function would also be made possible, according to the company, using optical character recognition (OCR). In their demos and promotional videos, Axon depicted its vision for how these forms of automation would work, showing speech-to-text automatically transcribing voices into words and OCR automatically scraping information from people's identification documents when held up in front of officers' body cameras. Of course, while automated transcription and OCR have seen great improvements, their use would still require reviewing and editing. This inconvenient problem underscores the way that body cameras were not eliminating but instead increasing the reporting and data-entry demands of police work.

The third application that Smith mentioned, *automated reporting*, was more of a catchall concept to encompass a broad range of possibilities. According to Smith, automated transcription would "eliminate the heads-down hand-written notes so officers can engage and empathize with the community"; the aim of automated reporting likewise was "to populate factual records directly from video and audio, so officers can spend time serving the community."⁵¹ The humanistic message was consistent with the one conveyed in Axon's promotional video (discussed in Chapter 3), claiming that AI technology would allow officers to "focus on people not paperwork."

The suggestion that bureaucratic labor is not *real* police work also served the company's interests in capturing police records management systems as a proprietary platform. Once again, we encounter the big promise that the company's technology will save labor, while in reality, Axon's business model depends not on replacing police work but on leveraging its surplus value. (Recall the subtitle of Axon's bar graph discussed in Chapter 3: "Revenue Recognition and Cash Flow per Officer.") The physical labor of the police rank-and-file *generates* the video and their digital labor *labels* it, making industry claims about the labor management benefits of body-worn cameras and their back-end systems even more gulling.

Axon's CEO emphasized his company's ethical orientation to its AI work, noting that Axon would establish an AI ethics board that would advise the AI team. There were ethical lines the company would draw: "An example workflow we might address is speeding up supervisor review of footage. An example decision that is outside our scope is inferring criminality."[52] Smith did not elaborate on what he meant by "inferring criminality," but one assumes he meant making conceptual leaps from the bodies and behaviors represented in video to claims about the inherent criminal proclivities of individuals or groups. If so, the company would be wise to avoid such dubious avenues for AI development. But the fact that Axon elsewhere posited "crime analysis" as among its platform value propositions suggests that "inferring criminality" would be hard to rule out from "Axon's AI work."[53]

The potential to "speed up supervisor review of footage" and the bigger promise to give law enforcement "complete analytics of their data" raised thorny issues that Axon's police-facing communications carefully tried to navigate: the intention was not only to introduce more automation into police reporting but to amplify the capacities of police leadership to monitor and manage the rank-and-file. This was one of the main promises being made about machine learning applied to bodycam video: helping police managers keep very close track of police patrol officers, analyzing and evaluating their behavior, less to ensure humane policing than to manage police patrols more effectively (although no doubt reducing police use-of-force was a managerial priority). At Axon Accelerate 2017, the company gave examples of how machine learning algorithms could identify when officers were not following policy, such as failing to activate their body cameras or do equipment checks.[54] Machine learning algorithms could be trained to track good behavior as well, such as identifying officers adept at de-escalation.

This managerial logic of labor surveillance and the apparent need to make use of bodycam and other police video *in its totality*, including the vast quantities of video sitting idly in storage, was also evident in the business model of another startup company called Truleo. In 2021, Truleo launched a service for law enforcement agencies that promised to process the entirety of their bodycam video datasets using natural language processing (NLP). The company's "Truleo Lifecycle Diagram" explained that "body cameras do not deliver on the problem of accountability or transparency because less than 1 percent of footage is reviewed." It further explained that "Truleo automatically processes 100 percent of BWC [body-worn camera] data and produces timely, actionable reports." Truleo software was designed so that a supervisor reviews the reports and then either rewards good behavior or "detects and intervenes [on] risky officer behavior."[55]

Truleo's NLP system targeted speech and language in bodycam recordings rather than the visual images. Here again, making the video useful meant processing recorded sound and language, not just images. The company indicated that the Truleo system performed sentiment analysis using NLP, identifying moments of high risk by analyzing language, such as the use of profanity. Individual officers would be assigned risk scores based on sentiment analysis of their words, and specific incidents would be automatically flagged for supervisor review. The company claimed that the technology could distinguish the voices of different individuals rather than simply translating speech-to-text in a continuous way, and that it would focus on the officers' voices, not those of civilians.[56]

The police departments experimenting with Truleo's NLP system for processing their entire bodycam video catalogs predictably brought on strong opposition from police unions, leading at least two of Truleo's client police departments to cancel their contracts with the company.[57] Truleo CEO and cofounder Anthony Tassone said that by ceding to union pressure, "they've gone back to status quo, which is to review practically none" of the bodycam videos.[58]

Companies and liberal police reformers alike lament the strength of police unions and their ability to successfully push back against the introduction of new technologies that promise to facilitate more intensive labor management. The collective power of police unions has been an obstacle to liberal reforms as well as the aims of the defunding and abolitionist movements. But police union opposition to more intensive oversight technologies also pushes against the individualization of responsibility for police violence, which has always been a convenient way of avoiding policing's structural problems. It is also pushes against the idea that police violence has a market-based technological solution in the form of subscription-based services that provide recurring revenue to IT companies. Police technology companies view opposition from police unions as risk factors affecting their business plans and potential profitability, much like the calls to "defund the police."

Despite the Axon CEO's claim that his company would be breaking from speculation about AI and moving forward with a roadmap of concrete applications, there remained much gesturing to the technology's future potential. There was always an implied promise of other wide-ranging possibilities for what insights might be gleaned from the video datasets using machine learning. Video AI promised to generate a wide range of insights from all the information "not being taken advantage of" because there was far too much video to review. The repeated suggestion was that video AI would have the ability to process the *totality of the video*. It would be able to view and listen to *all of it*, extracting the relevant *moments* and identifying *patterns* and in this way would generate more knowledge for the police and more value for the company. Machine learning algorithms presumably analyze datasets completely, exhaustively doing what would be far too exhausting for humans to do and, in fact, what humans would not be capable of doing even in great numbers, given the calculative capacity required. In the 1990s, sociologist William Bogard coined a term for this promise of complete technological perception: *the simulation of surveillance*, referring to the convergence of an "imaginary of surveillant control" with "the effort to push surveillance technologies to their absolute limit."[59] In the twenty-first century, companies have increasingly outsized roles and vested interests in creating imaginary needs for totalizing forms of police surveillance, including the twin objectives of crime control and police labor management.

Generative Video AI, Deepfakes, and "User Engagement"

If video AI refers to automated video processing and analysis, another approach known as *generative video AI* uses deep learning techniques to synthesize audiovisual material. We are now confronted by the seemingly imminent spread of "deepfakes," synthetic or altered videos produced with deep learning technology that have the realist aesthetics of regular video recordings. Generative video AI can be used to create videos in which people appear to say things that they never said, which of course requires voice synthesis as well as image manipulation. Common early uses of generative video AI are faked porn videos in which individuals' faces are replaced with someone else's without their consent. More optimistically, artists and other producers of culture can create new aesthetic forms by decomposing and recombining patterns and themes from existing works.[60]

The creative and labor-saving benefits of generative AI are the virtues that the tech industry promotes in their video AI imaginaries. In 2023, countless AI image generators were being offered online by tech companies, all promising to empower and unleash creativity and productivity. "The Best Video AI Generators in 2023," as listed at *Zapier*, included AI video editors and productivity apps geared toward commercial and marketing uses, always with a nod toward productivity and radical creative potential as the ultimate benefits.[61] A video describing DALL-E 2 concluded with a promise to "amplify your creative potential." Google described "Bard," its early experiment in generative AI, as "your creative and helpful collaborator, here to supercharge your imagination, boost your productivity, and bring your ideas to life."[62]

We should obviously be skeptical of this hyperbolic promotional language, but they are nonetheless powerful and self-serving industry claims. In the creative and social media marketing industries, there is considerable pressure to produce ever-more content to capture and monetize people's attention. In addition, absent from the tech-fetishistic marketing imaginaries is any mention of the new waves of epistemic confusion and chaos that AI video generators are virtually guaranteed to unleash, or the fuel they promise to throw on the fire of post-truth politics. Improvements in the speed and fidelity of generative video AI carry with them the specter of pervasive confusion about what is real and what is not, making everything recorded in video deniable—a grave problem in the domain of election campaigns, human rights, and violent conflicts.

In legal settings, videos tend to get more scrutiny than they do on the Internet, and trained video analysts are usually able to determine if videos have been altered or faked. Nonetheless, the legal domain has already seen incidents of the "deepfake defense," where videos that have not been altered are claimed to be deepfakes.[63] For example, Elon Musk's lawyers experimented with the deepfake defense in a case against his company brought by a family of a man who died in a collision while sitting in the driver's seat of a Tesla in self-driving mode. Musk's lawyers suggested that a video of Musk proclaiming the safety of self-driving Teslas could have been faked. The deepfake defense was also tried by lawyers for the rioters who stormed the Capitol building on January 6, 2021. Videos showing them violently clashing with the Capitol police, or even being there at all, could be deepfakes, so said their attorneys. This line of legal argumentation was rejected by the presiding judges in both cases, which seems promising only if we dismiss the inverse possibility of judges rejecting the deepfake defense when video evidence is in fact the product of generative video AI.[64]

What the ensuing cat-and-mouse game of video manipulation and verification techniques means for law, politics, journalism, and human rights is clearly worrisome. Given an impending avalanche of synthesized videos, computer scientists have proposed the use of automated tools to do the epistemic work of identifying manipulated content.[65] Yet computational tools that distinguish faked from unfaked videos cannot resolve the problems of trust that course through our perceptual entanglements with media and through the fractured media and political landscape. An indistinguishable line between reality and realism is arguably one of modern media's defining aesthetics, making something like generative video AI a predictable point on a media-technological trajectory. In fact, both the technology and discourse seem oddly reminiscent of the debates about Photoshop and computer-generated imagery in cinema in the 1980s. As Sun-ha Hong has argued, we seem to be stuck in a repetitious reimagining of the future, keeping modern society in a kind of stasis even in the face of what appears to be constant technological change.[66] In this context, distinguishing between faked and unfaked videos, while important, is insufficient. It is more important to better understand what the tech industry gains from the infrastructures and imaginaries of AI, who is paying for their gains, and what is being lost.

There is an obvious trajectory for the uses of generative video AI. The analysis of affect using video AI has the aim of applying analytic insights to manipulate people's emotional responses to media, or what is generally called "user engagement." In the gambling machine industry, Natasha Dow Schüll explains, this is referred to as "time on device."[67] Although it would be a formidable technical challenge, it is not hard to imagine a form of generative video AI that creates synthetic videos in response to people's emotional reactions in real time, in a feedback loop of affect analysis and content generation. This scenario would be a holy grail of user engagement, applied to video games, porn videos, and other media forms that rely on realist video aesthetics. Perhaps synthetic video AI will find an application in recruitment and training materials for the police. There is now much talk of "millennial police recruitment" (i.e., how to attract millennials to the profession of policing),[68] something in which companies like Axon have a vested interest, given that their revenue recognition and cash flow model is measured "per officer," rather than on any real or imagined properties of video AI. In the case of video curation for user engagement, the question is not just what gets programmed into *algorithms* but what gets programmed into *people*. Shifting focus from the content to the context of use, we find not just the synthesis of videos but also the synthesis of human and computational forms of perception.

Conclusion

In this chapter, I have argued that video AI, like AI in general, is as imaginary as it is infrastructural, and the imaginaries play a crucial, performative role in the trajectories of the technological projects carried out under its label. The development of video AI has been driven to a great extent by the aims of the Big Tech companies to expand the capacities of their proprietary platforms. AI and video AI are fundamentally scale-building projects made up of many computational experiments and technical systems in perpetual development, designed principally for large-scale, capital-intensive uses. A big claim about machine learning is that it provides complete analytics of data—that is, the analysis of vast datasets in their totality. But just as there is no such thing as "raw data," there is no such thing as "complete analytics."[69]

One primary early use-case for video AI is for policing and security, and more specifically, the efforts of private enterprise to capture police IT systems as sources of revenue and market value. Video AI is a part of the structural changes in policing and security described in Chapter 3, in which companies integrate their branded proprietary edge devices and platforms into the everyday workings of law enforcement agencies through their information and logistical systems. If the demands of profit-making are shaping the development of video AI, so are the demands of policing and security. We see this perhaps most clearly in the way the founders of the computer vision company Dextro described their enthusiasm about the opportunity to work with the labeled dataset of bodycam video that was accumulating on the Axon platform. Storehouses of recorded surveillance and dashcam and bodycam footage converge with other sources of data as the domain of experimentation in video analytics, embedding the carceral logics of policing into the epistemic machinery of video AI.

Video AI promises to solve a great many problems, improving the way audiovisual media are processed and analyzed in the vast array of contexts now saturated with cameras. Some form of automation is the overdetermined outcome of the video avalanche and the need to address the problems and exploit the opportunities that ever-growing volumes of video have created. This video is not empty of content; it contains a large swath of human activities, from exchanges between loved ones to large-scale acts of violence committed by armed forces. How to make sense of it all and sort through it is an undertaking with profound social and ethical implications. Who does it and how should be a matter of extreme care, deliberation, and input from the many constituencies affected by these projects. That any company or industry would do it with legal carte blanche should be unthinkable rather than the obvious, unquestioned path.

The tech industry makes heavy use of an ethics of care in its marketing and branding materials, claiming to be vested in the overall benefit of humanity. But just as it is a powerful misconception to see AI and data as empty of content, it is likewise a mistake to see companies developing these technologies as driven or constrained by the ethical principles alluded to in their communications. These market actors cannot act for long on any motivations that challenge the religion of growth. Perhaps some form of video AI could be developed independently of the platform business model and separately from the logistical needs of policing and security, but that is not the most consequential form of video AI being developed in the current AI era. We cannot understand real-world applications of artificial intelligence, machine learning, or video AI without attention to how these technologies are both imagined and physically built by companies that are laser-focused on scale, growth, and market dominance.

Conclusion

Putting Policing in a Different Frame

Questions That Remain

This book aims to fill a gap in the critical literature on policing and security regarding their deepening entanglements with audiovisual media and the platform economy. I have barely scratched the surface of the complex set of developments that took place in the first two decades of the twenty-first century in the media infrastructures of public and private policing. Many questions remain to be answered about key issues raised: the structuring tensions between the corporate strategies of tech companies and the social functions of policing as defined by the state and the police themselves; the extent to which corporations are taking on and intensifying the functions of policing at this phase of modern capitalist development; the importance of policing in the development of data analytics; and, of course, questions about video and the perceptual systems that perpetuate and contest police violence.

There are a variety of valid critiques that can be leveled against this book. Police scholars may object that I have not given police actors themselves enough attention, skewing the analysis so that corporations appear to have more influence on the police than they do. And I have considered only a small number of companies, largely ignoring significant players like Palantir and IBM. Critical data studies scholars may argue that by focusing on video, the book misses important ways that police power now relies on other forms of data and data analytics. Still another objection concerns the insufficient attention given to the structural racism of policing and the criminal legal system and the role of both in enforcing and reproducing white supremacy and racial capitalism. And I have given only a minor nod to the central role that video plays in human rights and anti-racist activism, presenting a bleak picture of the intensification of police power without offering solutions or counterstrategies. Each of these valid criticisms points to questions that are either in need of further study or issues that other critical scholars of policing have already addressed at some length (or both).

In this concluding discussion, I revisit some questions this book raises but does not fully answer concerning the relationship between video evidence and aesthetics, the challenges of analyzing surveillance infrastructures at a scale adequate to the stakes, the influence of policing on the development of video analytics, and the connections between the police surveillance economy and what abolitionists have called the prison-industrial complex.

Video Evidence and Police Aesthetics

One important question that requires more examination concerns the overlapping aesthetic, evidentiary, and logistical uses of video evidence. How are video's formal aesthetics relevant to its evidentiary and logistical uses? What are the aesthetic "afterlives" of video evidence?[1] How do the logistical uses of video allow "forensic aesthetics" and sensemaking to travel into other sites of media perception and interpretation? How do we make sense of the manner in which video's formal aesthetics mediates between reality and realism, implanting in perception, memory, and imagination in a way that dissolves the distinction?

The effective use of video for policing and security is not limited to any factual evidence that video recordings contain, but instead extends to the powerful, largely unconscious and immeasurable effects that video's realist aesthetics have on perception. If by aesthetics we mean to refer "not in the first place to art, but . . . the whole region of human perception and sensation," as the philosopher Terry Eagleton argued, then aesthetics are inherent in all forms of media and mediated experience.[2] In her study of the Soviet secret police, Cristina Vatulescu uses the term "police aesthetics" to theorize the overlaps and exchanges she observed between the secret police files and the literature and film of the period.[3] Vatulescu borrows the term "police aesthetics" from the Russian poet Osip Mandel'shtam, who paid close attention to "the self-presentation of the police through dress, parades, and the fashioning of the agent's body."[4] The police aesthetics of the Soviet period was not confined to obvious symbolic displays of police power but "instead seep[ed] in where one might expect it least."[5] It pervaded people's daily lives, the "psyches of little boys," and the sphere of cultural production.

As I discussed in Chapter 3, the aesthetics of twenty-first-century policing pervade the marketing materials and corporate branding of the technology company Axon Enterprise. Axon carefully designs it branded technologies and emotional appeals so that its corporate identity blends into the logistical and bureaucratic systems of policing. The black plastic, Glock-like aesthetics of the body camera pairs well with the fashion style of the police uniform and other attachments, including weapons, radios, and tasers. The yellow Axon triangle logo is imprinted on the upper right corner of bodycam videos, placed next to the time-date stamp and other information to convey a temporal and operative aesthetics. The screen interface of the police records management system also has a purposefully designed software aesthetic that is now embedded in the digital labor of police work.

The formal aesthetics of bodycam and surveillance videos differ from Axon's branded police aesthetic. These videos have a gritty realist aesthetic, deriving from their embodied conditions of production. They are "poor images,"[6] depicting awkward angles and distortion from camera motion and noise. Police aesthetics are imprinted in their conditions of production, as well as in the ways they get analyzed by trained forensic experts, and in their contexts of display on screens in the legal system and beyond.[7] Police bodycam videos are also "operative images"[8] that often closely resemble the formal aesthetics of first-person shooter video games.

While the evidentiary uses of video are assumed to be divorced from aesthetic concerns, the status of video as evidence is inseparable from its aesthetics. If video forensics is concerned with exploiting the evidentiary potential of recorded video, it is the formal aesthetics of video recordings that must be examined, enhanced, perceived, and explained. Eyal Weizman has argued that "forensics is an *aesthetic* practice, because it depends on both the modes and the means by which reality is sensed and presented publicly."[9] Video forensics involves techniques that give video recordings an aesthetics of objectivity, but the aesthetic practices of video forensics are intertwined with the logistics of police perception.

Vatulescu extends the concept of police aesthetics to include ways that the Soviet secret police represented both themselves and the people whose activities were documented in their textual and visual artifacts—notably, in the *police files*. If the media form of the police file is changing to include video, so is the entire form of the police filing system. How do we understand the powerful effects of police aesthetics as police evidence and recordkeeping systems are redesigned to encompass more media forms? The changing form of the police record to include video forces us to consider what aesthetic and perceptual work police records do *at scale*, shaping the logistics of police perception and extending it into other domains of media attention.

The Scale (of the) Problem

Implied in the term "avalanche" is the idea of scale. An avalanche of video is a large amount, the result of the spatial diffusion of cameras and the construction of large-scale infrastructures that store and circulate video. What means do we have for understanding the changing *scale* of video surveillance infrastructures? How do those changes affect the pace, scale, and pattern of policing, security, and other uses of surveillance?

Studying large-scale video infrastructures poses conceptual and methodological problems. If scale is challenging to build, it is also challenging to analyze, not only because it is a large and unwieldy object of analysis but also because it is not an object but a *process*. In the process of assembling scale, many actors are engaged in many scalar projects, loosely or tightly connected to one another. In "Anatomy of an AI system," Kate Crawford and Vladan Joler observe that "the scale required to build artificial intelligence systems is too complex, too obscured by intellectual property law, and too mired in logistical complexity to fully comprehend in the moment."[10] "The scale of the system is almost beyond human imagining," they write. "How can we see it, to grasp its immensity and complexity as a connected form?"[11] Their effort to grasp the scale of AI includes the design of a graphical, anatomical map and a series of vignettes offering snapshots of some of the objects and physical sites that make up Amazon's extractive system. The vignettes also include conceptual diagrams to make sense of scale. Reading their map from left to right, "the story begins and ends with the Earth, and the geological processes of deep time"; reading it top to bottom, it "begins and ends with a human."[12] The scale of their map makes it hard to read, rendering each of its elements into tiny icons.

James Rule tied the twentieth-century growth of bureaucratic recordkeeping systems to the increasing scale of modern societies. The cohesiveness of large-scale social systems depended, Rule argued, on the development of effective forms of social control, which required ways of enforcing rules at scale. Rule conducted studies of five separate public and private bureaucratic surveillance systems in the United States and the United Kingdom in the late 1960s and early 1970s, providing a snapshot of these systems on the cusp of computerization, including criminal records, vehicle and driver's licensing systems, national insurance in Britain, consumer credit reporting in the United States, and the BankAmericard system, which later became Visa. At the time, he could still examine them as separate systems in a way that would much more difficult today. Without systems of social control, Rule argued, fault lines emerge and social cohesion breaks down. But social control creates its own fault lines, which can lead to escalating systems of control, building the scale of surveillance infrastructures and breaking down the boundaries between them. A central question for social and political theory has long concerned whether democracy is possible in large-scale complex societies.

The problem of scale is not new, nor is it exclusive to computing or surveillance infrastructures. Chandra Murkerji provides a study of early modern scale-building in her book on the Canal du Midi, built in France in the seventeenth century under the Sun King.[13] There we see how an engineering project of that scale was a logistical challenge, and the impossible engineering feat of building the Canal du Midi was an exercise in logistical power. It never worked perfectly, and it was never perfectly built, but that did not prevent it from working its logistical magic, shifting the balance of power from personal to impersonal rule. The Canal automated power in part by accelerating the pace of circulation of people and goods and extending the distance that they traveled. Once it was carved into the landscape, its power was virtually impossible to contest. It exercised a form of logistical power that operated automatically through its durable infrastructure and the way it reshaped the landscape and the built environment.

Artificial intelligence (AI) and video AI are problems of scale. They are also solutions to scalar problems, especially the scalar problem of analyzing large volumes of data. AI, machine learning, and computer vision are technical processes and methods of data analysis that *require* scale; they are being made possible by large-scale computing infrastructures. At the same time, large-scale computing infrastructures and growing volumes of data *create the need* for these automated, scalar analytic systems because these infrastructures require more and more automation of data processing in order to function. Artificial intelligence, as we use the term now, refers to the particular forms of automation that are being designed into large-scale computing infrastructures to allow them to function and grow in scale. As they have grown in scale, computing infrastructures have exercised forms of logistical power that are very difficult to contest.

Although they are not one and the same, the growth imperatives of computing are attuned to the growth imperatives of capitalism, and vice versa. At this stage in both these growth-driven processes, they are completely interdependent. AI technology has the logics and technical demands of financialization woven into its infrastructures and imaginaries. Digital platforms are scalar projects of industrial actors. Inherent in the platform business model and in the construction of digital platforms is the imperative to expand and extend the reach of the platform, to create network effects by bringing more users onto the platform. At the heart of the platform business model is a process of perpetual scaling up and reconfiguring, automation and acceleration, all in pursuit of the destructive ambition of exponential growth without material constraints.

The tech industry likes to portray itself as having all the solutions, but this industry, in alliance with finance, is in many ways responsible for the scale of the problems we are facing. They are powerful actors building large-scale infrastructures that marry knowledge production with wealth accumulation. They demand computational training from universities and then grab the best-trained computational minds to put them to use for building large-scale data extraction and processing systems that serve the growth of the tech and finance industries first and foremost. These industries operate as if their growth can occur indefinitely, and they posit that infinite growth as virtuous. When Sandy

Parakilas, senior product manager for privacy at Apple, joined Facebook as operations manager in 2011, Facebook's orientation program conveyed a singular theme, as he explained to writer Evan Osnos.[14] The message was: "We believe in the religion of growth." At the apex of Facebook's religious order was its "growth team," which the company loaded with "all the smartest minds," who in turn "focused on doing whatever they can possibly do to get those growth numbers up." Axon Enterprise and its competitors have adopted a similar approach in their efforts to dominate and grow the police surveillance economy.

One of the obstacles to realizing the police platform business model (discussed near the end of Chapter 4) was the competition for the "AI vanguard," what Shoshana Zuboff has referred to as an "arms race" for human capital trained in the language and science of computation.[15] While elite tech workers are undoubtedly attracted to jobs based on the compensation packages that potential employers can offer them, there are other incentives and disincentives that define the range of motivations among this group. Imagine if all the well-trained minds got to work building more sustainable and equitable worlds? Of course, equally important is the question of how people without computer science degrees can participate in what Lisa Parks calls "the politics of infrastructure intelligibility."[16] In other words, how can infrastructures be made more intelligible to citizens whose lives are shaped by them so that they can participate in the politics that shape infrastructures rather than simply being passively affected by them?

The Carceral Perspective of Video AI

Another question this book raises that it does not adequately answer concerns the role that policing plays in the development of video AI. How far does policing's influence on the development of video analytics go? To what extent are computational systems being taught to perceive the world from the carceral perspective of policing, like automated police hammers that see criminal nails everywhere?

Critical studies of "predictive policing" have tried to understand how the "dirty data" of policing gets baked into predictive algorithms. A body of critical research has done the important work of historicizing the predictive policing paradigm,[17] examining its racial and other biases,[18] theorizing its novel logic of preemption,[19] identifying its faulty premises and circular logics,[20] and offering ethnographic insights into the ways predictive policing gets developed and applied.[21] The focus of this important literature on the design and application of predictive policing is essential, but it has left largely unexamined the business models of the companies supplying these systems to police departments.

The critical literature on predictive policing also seems disconnected from debates about the "new visibility" of policing that has resulted from the spread of smartphones and social media. Research that looks at datafied policing largely ignores the ubiquity of video, despite its embedded role in policing's logistical and bureaucratic systems. Policing and security are deeply entangled with video technology, and video is now a digital medium and field of data where much experimentation with data analytics and machine learning occurs. Why and how images and videos get labeled the way they do is an important question, and every study that opens the lid on training data like ImageNet finds deeply problematic labeling patterns.[22] These patterns are not errors or aberrations but extensions of existing ways of perceiving the world. They will never be scrubbed out of the training datasets or out of machine learning algorithms.

The question of what perceptual orientations and assumptions get designed into algorithms is an important one, but it is also critical to understand the way algorithms get woven into the world and into the ways the world is perceived. In *Cloud Ethics*, Louise Amoore argues that "the conditions of an algorithm's emergence" are always necessarily "a composite of human-algorithm relations" and so, by definition, ethical and political.[23] Algorithms are "composite creatures" and "generative agents" that come into being and have effects only in their experimental engagement with the world.[24] She uses the camera metaphor of "apertures" to describe the power of algorithms "to perceive and distill something for action."[25] Algorithms cannot be abstracted and examined as bounded objects because they are already fully entangled in perception and action. And as they model actions to try to reduce uncertainty, they introduce more vectors of causality. It is important to understand not only what gets programmed into algorithms and AI but also what gets programmed into *people* and their conditions of life.

Admittedly, I have no idea how to measure the extent of policing's influence on video analytics, although I am confident that without the use-cases of policing and security, video AI would be taking different forms than it is. It may not be possible to track what machine learning algorithms do with the video avalanche, since even data scientists cannot say for sure how the algorithms generate their results. If algorithms provide partial accounts of themselves as they weave into the world, as Amoore suggests, it may not be necessary to examine their source code to understand how they work. The math may not be that revealing. The hope is that AI will see and hear things that humans fail to perceive, like cancer cells or people intent on causing harm. Could video AI make the police more humane and people-focused, as the company Axon claims in their panoramic visions of the future of policing? It is interesting that this promise is inextricably tied to relieving police officers of their labor burdens—an acknowledgment that police are doing too much of the wrong kind of work. It is unfortunate that it is an unreliable and dubious claim. Even so, I remain convinced that corporate messaging is more powerful than social research acknowledges, and that studies of technology ignore it to the detriment of understanding. Video AI is both infrastructure and imaginary, both a technological project and a work of cultural production, and its realization is deeply dependent on both.

The Challenges of Scaling Back

The scalar project of platform building points to another question left unexamined in this book: If platform capitalism is reconfiguring policing by capturing its data and logistical systems, what does this suggest for what prison abolitionists call "the prison-industrial complex"?

Critiques of policing and police technologies are at the heart of antiracist scholarship and activism, where much of the discussion leads to police and prison abolition. Scholar Jackie Wang suggests a "carceral continuum" from prisons to algorithmic policing to the debt economy.[26] The continuum includes predatory lending—"the extension of credit as a method of dispossession."[27] And it includes forms of "parasitic governance," such as the use of police by municipalities to loot the residents of poor communities.[28] This occurs through predatory fines and fees as well as the more devastating practice of civil asset forfeiture. (Recall that companies like Axon see policies limiting civil forfeiture as "risk factors" that would adversely impact their ability to realize their revenue models.) The carceral continuum is so deeply entangled with "the dynamics of late capitalism" that Wang calls it "carceral capitalism."[29]

Wang's theory of carceral capitalism is different from what geographer and prison abolitionist Ruth Wilson Gilmore calls the "Golden Gulag," where "golden" refers not to capital but to the "Golden State" of California.[30] Gilmore examines the "astonishing prison growth"—the prison building boom—that occurred in California beginning in the early 1980s, asking why it happened and challenging many of the prevailing explanations, especially those that point to high crime rates. "The prison fix," Gilmore argues, was a four-prong story: first, how prison building was *financed*; second, how the prisons were *physically located*; third, the *amplified criminalization* that filled the prisons and provided the basis for claiming future need for capacity; and fourth, the *industrialization of the system of punishment*.

Gilmore's account of California's prison building boom and Wang's explanation of the carceral continuum offer two different accounts, but both are useful for understanding the logistical power of scale-building. An abolitionist perspective requires asking what it would mean to scale back carceral infrastructures, including but not limited to shutting down prisons. It must also include reversing the corporate capture of police records management systems, for example. As Ruha Benjamin writes, "the sticky web of carcerality" extends well beyond the prison walls "into the everyday lives of those who are purportedly free, wrapping around hospitals, schools, banks, social service agencies, humanitarian organizations, shopping malls, and the digital service economy."[31]

A big challenge for dismantling the carceral infrastructure is the growing scale of private policing in the service of corporate expansion. Defunding the police is a tricky proposition given the tendency of private security to flood into spaces where public policing falls short of the needs of powerful interests. If the security technology industry is adept at video surveillance infrastructure development, it is also proficient at using video to build industry's branded cultural imaginaries of policing and security. Business-to-business video advertising pervades the Internet, accessible on corporate websites and video-sharing platforms. Although any specific category of video production is diminished in significance by the avalanche of online media, business-to-business video advertising is a major form of contemporary cultural production, almost entirely ignored in media and cultural analysis today. In Chapter 3, I describe at length one example that offers a panoramic projection of the "Axon Network" in action. The text of another promotional video, this one found at the website of Motorola Solutions, offers a techno-imaginary of security that is completely scrubbed of the police:

> What if safety, efficiency, and productivity were deeply connected? That the technologies that make us safer could also make us better at everything they do? Smarter and faster, more focused and aware, more connected and resilient, more accurate and fair? It's a reinvention of what safety can achieve, from everyday operations to your overall mission. We've made it real by building the first technology ecosystem that unifies voice, video, data, and analytics on a single platform. Technologies that communicate with each other, learn from each other, information that flows freely from cameras to radios, from smart devices to command centers. Intelligence that advances outwards, giving you eyes and ears where you've never had them before, addressing the industry challenges of today with an eye toward the future. It's time to know more of what's happening. To put people where they're needed most. To get ahead of events before they unfold. To start evolving without limits, disruption or downtime. It's time to reimagine what safety can do.[32]

If there was any question about the idealizing work that corporate imaginaries perform, the text of this video should dispel it. As Walter Benjamin said about Filippo Tommaso Marinetti's "Futurist Manifesto," it has the virtue of clarity.[33] Marinetti outwardly proclaimed the aesthetic beauty of industrial warfare. Motorola Solutions would have its audience believe in a world where safety, efficiency, and productivity converged into singular systems of perfect control, presenting this world as a techno-spiritual utopia. Having eyes and ears in all new places is something for security firms to dream of, and evolving without limits is the ultimate virtue bestowed by the gods of corporate security. The text, just one of many like it, takes "the kinder, gentler gaze of Big Brother"[34] to new heights, calling for a whole new futurist aspirational philosophy of "safety, efficiency, and productivity" based on unifying voice, video, data, and analytics on a singular platform.

Motorola Solution's advertising copy may very well be the product of an auto-text generator like ChatGPT, algorithmically recycling a new combination of phrases from an existing corpus of tired techno-imaginaries. The glossy visuals likewise could easily be assembled by a nonhuman synthetic video editor. The text makes heavy use of "us," "we," and "you" as pronouns to express corporate personhood. This powerful large-scale actor is found everywhere in the understudied, underestimated world of corporate marketing, branding, and public relations. It is also being enshrined in law, most notably in the U.S. Supreme Court's disastrous 2010 decision in *Citizens United v. Federal Election Commission*, giving corporations a First Amendment right to make unlimited political contributions. They also have extensive rights to privacy.

There is "a profound violence in the algorithm's foreclosure of alternative futures," as Amoore concludes in *Cloud Ethics*.[35] AI is simultaneously technological infrastructure and technocultural imaginary, and algorithms weave their way through both. This process of technical, perceptual, and cultural integration may be consistent in some ways with the old media of realist cinema and television. But as objects to think with, new technologies can also make obscured media logics more apparent. As Benjamin famously taught us, mechanical reproduction both destroyed and made evident the aura of original artworks. Computers' capacity to process large volumes of video and autonomously remix videos from existing video datasets may have more to tell us about the way perception, cognition, memory, and imagination are entangled with media. The big challenge will be how to use this knowledge for more humane, ethical, and equitable world-building.

It is challenging to make ethical and political interventions when the tech industry moves so fast and breaks so many things. Ethical discussions seem always to be in reactive mode, responding to decisions and changes already occurring. In "What Privacy Is For," Julie Cohen makes the normative case for the right to privacy conceived as "breathing room," making an appeal for the vital importance of spaces and times that are free of the extractive and analytic interventions of Big Data.[36] In *Crisis Vision*, Torin Monahan suggests the need for an ethics of "collective opacity" in contrast to liberal individual claims to privacy.[37] In *Cloud Ethics*, Louise Amoore insists that allowing for "the opaque and unknowable nature" of every kind of acting subject is a vital precondition for the very possibility of "ethicopolitical life."[38] The critical need for breathing room and opacity from perpetual surveillance, as collective social goods, are things we already know are needed for democratic political life. We also know that neither the police nor the tech industry will willingly provide them. As Ruha Benjamin explains, dismantling the carceral continuum—that sticky web that extends beyond prisons, weaving into many other domains of life—requires imagining and building not just one but "a *continuum* of alternatives."[39]

ACKNOWLEDGMENTS

The research that would eventually lead to this book began over a decade ago, so I have so many people to thank. I have also aged during this time, and my memory is not what it once was, so I am certain there are others who helped me along the way that I have neglected to mention. My sincere gratitude to those I forgot!

Two people who deserve special mention are Olga Kuchinskaya and Jonathan Sterne, who read the full manuscript and offered extremely helpful guidance. This book is the product of many conversations and feedback sessions with Olga, as well as group discussions with Lilly Irani, Chandra Mukerji, Fernando Domínguez Rubio, and Christo Sims. Yelena Gluzman helped immensely with early drafts of the chapter on Target Corp. Other writing comrades who helped me move the needle forward are the cadre I like to call "the Australians," even though they are not all from Australia, including our fearless leader Brian Martin, Tonya Agostini, Paula Arvela, Anu Bissonauth-Bedford, Jungmin Choi, Emily Herrington, Anneleis Humphries, Anita Johnson, Timothy Johnson-Newell, Olga Kuchinskaya (again!), Julia LeMonde, Erin Twyford, Jody Watts, and Qinqing Xu.

Heartfelt thanks go to *all* my colleagues in the Communication Department and the Science Studies Program at the University of California San Diego for being who you are and doing what you do. Extra hugs to those who read parts of this work and gave me feedback, including the people named above as well as Val Hartouni and Gary Fields. I would not have finished this work, nor would I still be an academic, without the overwhelming support and friendship of Amy Binder, Boatema Boateng, Natalia Roudakova, and Elana Zilberg.

I also wish to thank Patrick Anderson, Mark Andrejevic, Peter Asaro, Christina Aushana, Matilde Córdoba Azcárate, Toby Beauchamp, Marisa Brandt, Jack Bratich, Colin Burke, Lisa Cartwright, Julie Cohen, Kim Clark, Michael X. Delli-Carpini, Huub Dijstelbloem,

Laura Earl, Keli Gabinelli, Cathy Gere, Brian Goldfarb, Dan Hallin, Ari Heinrich, Mark Hineline, Sun-ha Hong, Caroline Jack, Caren Kaplan, Allan Klima, Amanda Lagerkvist, Marie Leger, Elizabeth Losh, Shoshana Magnet, Lev Manovich, Tara McPherson, Toby Miller, Kathryne Metcalf, Cameron McCarthy, Kelli Moore, Torin Monahan, Bryce Newell, Lisa Parks, Sandra Ristovska, Craig Robertson, Pepe Rojo, Carrie Rentschler, Perrin Selcer, David Serlin, Akshita Sivakumar, Patrick Brian Smith, Lian Song, Anna Starshinina, Mitali Thakor, Matilda Tudor, Angharad Valdivia, Cristina Visperas, Jonathan Walton, Andrew Whitworth-Smith, Dean Wilson, Wendy Wong, Emily York, Barbie Zelizer, and the late Anita Schiller. Many thanks go to Eric Zinner and Furqan Sayeed at New York University Press, and to my production editor, Abigail Michaud, as well as the forensic video analysts who generously gave me their time, despite their intense workload.

Finally, so much credit and gratitude go to my family, including Casper, and especially my brilliant husband Greg Barrett, whose outpouring of love, encouragement, and endless curiosity keeps me going. This book is for him.

NOTES

INTRODUCTION

1 "Glossary," Scientific Working Group on Digital Evidence, accessed January 15, 2023, www.swgde.org.
2 Brown, *In the Ruins of Neoliberalism*. The language of a "dual structure" of public and private policing is from Spitzer, "The Political Economy of Policing," 587.
3 Hacking, *The Taming of Chance*, 2.
4 On Francis Galton's statistical analysis of criminal bodies, see Sekula, "The Body and the Archive."
5 Hacking, *The Taming of Chance*, 4.
6 Muhammad, *The Condemnation of Blackness: Race, Crime, and the Making of Modern Urban America*.
7 Ibid., 33–34.
8 As Khalil Gibran Muhammad explains (*The Condemnation of Blackness*, 58), there was just as much crime committed by whites, but it was never deemed to be a measure of whiteness, inherent in the white race. These deeply flawed statistical claims were used as justification for second-class citizen status and supported the successful argument against reparations. However, statistics were also marshaled to make counterarguments and to reveal systemic antiblack racism. Muhammad discusses Ida B. Wells's use of statistics in her writings about lynching. Lynchings were widely assumed to be a form of "popular justice" meted out to Black men accused of raping white women. Wells used printed numbers to show that most lynchings did not involve charges of rape. Unfortunately, her writings did not have the weighty power and authority of the criminal legal infrastructure behind them.
9 Hacking, *The Taming of Chance*, 2.
10 Amoore, *Cloud Ethics*, 33, 42.
11 Ibid., 42.
12 Crawford, *Atlas of AI*, 95.
13 On datafied policing, see Andrejevic, "To Preempt a Thief"; Brayne, *Predict and Surveil*; Ferguson, *The Rise of Big Data Policing*; Richardson, Schultz, and Crawford, "Dirty Data, Bad Predictions"; Sheehey, "Algorithmic Paranoia"; Završnik, *Big Data, Crime and Social Control*; Moses and Chan, "Algorithmic Prediction in Policing"; McQuade, "World Histories of Big Data Policing."
14 Jonathan Sterne describes the MP3 as a "container technology" for sound, a term that he borrows from Lewis Mumford. See Sterne, "The MP3 as Cultural Artifact," 827. See also Sterne, *MP3*.

15 Birze, Regehr, and Regehr, "Video Playback, Affective Witnessing, and the Mobility of Trauma."
16 Dextro, "Sight, Sound & Motion," *Medium*, September 21, 2015, https://medium.com.
17 Dextro, "Security Video Monitoring," accessed May 15, 2017, www.dextro.co.
18 Benjamin, "The Work of Art in the Age of Mechanical Reproduction," 229–230.
19 As Dan Hallin has argued, there are not one but many different forms of mediatization. See Hallin, "Mediatization, Neoliberalism, and Populisms." See also Esser and Strömböck, *Mediatization of Politics*; Hjarvard, *The Mediatization of Culture and Society*; Lundby, *Mediatization of Communication*; Schulz, "Reconstructing Mediatization as an Analytical Concept"; Hepp, *Cultures of Mediatization*; Cottle, *Mediatized Conflict*.
20 Hayles, *Unthought*, 3, 11.
21 McCosker and Wilken, *Automating Vision*.
22 Caldwell, *Production Culture*.
23 Bourdieu, "Rethinking the State," 17.
24 Wacquant, *Punishing the Poor*, xi. Italics in the original.
25 Readers may notice the echo of Marshall McLuhan's "The Medium Is the Message."
26 This is the argument made in Hall et al., *Policing the Crisis*.
27 Linnemann, *Meth Wars*.
28 Ibid., 221–222.
29 Aushana, "Seeing Police."
30 C. Wilson, *Cop Knowledge*, 16.
31 Virilio, *War and Cinema*. See also the chapter on "Film" in Kittler, *Gramophone, Film, Typewriter*.
32 Peters, *The Marvelous Clouds*, 37.
33 Rossiter, *Software, Infrastructure, Labor*, xv.
34 Mukerji, "The Territorial State as a Figured World of Power," 402.
35 Mukerji, "The Territorial State as a Figured World of Power."
36 "Logistics per se has not been ignored by social theorists, simply blurred with strategics in both Marxist and Foucauldian ways," writes Mukerji (*Impossible Engineering*, 216).
37 Reeves and Packer, "Police Media: The Governance of Territory, Speed, and Communication."
38 Shapiro, *Design, Control, Predict*. See also D. Wilson, "Predictive Policing Management"; D. Wilson, "The New Platform Policing."
39 Manning, "Producing Drama."
40 Manning, "Producing Drama," 239.
41 Ibid.
42 Zuboff, *The Age of Surveillance Capitalism*, 115.
43 See also D. Wilson, "The New Platform Policing"; D. Wilson, "Predictive Policing Management"; Iliadis and Acker, "The Seer and the Seen"; S. Wood, "Policing through Platform"; Bratich, "Adventures in the Public Secret Sphere."

44 Cohen, "Law for the Platform Economy."
45 As Dean Wilson ("Platform Policing and the Real-Time Cop," 74) states, "Increasingly interpolated by the value seeking mechanisms of surveillance capitalism, police organizations are reimagined as both customers of technology and as producers of surplus value."
46 In the modern period of capitalist development, Steven Spitzer has argued, "socialized policing has neither been as one-sided nor complete as it initially appeared. In fact, what we find is not a single structure of public policing devoted to the tasks of crime control, but a dual structure comprised of both private and public forms" (Spitzer, "The Political Economy of Policing," 586–587).

Ian Loader writes, "We are living in the midst of a potentially far-reaching transformation in the means by which order and security are maintained in liberal democratic societies, one that is giving rise to the fragmentation and diversification of policing provision, and ushering in a plethora of agencies and agents, each with particular kinds of responsibility for the delivery of policing and security services and technologies.... We inhabit a world of plural, networked policing" (Loader, "Plural Policing and Democratic Governance," 324–325).

Writing in 2000, Loader noted that the "protection of person and property is now less and less the exclusive province of the public police, and is increasingly being delivered by a plethora of public, commercial and voluntary bodies." (Loader, "Consumer Culture and the Commodification of Policing and Security," 374). Loader suggested that policing and security were increasingly commodified, rethinking the logic of consumption. A 2010 study reprised this inquiry into security as a form of commodity consumption; see Goold, Loader, and Thumala, "Consuming Security?"
47 Spitzer, "The Political Economy of Policing."
48 Reeves, *Citizen Spies*.
49 Spitzer, "The Political Economy of Policing," 576.
50 Ibid., 577.
51 Ibid.
52 Ibid.
53 On the proliferation of hybrid public-private security assemblages, see Schuilenburg, *The Securitization of Society*. For ethnographies of the widely varying spatial assemblages security takes, see Low and Maguire, *Spaces of Security*. See also Wakefield, *Selling Security*; O'Connor, et al., "Seeing Private Security Like a State."
54 D. M. Wood, "A New 'Baroque Arsenal'?"
55 Goold, Loader, and Thumala, "The Banality of Security."
56 "U.S. Video Surveillance System Market Size and Share Analysis," *Mordor Intelligence*, accessed July 22, 2024, www.mordorintelligence.com/.
57 "Video Surveillance Market," *Markets and Markets*, accessed July 22, 2024, www.marketsandmarkets.com.
58 Steve Lasky, "Canon to Acquire Milestone Systems," *Security Infowatch*, June 13, 2014, www.securityinfowatch.com.

59 "Moments That Made Us," Axis Communications, accessed January 15, 2023, www.axis.com.
60 Paul Rothman, "Canon to Acquire Axis," *Security Infowatch*, February 10, 2015, www.securityinfowatch.com.
61 Quoted in Rothman, "Canon to Acquire Axis."
62 Bratich, "Adventures in the Public Secret Sphere," 16; Dunworth, "Information Technology and the Criminal Justice System."
63 Motorola Solutions, Inc., "Evidence: Build a More Complete Law Incident," accessed April 16, 2021, www.motorolasolutions.com.
64 Motorola Solutions, Inc., "Records and Evidence Management," accessed April 16, 2021, www.motorolasolutions.com.
65 D. Wilson, "Predictive Policing Management"; D. Wilson, "Platform Policing and the Real-Time Cop"; Shapiro, "Predictive Policing for Reform?"; Shapiro, *Design, Control, Predict*.
66 Dean Wilson ("Predictive Policing Management") has argued that predictive policing is continuous with the business management models that have been part of recommendations for police reforms since the 1920s in the United States.
67 D. Wilson, "Predictive Policing Management."
68 Willis, Koper, and Lum, "Technology Use and Constituting Structures," 484.
69 Schrader, *Badges without Borders*.
70 Ristovska, *Seeing Human Rights*.
71 Richardson, "Bearing Witness While Black"; Richardson, *Bearing Witness While Black: Smartphones, African Americans and the New Protest #Journalism*.
72 Kuchinskaya, *Networked Movements and Technological Innovation*. These three dimensions of media-technological change—"pace, scale and pattern"—are taken from Marshall McLuhan's "The Medium Is the Message." McLuhan was a media scholar with a dubious record on questions of race and racism. The Black studies scholar Armond R. Towns has critiqued and appropriated McLuhan's materialist media theory to develop an alternative Black media epistemology. See Towns, *On Black Media Philosophy*.
73 Kumanyika, "Livestreaming in the Black Lives Matter Network."
74 Goldsmith, "Policing's New Visibility."
75 Here, of course, I am paraphrasing a famous line from Dr. Martin Luther King Jr.'s "Remaining Awake through a Great Revolution" speech, delivered at the National Cathedral, March 31, 1968.
76 Petersen, "Ubiquitous Video, Objectivity, and the Problem of Perspective in Digital Visual Evidence."
77 Sacharoff and Lustbader, "Who Should Own Police Body Camera Videos?"
78 Newell, *Police Visibility*.
79 Owens, "Violence Everywhere." Rasul Mowatt asks, "With the proliferation of videos that are taken from a scene, posted, shared, have we truly become more engaged citizens, staunch activists, and effective community organizers? Or has a kind of passive activism set in, where people copy and paste links and make

statements of outrage on social media, while in the offline world 'nothing changes at all'?" Mowatt, "Black Lives as Snuff," 777.
80 Wood and Ball, "Brandscapes of Control?"
81 "PA Turnpike History," accessed September 15, 2023, www.paturnpike.com.
82 Foucault, "On Popular Justice: A Discussion with Maoists," 34.
83 Ibid., 15.
84 Ibid., 22–23.

CHAPTER 1. "GRAINY TO GUILTY"

1 News coverage was extensive. See, for example, Peter Williams, "Department Store Camera May Hold Important Clues," *NBC Nightly News*, April 17, 2013; Kate Dailey, "The Boston Marathon Bomber," *BBC News Magazine*, accessed April 18, 2013, www.bbc.com; Hodson, "AI Could Help Investigation of Boston Marathon."
2 Madrigal, "#BostonBombing." See also Nhan, Huey, and Broll, "Digilantism."
3 Hodson, "AI Could Help Investigation of Boston Marathon."
4 Brian Ross, "'5 Days': The Hunt for the Boston Marathon Bombers," *ABC News*, April 18, 2016.
5 Michiko Kakutani, "Unraveling Boston Suspects' Online Lives, Link by Link," *The New York Times*, April 23, 2013, www.nytimes.com.
6 Winner, "Who Will We Be in Cyberspace?"
7 Neal Feigenson and Christina Spiesel call this "naïve realism" (Feigenson and Spiesel, *Law on Display*).
8 Google, "Video AI," accessed February 10, 2024, https://cloud.google.com/video-intelligence.
9 Zuboff, "Big Other," 86.
10 Mnookin, "The Image of Truth"; Sekula, "The Body and the Archive"; Tagg, *The Burden of Representation*.
11 U.S. Bureau of Justice Assistance, *Video Evidence*.
12 iNPUT-ACE, "6 Key Trends in Video Evidence," accessed March 4, 2023, https://input-ace.com.
13 On the importance of media forensics and the materiality of evidence in the human rights context, see Weizman, *Forensic Architecture*; Schuppli, *Material Witness*.
14 C. Wilson, *Cop Knowledge*.
15 Siegel, *Forensic Media*, 6.
16 Weizman, *Forensic Architecture*.
17 Sheers, "Video Forensics."
18 Levin, "Rhetoric of the Temporal Index," 592. The "indexical" status of signs refers to their presumed ability to stand unequivocally for an existing material thing as a *matter of fact*, through a direct, physical connection. Canonical work on indexicality in semiotics is associated with the philosopher Charles Sanders Peirce. See, for example, Peirce, *Charles S. Peirce*. In his history of motion picture evidence in the U.S. courts, Louis-Georges Schwartz argues that "in *court*, the cinema of indexicality is not the same as film theory. In cinema such indexicality is an

implicit result of the medium itself and works to give the spectator an impression of reality. In court, film's indexicality is a result of the combination of a particular image and the testimony authenticating it, making the process of creating a particular image explicit. Evidentiary film's indexicality functions to purvey the facts of an event to the jury" (Schwartz, *Mechanical Witness*, 9. Emphasis in the original). I do not agree with Schwartz that in court proceedings, motion-picture evidence functions solely to purvey facts, although of course that is always the explicit claim.

19 Sharma, *In the Meantime*.
20 Goodwin, "Professional Vision."
21 Peter Marshall, "Victim of CCTV Murder Evidence Error Speaks Out," *BBC Newsnight*, July 13, 2009, https://news.bbc.co.uk/.
22 Quoted in Marshall, "Victim of CCTV Murder Evidence Error Speaks Out."
23 Nico Bento eventually won a libel case against the Bedford Police. "Man Cleared of Bedford Lake Murder Wins Libel against Police," *BBC News*, June 1, 2012, www.bbcnews.com. According to the BBC, Casey Caudle committed suicide. Marshall, "Victim of CCTV Murder Evidence Error Speaks Out."
24 Marshall, "Victim of CCTV Murder Evidence Speaks Out."
25 U.S. Bureau of Justice Assistance, *Video Evidence*.
26 National Research Council, *Strengthening Forensic Science in the United States*, 5–6.
27 Edmond, "Legal Versus Non-Legal Approaches to Forensic Science Evidence."
28 Gilligan, "States Struggle with Rape Kit Backlog Despite Funding Efforts."
29 Wright, Heynen, and van der Meulen, "'It Depends on Who You Are, What You Are.'"
30 For one study on the way police in Canada systematically failed to investigate cases of missing and murdered women from Indigenous and other marginalized groups, see Oppal, *Forsaken: The Report of the Missing Women Commission of Inquiry*.
31 Brown, *Dark Matters*; Brucato, *Race and Police*; Hadden, *Slave Patrols*; Parenti, *The Soft Cage*.
32 Ruha Benjamin argues that new technologies of automation in policing have similar racist consequences as did Jim Crow laws, creating "the New Jim Code" under the cover of technical neutrality. Benjamin, *Race after Technology*, 5.
33 U.S. Bureau of Justice Assistance, *Video Evidence*. Videos recorded in proprietary formats can be difficult if not impossible to play back using any device or codec other than those of the original recordings.
34 "Video Surveillance History, 2000–2024," *IPVM*, May 25, 2023, https://ipvm.com.
35 Video surveillance as a service provides "live viewing, analytics and storage solutions for a monthly price" (Thorpe, "The Rise of Video Surveillance as a Service").
36 Honovich, "Hostage as a Service (HaaS)—Meraki, Rhombus, and Verkada."
37 Honovich, "2030."
38 In addition, the year 2021 saw the launch of a record number of video surveillance startup companies, each attempting to create their own proprietary and profitable technologies, many of them recognizing that getting acquired by a larger tech

firm would be the most viable outcome. "64 Video Surveillance Startups Directory 2021," *IPVM*, May 7, 2021. https://ipvm.com.
39 Axon Enterprise, "Introducing Axon Investigate," October 27, 2022, www.axon.com.
40 Ibid.
41 Ristovska, *Seeing Human Rights*.
42 Weizman, *Forensic Architecture*, 10.
43 Gates, "*Day of Rage*"; Bjerknes, "Images of Transgressions"; Ristovska, "Open-Source Investigation as a Genre of Conflict Reporting"; Müller and Wiik, "From Gatekeeper to Gate-Opener."
44 Weizman, *Forensic Architecture*, 20.
45 Daston and Galison, *Objectivity*, 43.

CHAPTER 2. "A HIGH-TECH COMPANY MASQUERADING AS A RETAILER"

1 Charles Duhigg, "How Companies Learn Your Secrets," *New York Times Magazine*, February 16, 2012, www.nytimes.com.
2 Quoted in Sarah Bridges, "Retailer Target Branches Out into Police Work," *Washington Post*, January 29, 2006, www.washingtonpost.com.
3 Brekke, "When Risks Go Up and Resources Go Down, the Game-Changer Is Partnerships."
4 Jenn Abelson, "Target Goes High-Tech to Stop Increasingly Savvy Thieves," *Boston Globe*, December 10, 2011.
5 Kevin Plante, quoted in Abelson, "Target Goes High-Tech." See also Bob Giles, "Minneapolis' SafeZone." *SecurityInfowatch*, April 18, 2012, www.securityinfowatch.com.
6 Kaveh Waddel, "CSI: Walmart," *The Atlantic*, April 3, 2017, www.theatlantic.com.
7 Walby, Lippert, and Luscombe, "The Police Foundation's Rise: Implications of Public Policing's Dark Money."
8 Zuboff, *The Age of Surveillance Capitalism*.
9 Rowley, *On Target*.
10 Target Corp., "Target through the Years," *A Bullseye View*, accessed September 2, 2021, https://corporate.target.com/; Target Corp., *2020 Annual Report*, 2020, https://corporate.target.com/annual-reports/2020.
11 Brad Brekke, quoted in Giles, "Minneapolis' SafeZone."
12 Wood and Ball, "Brandscapes of Control?"
13 R. H. Williams, *Dream Worlds*.
14 Turow, *The Aisles Have Eyes*.
15 Wood and Ball, "Brandscapes of Control?" 48.
16 Target Corp. *Target 2017 Annual Report*, https://corporate.target.com.
17 According to the Indeed online career guide, loss prevention is defined as "any organizational activity that is specifically implemented to minimize preventable losses . . . as a result of purposeful or accidental actions on behalf of customers, employees or other individuals who interact with the business" ("What Is Loss Prevention? Tips and Examples," *Indeed*, December 28, 2023, www.indeed.com).

18 Goold, Loader, and Thumala, "The Banality of Security."
19 Hacking, *The Taming of Chance*, 2.
20 McCarthy, *Ambient Television*; Spiegel, *Make Room for TV*.
21 Abelson, "Target Goes High-Tech."
22 Giles, "Minneapolis' SafeZone."
23 Ibid.
24 Ibid.
25 Abelson, "Target Goes High-Tech."
26 Ibid.
27 Quoted in Giles, "Minneapolis' SafeZone."
28 Abelson, "Target Goes High-Tech."
29 Bridges, "Retailer Target Branches Out into Police Work."
30 Quoted in B. Williams, "Target's State-of-the-Art Forensics Lab."
31 Quoted in Giles, "Minneapolis' SafeZone."
32 These images were also posted on the website of *SecurityInfowatch*, April 18, 2012, www.securityinfowatch.com.
33 Fujio Mitarai, quoted in Rothman, "Canon to Acquire Axis."
34 Quoted in Giles, "Minneapolis' SafeZone."
35 Ibid.
36 Quoted in Mary Ellen Egan, "CSI: Target," *Forbes*, April 3, 2008, www.forbes.com.
37 Peterson and Hickman, "Census of Publicly Funded Forensic Crime Laboratories, 2002."
38 B. Williams, "Target's State-of-the-Art Forensics Lab."
39 Egan, "CSI: Target."
40 Ibid.
41 B. Williams, "Target's State-of-the-Art Forensics Lab."
42 Target Corp., "An Unexpected Career: Target's Forensic Services Laboratory," February 15, 2012, https://corporate.target.com.
43 Ibid.
44 Egan, "CSI: Target." This forensic analyst appears in the 2008 Errol Morris documentary *Standard Operating Procedure*, about the Abu Ghraib prison investigation, where he explains the process of photo evidence analysis using both the content of images and the metadata attached to them.
45 Egan, "CSI: Target."
46 Bridges, "Retailer Target Branches Out into Police Work."
47 Egan, "CSI: Target."
48 B. Williams, "Target's State-of-the-Art Forensics Lab."
49 Rob Allen, quoted in B. Williams, "Target's State-of-the-Art Forensics Lab."
50 Quoted in Bridges, "Retailer Target Branches Out into Police Work." Although Garvis was perhaps merely making an analogy, his equation of human beings with inventory was a revealing expression of the way twenty-first-century crime management continued the long afterlife of slavery.

51 Michelle Woo, "What Happened When I Stole from Target: A Former Shoplifter Tells His Story," *Reddit Upvoted* (blog), January 13, 2016, https://redditblog.com/r/Upvoted/.
52 Ibid.
53 National Retail Federation, "2023 Retail Security Survey: The State of National Retail Security and Organized Retail Crime," September 26, 2023, https://cdn.nrf.com/.
54 Rebecca Ballhaus and Shalini Ramachandran, "Ben Dugan Works for CVS. His Job Is Battling a $45 Billion Crime Spree," *Wall Street Journal*, September 14, 2021.
55 Ibid.
56 Haurek, quoted in Ballhaus and Ramachandran, "Ben Dugan Works for CVS."
57 Jerry Iannelli, "Big Retail Chains Are Manufacturing a Shoplifting 'Crisis,'" *The Appeal*, November 9, 2020, https://theappeal.org.
58 Courtney Reagan, "Retail Theft Isn't Actually Increasing Much, Major Industry Study Finds," *CNBC*, September 26, 2023, www.cnbc.com.
59 Hayes, "Retail Theft."
60 Smith and Clarke, "Shoplifting of Everyday Products That Serve Illicit Drug Uses."
61 In their study of shoplifting by drug users, Gail A. Caputo and Anna King found that women in particular understood shoplifting as a form of work. See Caputo and King, "Shoplifting by Male and Female Drug Users." See also Caputo and King, "Shoplifting"; Caputo, *Out in the Storm*.
62 Quoted in B. Williams, "Target's State-of-the-Art Forensics Lab."
63 Brad Brekke, "Spotlight on Public/Private Initiative: Target & Blue," Security Executive Council, 2007, www.securityexecutivecouncil.com.
64 Ibid.
65 Ibid.
66 Target Corp., "Target Public Safety Grants," *A Bullseye View*, accessed July 12, 2020, https://corporate.target.com.
67 Bridges, "Retailer Target Branches Out into Police Work."
68 Ibid.
69 Ibid.
70 Ibid.
71 "PERF and Target Announce Project to Promote Police Foundations," *Subject to Debate: A Newsletter of the Police Executive Research Forum* 24, no. 11 (December 2010): 6
72 Michigan Public Radio described the National Police Foundations Project as "a federally funded effort to help law enforcement agencies set up foundations," which in turn would "make it easier for public law enforcement agencies to receive private contributions," but it failed to note that Target Corp. was also centrally involved (B. Williams, "Target's State-of-the-Art Forensics Lab").
73 B. Williams, "Target's State-of-the-Art Forensics Lab."
74 Pamela Delaney, quoted in B. Williams, "Target's State-of-the-Art Forensics Lab."

75 Ali Winston and Darwin Bond Graham, "Private Donors Supply Spy Gear to Cops," *ProPublica*, October 13, 2014, https://propublica.org.
76 Ibid.
77 Ibid.
78 Walby, Lippert, and Luscombe, "The Police Foundation's Rise."
79 Ibid.
80 Peter Waldman and Laruen Etter, "How Target Got Cozy with the Cops, Turning Black Neighbors into Suspects," August 25, 2021, *Bloomberg Businessweek*, www.bloomberg.com/.
81 Ibid.
82 Ibid.
83 Michael Hickins, "What Is Retail Analytics? The Ultimate Guide," *Oracle*, March 17, 2023, www.oracle.com/retail/what-is-retail-analytics/.
84 Ibid.
85 Ibid.
86 Turow, *The Aisles Have Eyes*, 18.
87 Axis Communications, "Store Optimization," *Axis.com*, accessed February 25, 2022.
88 Ibid.
89 Stephanie Miles, "Analytics from Surveillance Footage," *Street Fight*, May 13, 2014, https://streetfightmag.com.
90 Axis Communications, "Retail," *Axis.com*, accessed February 25, 2022.
91 See Huberman, "Amazon Go, Surveillance Capitalism, and the Ideology of Convenience."
92 Apple Privacy, email message to author, August 19, 2024.
93 According to Shoshana Zuboff, "Surveillance capitalism lays claim to [decision rights regarding when to disclose information]. The typical complaint is that privacy is eroded, but that is misleading. In the larger societal pattern, privacy is not eroded by redistributed, as decision rights over privacy are claimed for surveillance capital" (Zuboff, *The Age of Surveillance Capitalism*, 90). "The intentional work of hiding naked facts in rhetoric, omission, complexity, exclusivity, scale, abusive contracts, design, and euphemism is another factor that helps explain why during Google's breakthrough to profitability, few noticed the foundational mechanisms of its success and their larger significance" (Zuboff, *The Age of Surveillance Capitalism*, 91).
94 McCarthy, *Ambient Television*.
95 Brekke, "When Risks Go Up and Resources Go Down."
96 Ibid.
97 Nadler, Crain, and Donovan, "Weaponizing the Digital Influence Machine."

CHAPTER 3. "STORAGE COSTS SET TO SKYROCKET"

1 Zuboff, *The Age of Surveillance Capitalism*.
2 Mearian, "As Police Move to Adopt Body Cams, Storage Costs Set to Skyrocket."
3 U.S. Bureau of Justice Assistance, *Public Safety Primer on Cloud Technology*, 2.
4 Ibid., 4.

5 Fan, *Camera Power*, 204–206.
6 Newell, *Police Visibility*.
7 Goldsmith, "Policing's New Visibility."
8 Stacy Wood ("Policing through Platform") similarly focuses on the imaginaries of police work that Axon promotes, examining the promises the company makes in its promotional videos. Wood analyzes Axon through the lens of platform studies, including the analysis of "convergences between design, technological affordances, and ideology," and examines the porous boundaries between law enforcement and the companies that service them, focusing on Axon. Dean Wilson ("Platform Policing and the Real-Time Cop," 70) also focuses "the imaginaries of real-time platform policing rather than the contingent and mutable unfolding of such imaginaries within specific contexts."
9 Virilio, *War and Cinema*.
10 See Sekula, "The Body and the Archive"; Tagg, *The Burden of Representation*.
11 See Gunning, "Tracing the Individual Body: Photography, Detectives, and Early Cinema."
12 New York City Municipal Archives, "New York Police Department Surveillance Films," REC0063-RG 062, 1960–1980, https://a860-collectionguides.nyc.gov.
13 Rosenblatt, Cromartie, and Firman, *The Impact of Video Evidence on Modern Policing*.
14 D. Wilson, "Predictive Policing Management."
15 Poli, "Development and Present Trend of Police Radio Communications."
16 D. Wilson, "Predictive Policing Management," 141.
17 Rule, *Private Lives and Public Surveillance*, 87–88.
18 Seo, *Policing the Open Road*; Sorin, *Driving While Black*; Livingston and Ross, *Cars and Jails*.
19 Friedberg, *The Virtual Window*. Aushana, "Seeing Police."
20 Hallett and Powell, "Backstage with 'COPS'" 104.
21 Ibid., 111.
22 Ibid., 115.
23 Jackie Wang (*Carceral Capitalism*, 132) refers the municipal fines and legal fees levied on Black folks as the "racial surtax."
24 On "viewfinderlessness," see Cartwright and Rice, "My Hero."
25 Loader, "Policing and the Social"; Mawby, *Policing Images*; Manning, *Policing Contingencies*.
26 Ericson and Haggerty, *Policing the Risk Society*.
27 Goldsmith, "Policing's New Visibility."
28 Trottier, "'Fear of Contact'"; Trottier, "Vigilantism and Power Users"; Trottier, "Policing Social Media"; Bullock, "The Police Use of Social Media."
29 Wall and Linnemann, "Staring Down the State."
30 A number of scholars have explained the phenomenon of police body cameras as a recursive battle between cell phone-wielding publics and the police. See Bock, *Seeing Justice*; and Fan, *Camera Power*.

31 Bryce Newell (*Police Visibility*, 48) argues that police adoption of body cameras is reconfiguring the information politics of law enforcement and police-citizen relations, creating new forms of "collateral visibility" and necessitating policy that protects citizens' rights, including their right to record the police and to hold the state accountable.

32 Again, there are important exceptions, including S. Wood, "Policing through Platform," and D. Wilson, "Platform Policing and the Real-Time Cop."

33 Michael Joseph Gross, "Shock & Ow!" *GQ*, July 5, 2010, www.gq.com; Quentin Hardy, "Taser's Latest Police Weapon: The Tiny Camera and the Cloud," *New York Times*, February 21, 2012. According to the Associated Press, the U.K. Home Office reported that police in Plymouth had begun experimenting with body cameras in 2007, but they did not name the supplier. The Association of Chief Police Officers was not entirely receptive to body cameras, issuing a statement that "we need to guard against creating an expectation that all police activity ought to be supported by the use of digital recording technology." See "Britain Straps Video Cameras to Police Helmets." *NBC News*, July 13, 2007, www.nbcnews.com/.

34 Morozov, *To Save Everything, Click Here*.

35 The criminologists Jude McCulloch and Dean Wilson borrowed the term "pre-crime" from *Minority Report* to diagnose the new orientation to policing that took shape in the post-9/11 context, stressing the importance of *imagination* to this emerging paradigm of criminal justice. In the pre-crime approach to police management, they argue, the pivotal role of imagination is masked behind an objective veneer of data science and mathematical calculation. For them, predictive policing is the application of the computational tools of predictive analytics to the pre-crime project; it is the technology that makes the preemptive logics of pre-crime possible. But, according to their study, the key to understanding predictive policing, as well as other future-facing claims being made about police technoscience, is the inseparability of the imagination from actual police practice. Crime dramas, including science-fiction scenarios about predicting and controlling the future, have made a special impression on reality. To paraphrase Donna Haraway, the boundary line between science fiction and social reality is an optical illusion (Haraway, "A Manifesto for Cyborgs"). Cultural imaginaries of policing play an important role in defining what is thought to be desirable and possible in the domain of police technoscience. See McCulloch and D. Wilson, *Pre-crime*. For another argument about the relevance of *Minority Report* to debates about predictive policing (focusing on their fundamentally racist and racializing logics), see Scannell, "This is Not *Minority Report*."

36 Latour, *Reassembling the Social*.

37 Ibid., 189.

38 Parks and Starosielski, *Signal Traffic*, 1.

39 Moore, *Legal Spectatorship*.

40 On "material semiotics," see Haraway, "Situated Knowledges"; Law, "Actor Network Theory and Material Semiotics."

41 MLive, "Grand Rapids Police Stop 5 Unarmed Black Youth at Gunpoint," April 20, 2017, www.youtube.com/watch?v=_ONict5F3w4.
42 Goodman and Parisi, "Machines of Memory."
43 Parisi and Goodman, "Mnemonic Control," 173.
44 Goodman and Parisi, "Machines of Memory," 345.
45 This was also true of technologies of household automation. See Cowan, *More Work for Mother*.
46 Sterne and Razlogova, "Tuning Sound for Infrastructure," 1.
47 Muniesa, Millo, and Callon, "An Introduction to Market Devices," 2.
48 MacKenzie, *An Engine, Not a Camera*.
49 See Sturken, "Advertising and the Rise of Amateur Photography."
50 Axon Enterprise, "Axon Reports Second Quarter Results; Software Annual Recurring Revenue of $93 Million," press release, August 7, 2018. https://investor.axon.com/press-releases.
51 Ibid.
52 Srnicek, *Platform Capitalism*, 44.
53 Ibid., 45.
54 Ibid., 48.
55 Ibid., 47.
56 Willis, Koper, and Lum, "Technology Use and Constituting Structures," 484. For further discussion of police RMS, including the companies that dominate the RMS market, see S. Wood, "Policing through Platform."
57 See, e.g., Rule, *Private Lives and Public Surveillance*.
58 Ericson and Haggerty, *Policing the Risk Society*, 446.
59 S. Wood, "Policing through Platform."
60 Willis, Koper, and Lum, "Technology Use and Constituting Structures," 492.
61 Motorola Solutions, "Evidence: Build a More Complete Law Incident," accessed April 16, 2021, www.motorolasolutions.com.
62 Motorola Solutions, "Records and Evidence Management," accessed March 21, 2022, www.motorolasolutions.com.
63 Gilmore, *Golden Gulag*, 100.
64 See Jillian Forstadt, "Proposal to Expand Pittsburgh Police's Body- and Dash-Camera Contract Means Rising Costs," 90.5 WESA, June 22, 2023, www.wesa.fm.
65 Mayor's Press Office, "Body Worn Cameras Expansion Completed—One Year Ahead of Schedule," press release, December 10, 2017, www.chicago.gov.
66 Axon Enterprise, "Axon Acquires VIEVU Camera Subsidiary from the Safariland Group and Announces Strategic Long-Term Holster Partnership," press release, May 4, 2018, https://investor.axon.com.
67 U.S. Federal Trade Commission, "FTC Challenges Consummated Merger of Companies That Market Body-Worn Camera Systems to Large Metropolitan Police Departments," press release, January 3, 2020, www.ftc.gov.
68 "*Axon Enterprise, Inc. v. FTC*," *Harvard Law Review*.
69 "*Axon Enterprise, Inc. v. FTC*," *Harvard Law Review*.

70 As Ruha Benjamin writes (*Race after Technology*, 167), "A key tenet of prison abolition is that caging people works directly against the safety and well-being of communities because jails and prisons do not address the underlying reasons why people harm themselves and others—in fact they exacerbate the problem by making it even more difficult to obtain any of the support needed to live, work, and make amends for the harms committed."
71 Axon Enterprise Inc., *Form 10-K 2017*. Scottsdale, AZ: Axon Enterprise Inc., 2017, 14.
72 Ibid., 15.
73 Stillman, "Taken"; Knepper et al., *Policing for Profit*; MacDougall, "Police Say Seizing Property without Trial Helps Keep Crime Down. A New Study Shows They're Wrong."
74 Zuboff, *The Age of Surveillance Capitalism*, 189.
75 Mitchell, "Uber Eats."

CHAPTER 4. "OUR MACHINES WATCH SO YOU DON'T HAVE TO"

 1 Mearian, "As Police Move to Adopt Body Cams, Storage Costs Set to Skyrocket."
 2 Srnicek, *Platform Capitalism*, 101.
 3 O'Mahony, et al., "Computer Vision for 3D Perception," 789.
 4 Dreyfus, *What Computers Still Can't Do*.
 5 Richardson, Schultz, and Crawford, "Dirty Data, Bad Predictions"; Benjamin, *Race after Technology*; Scannell, "This is Not *Minority Report*"; Buolamwini, *Unmasking AI*; Mirzoeff, "Artificial Vision, White Space and Racial Surveillance Capitalism."
 6 See Mitchell, "Uber Eats." In this article, Timothy Mitchell is making an argument about the modern shareholder corporation, not AI.
 7 Crawford and Joler, "Anatomy of an AI System."
 8 Lewis-Kraus, "The Great AI Awakening."
 9 The claim that AI has no historical precedents and that it is the last technology that humans will ever invent was made by Pascal Finette, the keynote speaker at the closing of the general session of Axon Accelerate 2017. You can find him expressing these ideas on his YouTube channel at PascalFinetteVideos.
10 McLuhan, "The Medium Is the Message."
11 Amoore, *Cloud Ethics*.
12 Zuboff, *The Age of Surveillance Capitalism*.
13 Cohen, "Law for the Platform Economy."
14 Jordan, "Artificial Intelligence—The Revolution Hasn't Happened Yet."
15 Ibid.
16 Ibid.
17 Hayles, *How We Think*, 32.
18 Ibid, 3.
19 Chace, "Has There Been a Second AI Big Bang?"; Lewis-Kraus, "The Great AI Awakening."
20 Frederic Lardinois, "Google's New Machine Learning API Recognizes Objects in Videos," *Tech Crunch*, March 8, 2017, https://techcrunch.com.

21. Google, "Python Client for Video Intelligence API," accessed July 19, 2024, https://cloud.google.com.
22. This definition of API comes from Martin Reddy, *API Design for C++* (Amsterdam: Elsevier, 2011): 1.
23. Lardinois, "Google's New Machine Learning API." Emphasis added.
24. Fei-Fei Li, "Announcing Google Cloud Video Intelligence API and More Cloud Machine Learning updates," *Google Cloud Blog*, March 8, 2017, https://cloud.google.com/.
25. Zuboff, *The Age of Surveillance Capitalism*, 74–97.
26. Kent Walker, "AI for Social Good in Asia Pacific," *The Keyword*, December 13, 2018, https://blog.google.
27. Browne, *Dark Matters*, 108–119.
28. Mirzoeff, "Artificial Vision, White Space and Racial Surveillance Capitalism," 1296.
29. See MacKenzie, *Inventing Accuracy*.
30. AWS, "Featured Rekognition Customers," accessed May 27, 2018, https://aws.amazon.com.
31. Matt Cagle and Nicole Ozer, "Amazon Teams Up with Government to Deploy Dangerous New Facial Recognition Technology," *ACLU*, May 22, 2018, www.aclu.org.
32. Ibid.
33. Robert McMillan, "The Incredible AI That Can Watch Videos and Tell You What It's Seeing," *Wired*, February 5, 2015, www.wired.com.
34. Derrick Harris, "A Startup Wants to Quantify Video Content Using Computer Vision," *GIGAOM*, December 29, 2014, https://gigaom.com.
35. Ben Dickson, "What Is Computer Vision?" *PC Magazine*, February 9, 2020, www.pcmag.com.
36. Klint Finley, "Can't Find the Good Stuff on Periscope? Maybe AI Can Help," *Wired*, May 5, 2015, www.wired.com.
37. Dextro, "Sight, Sound & Motion," *Medium*, September 21, 2015, https://medium.com.
38. Ibid.
39. Ibid.
40. Harris, "A Startup Wants to Quantify Video."
41. Ibid.
42. David Luan, quoted in Harris, "A Startup Wants to Quantify Video."
43. One of Luan's slides read: "Our vision is to eliminate paperwork with AI, while giving LE complete analytics of their data." See the video excerpt of his presentation, "Accelerate 2017 Recap," *Axon.com*, June 30, 2017. www.axon.com.
44. David Luan and Sanchit Arora, "We're Excited to Join Axon!" *Medium*, February 9, 2017, https://medium.com.
45. Goodwin, "Professional Vision."
46. Erin Fleischli, "Public Safety and Machine Learning," Axon Accelerate 2017, June 21, 2017.
47. Rick Smith, "Axon's AI Work: What's Ahead," *Axon.com*, May 5, 2017.
48. Ibid.

49 Newell, *Police Visibility*, 48.
50 Smith, "Axon's AI Work."
51 Ibid.
52 Ibid.
53 In a press release for investors, the company noted that "beyond incident reporting capability, we are also building out crime analysis, records review capability, and investigations and case tracking." See Axon Enterprise, Inc., "Axon Reports Second Quarter Results," August 7, 2018, https://investor.axon.com.
54 Fleischli, "Public Safety and Machine Learning."
55 Truleo Inc., "Truleo Lifecycle Diagram," accessed August 28, 2023, https://truleo.com.
56 According to Johathan Sterne and Mehak Sawhney ("The Acousmatic Question and the Will to Datafy," 299), "Voiceprints are not nearly as developed a science as fingerprinting, and within forensic science, there is still some disagreement as to what even constitutes them."
57 Melissa Santos, "Seattle Police Stop Using AI System to Analyze Bodycam Footage," *Axios.com*, February 14, 2023.
58 Laurence Du Sault, "Under Union Pressure, Vallejo Police Chief Ends Body Camera Analysis," *Open Vallejo*, July 9, 2023, https://openvallejo.org/.
59 Bogard, *The Simulation of Surveillance*, 4.
60 Manovich, "Separate and Reassemble." See also Zachary Small, "Black Artists Say AI Shows Bias, with Algorithms Erasing Their History," *New York Times*, July 4, 2023, www.nytimes.com.
61 For a critique of the secular virtue of productivity, see Gregg, *Counterproductive*.
62 Google, "Generative AI," accessed November 27, 2023, https://ai.google.
63 Shannon Bond, "People Are Trying to Claim Real Videos Are Deepfakes. The Courts Are Not Amused," *All Things Considered*, May 8, 2023, www.npr.org/.
64 It is not surprising that the "deepfake defense" has been leveraged to defend the aggressive masculinist strain of post-truth political performers. See Harsin, "Aggro-truth."
65 See Agarwal et al., "Detecting Deep-Fake Videos from Phoneme-Viseme Mismatches."
66 Hong, "Technofutures in Stasis."
67 Schüll, *Addiction by Design*, 3, 58–59.
68 Jim DeLung, "7 Focus Areas for Millennial Police Recruitment," *Axon.com*, February 20, 2019; Nicole Cain, "Recruiting and Hiring the Next Generation of Police Officers," *American Public University*, June 30, 2022, https://apu.apus.edu; Ben Langham, "Millennials and Improving Recruitment in Law Enforcement," *Police Chief Magazine*, May 24, 2017, www.policechiefmagazine.org; International Association of Chiefs of Police, "The State of Recruitment: A Crisis for Law Enforcement," accessed May 1, 2023, www.theiacp.org; "Adapting Police Recruiting Efforts for Millennials and Gen-Z," *Digital PD*, accessed May 1, 2024, https://thedigitalpd.com.
69 Gitelman, *"Raw Data" Is an Oxymoron*; Bowker, *Memory Practices in the Sciences*.

CONCLUSION

1. Biber, *In Crime's Archive*. Film studies scholars have examined the ways in which the aesthetics of surveillance video have been interwoven into cinema. See Levin, "Rhetoric of the Temporal Index"; Stewart, *Closed Circuits*; Zimmer, *Surveillance Cinema*; Wise, *Surveillance and Film*; Fang, *Arresting Cinema*.
2. Eagleton, *The Ideology of the Aesthetic*, 13.
3. Vatulescu, *Police Aesthetics*.
4. Ibid., 22.
5. Ibid.
6. Steyerl, "In Defense of the Poor Image." On the aesthetics of police body-worn camera video, see McKay and Lee, "Body-Worn Images." See also Stork, "Aesthetics, Politics, and the Police Hermeneutic."
7. Eyal Weizman (*Forensic Architecture*, 94) theorizes forensics as an aesthetic practice. He explains that aesthetics "traverses three sites of forensic operation, the field, the lab/studio and the forum," and operates in different ways in each of these sites. "Material aesthetics" occurs at the level of the field, or the scene of the crime, where "material objects—bones, ruins or landscapes—function as sensors and register changes in their environment." In the lab/studio, investigative aesthetics involves slowing down time and intensifying "sensibility to space, matter, and image." And in the forum, aesthetic practice occurs in the "modes of narration and the articulation of truth claims." See also Fuller and Weizman, *Investigative Aesthetics*.
8. Farocki, "Phantom Images," 17.
9. Weizman, *Forensic Architecture*, 94. Emphasis in the original.
10. Crawford and Joler, "Anatomy of an AI System," 24.
11. Ibid., 3.
12. Ibid., 6.
13. Mukerji, *Impossible Engineering*.
14. Osnos, "Can Mark Zuckerberg Fix Facebook Before It Breaks Democracy?"
15. Zuboff, *The Age of Surveillance Capitalism*, 189.
16. Parks, "Earth Observation and Signal Territories," 288.
17. McCulloch and Wilson, *Pre-Crime*; D. Wilson, "Predictive Policing Management."
18. Angwin et al., "Machine Bias"; Richardson, Schultz, and Crawford, "Dirty Data"; Ferguson, *The Rise of Big Data Policing*; Scannell, "This Is Not *Minority Report*"; Wang, "This Is a Story about Nerds and Cops."
19. Andrejevic, "To Preempt a Thief"; Hartcourt, *Against Prediction*; Sheehey, "Algorithmic Paranoia."
20. Shapiro, *Design, Control, Predict*; Moses and Chan, "Algorithmic Prediction in Policing."
21. Brayne, *Predict and Surveil*; Shapiro, *Design, Control, Predict*.
22. Crawford and Paglen, "Excavating AI"; Denton et al., "On the Genealogy of Machine Learning Datasets."
23. Amoore, *Cloud Ethics*, 9.
24. Ibid., 11–12.

25 Ibid., 16.
26 Wang, *Carceral Capitalism*, 85. See also Shedd, "Countering the Carceral Continuum."
27 Wang, *Carceral Capitalism*, 69.
28 Ibid., 77.
29 Ibid., 85.
30 Ruth Wilson Gilmore, *Golden Gulag*.
31 R. Benjamin, "Introduction," 2.
32 Motorola Solutions, "Safety Reimagined," accessed April 10, 2022, www.motorolasolutions.com.
33 W. Benjamin, "The Work of Art in the Age of Mechanical Reproduction."
34 Andrejevic, "The Kinder, Gentler Gaze of Big Brother," 251.
35 Amoore, *Cloud Ethics*, 161.
36 Cohen, "What Privacy Is For," 1906.
37 Monahan, *Crisis Vision*, 20.
38 Amoore, *Cloud Ethics*, 8.
39 R. Benjamin, "Introduction," 3.

BIBLIOGRAPHY

Agarwal, Shruti, Hany Farid, Ohad Fried, and Maneesh Agrawala. "Detecting Deep-Fake Videos from Phoneme-Viseme Mismatches," *2020 IEEE/CVF Conference on Computer Vision and Pattern Recognition Workshops*, Seattle, WA, 2020, 2814–2822. New York: Institute of Electrical and Electronics Engineers (IEEE).

Amoore, Louise. *Cloud Ethics: Algorithms and the Attributes of Ourselves and Others.* Durham, NC: Duke University Press, 2020.

Andrejevic, Mark. "To Preempt a Thief." *International Journal of Communication* 11 (2017): 879–896.

Andrejevic, Mark. "The Kinder, Gentler Gaze of Big Brother: Reality TV in the Era of Digital Capitalism." *New Media & Society* 4, no. 2 (2002): 251–270.

Angwin, Julia, Jeff Larson, Surya Mattu, and Lauren Kirchner. "Machine Bias." *ProPublica*, May 23, 2016. www.propublica.org.

Aushana, Christina. "Seeing Police: Cinematic Training and the Scripting of Police Vision." *Surveillance & Society* 17, no. 3/4 (2019): 367–381.

"Axon Enterprise, Inc. v. FTC." *Harvard Law Review* 137, no. 1, 2023. https://harvardlawreview.org

Benjamin, Ruha. *Race after Technology: Abolitionist Tools for the New Jim Code.* Cambridge: Polity, 2019.

Benjamin, Ruha. "Introduction: Discriminatory Design, Liberating Imagination." In *Captivating Technology: Race, Carceral Technoscience, and Liberatory Imagination in Everyday Life*, edited by Ruha Benjamin, 1–22. Durham, NC: Duke University Press, 2019.

Benjamin, Walter. "The Work of Art in the Age of Mechanical Reproduction." In *Illuminations*, edited by Hannah Arendt, translated by Harry Zohn, 217–252. New York: Schocken Books, 1939.

Biber, Katherine. *In Crime's Archive: The Cultural Afterlife of Evidence.* New York: Routledge, 2019.

Birze, Arija, Cheryl Regehr, and Kaitlyn Regehr. "Video Playback, Affective Witnessing, and the Mobility of Trauma: Video Evidence of Violent Crime in the Criminal Justice System." *Emotion, Space and Society* 47 (2023): 1–8.

Bjerknes, Fredrik. "Images of Transgressions: Visuals as Reconstructed Evidence in Digital Investigative Journalism." *Journalism Studies* 23, no. 8 (2022): 951–973.

Bock, Mary Angela. *Seeing Justice: Witnessing, Crime and Punishment in Visual Media.* Oxford: Oxford University Press, 2021.

Bogard, William. *The Simulation of Surveillance: Hypercontrol in Telematic Societies.* Cambridge: Cambridge University Press, 1996.

Bourdieu, Pierre. "Rethinking the State: Genesis and Structure of the Bureaucratic Field." Translated by Loïc J.D. Wacquant and Samar Farage. *Sociological Theory* 12, no. 1 (1994): 1–18.
Bowker, Geoffrey C. *Memory Practices in the Sciences*. Cambridge, MA: MIT Press, 2008.
Bratich, Jack. "Adventures in the Public Secret Sphere: Police Sovereign Networks and Communications Warfare." *Cultural Studies ↔ Critical Methodologies* 14, no. 1 (2014): 11–20.
Brayne, Sarah. *Predict and Surveil: Data, Discretion, and the Future of Policing*. Oxford: Oxford University Press, 2020.
Brekke, Brad. "When Risks Go Up and Resources Go Down, the Game-Changer Is Partnerships." In *Target's Safe City Program: Community Leaders Take the Initiative in Building Partnerships with the Police*, 24–25. Washington, DC: Police Executive Research Forum, 2010.
Brown, Wendy. *In the Ruins of Neoliberalism: The Rise of Antidemocratic Politics in the West*. New York: Columbia University Press, 2019.
Browne, Simone. *Dark Matters: On the Surveillance of Blackness*. Durham, NC: Duke University Press, 2015.
Brucato, Ben. *Race and Police: The Origins of Our Peculiar Institutions*. New Brunswick, NJ: Rutgers University Press, 2023.
Bullock, Karen. "The Police Use of Social Media: Transformation or Normalisation?" *Social Police and Society* 17, no. 2 (2017): 245–258.
Buolamwini, Joy. *Unmasking AI: My Mission to Protect What Is Human in a World of Machines*. New York: Random House, 2023.
Caldwell, John. *Production Culture: Industrial Reflexivity and Critical Practice in Film and Television*. Durham, NC: Duke University Press, 2008.
Callon, Michel, Yuval Millo, and Fabian Muniesa, eds. *Market Devices*. Oxford: Blackwell, 2007.
Caputo, Gail A. *Out in the Storm: Drug-Addicted Women Living as Shoplifters and Sex Workers*. Boston: Northeastern University Press, 2008.
Caputo, Gail A., and Anna King. "Shoplifting by Male and Female Drug Users: Gender, Agency, and Work." *Criminal Justice Review* 40, no. 1 (2015): 47–66.
Caputo, Gail A., and Anna King. "Shoplifting: Work, Agency, and Gender." *Feminist Criminology* 6, no. 3 (2011): 159–177.
Cartwright, Lisa, and D. Andy Rice. "My Hero: A Media Archaeology of Tiny Viewfinderless Cameras as Technologies of Intra-Subjective Action." *S&F Online* 13.3–14.1 (2016). https://sfonline.barnard.edu/.
Chace, Calum. "Has There Been a Second AI Big Bang?" *Forbes*, October 18, 2022. www.forbes.com.
Cohen, Julie. "Law for the Platform Economy." *U.C. Davis Law Review* 51 (2017): 133–204.
Cohen, Julie. "What Privacy Is For." *Harvard Law Review* 26, no. 7 (2013): 1904–1933.
Cowan, Ruth Schwartz. *More Work for Mother: The Ironies of Household Automation*. New York: Basic Books, 1985.

Crandall, Jordan. "Anything That Moves: Armed Vision." *CTHEORY* (1999): https://journals.uvic.ca.

Crawford, Kate. *Atlas of AI*. New Haven, CT: Yale University Press, 2021.

Crawford, Kate, and Vladan Joler. "Anatomy of an AI System: The Amazon Echo as an Anatomical Map of Human Labor, Data and Planetary Resources." AI Now Institute and Share Lab, September 7, 2018. https://anatomyof.ai.

Crawford, Kate, and Trevor Paglen. "Excavating AI: The Politics of Images in Machine Learning Training Sets," September 19, 2019. https://excavating.ai.

Cottle, Simon. *Mediatized Conflict*. Maidenhead, UK: Open University Press, 2006.

Daston, Lorraine, and Peter Galison. *Objectivity*. Princeton, NJ: Zone Books, 2007.

Denton, Emily, Alex Hanna, Razvan Amironesei, Andrew Smart, and Hilary Nicole. "On the Genealogy of Machine Learning Datasets: A Critical History of ImageNet." *Big Data & Society* 8, no. 2 (2021). https://journals.sagepub.com.

Dreyfus, Hubert. *What Computers Still Can't Do*. Cambridge, MA: MIT Press, 1992.

Dunworth, Terence. "Information Technology and the Criminal Justice System: An Historical Overview. In *Information Technology and the Criminal Justice System*, edited by April Pattavina, 3–28. Thousand Oaks, CA: Sage, 2005.

Eagleton, Terry. *The Ideology of the Aesthetic*. Malden, MA: Blackwell, 1990.

Edmond, Gary. "Legal Versus Non-Legal Approaches to Forensic Science Evidence." *International Journal of Evidence & Proof* 20, no. 1 (2016): 3–28.

Ericson, Richard V., and Kevin D. Haggerty. *Policing the Risk Society*. Toronto: University of Toronto Press, 1997.

Esser, Frank, and Jesper Strömböck. *Mediatization of Politics: Understanding the Transformation of Western Democracies*. New York: Palgrave, 2014.

Fan, Mary. *Camera Power: Proof, Policing, Privacy, and Audiovisual Big Data*. Cambridge: Cambridge University Press, 2019.

Fang, Karen. *Arresting Cinema: Surveillance in Hong Kong Film*. Redwood City, CA: Stanford University Press, 2017.

Farocki, Harun. "Phantom Images." *Public* 29 (2004): 12–22.

Feigenson, Neal, and Christina Spiesel. *Law on Display: The Digital Transformation of Legal Persuasion and Judgment*. New York: New York University Press, 2009.

Ferguson, Andrew. *The Rise of Big Data Policing: Surveillance, Race, and the Future of Law Enforcement*. New York: New York University Press, 2017.

Foucault, Michel. "On Popular Justice: A Discussion with Maoists." In *Power/Knowledge: Selected Interviews and Other Writings, 1972–1977*, edited by Colin Gordon, translated by Colin Gordon, Leo Marshall, John Mepham, and Kate Soper, 1–36. New York: Pantheon, 1980.

Friedberg, Anne. *The Virtual Window: From Alberti to Microsoft*. Cambridge, MA: MIT Press, 2009.

Fuller, Matthew, and Eyal Weizman. *Investigative Aesthetics: Conflicts and Commons in the Politics of Truth*. London: Verso, 2021.

Gates, Kelly. "*Day of Rage*: Forensic Journalism and the U.S. Capital Riot." *Media, Culture & Society* 46, no. 1 (2024): 78–93.

Gates, Kelly. *Our Biometric Future: Facial Recognition Technology and the Culture of Surveillance*. New York: New York University Press, 2011.
Gilligan, Chris. "States Struggle with Rape Kit Backlog Despite Funding Efforts." *U.S. News and World Report*, June 20, 2023. https://usnews.com.
Gilmore, Ruth Wilson. *Golden Gulag: Prisons, Surplus, Crisis, and Opposition in Globalizing California*. Berkeley: University of California Press, 2007.
Gitelman, Lisa, ed. *"Raw Data" Is an Oxymoron*. Cambridge, MA: MIT Press, 2013.
Goldsmith, Andrew John. "Policing's New Visibility." *British Journal of Criminology* 50 (2010): 914–934.
Goodman, Steve, and Luciana Parisi. "Machines of Memory." In *Memory: Histories, Theories, Debates*, edited by Susannah Radstone and Bill Schwarz, 343–359. New York: Fordham University Press, 2010.
Goodwin, Charles. "Professional Vision." *American Anthropologist* 96, no. 3 (1994): 606–633.
Goold, Benjamin, Ian Loader, and Angelica Thumala. "The Banality of Security: The Curious Case of Surveillance Cameras." *British Journal of Criminology* 53 (2013): 977–996.
Goold, Benjamin, Ian Loader, and Angelica Thumala. "Consuming Security? Tools for a Sociology of Security Consumption." *Theoretical Criminology* 14, no. 1 (2010): 3–30.
Gregg, Melissa. *Counterproductive: Time Management in the Knowledge Economy*. Cambridge, MA: MIT Press, 2018.
Gunning, Tom. "Tracing the Individual Body: Photography, Detectives, and Early Cinema." In *Cinema and the Invention of Modern Life*, edited by Leo Charney and Vanessa R. Schwartz, 15–45. Berkeley: University of California Press, 1995.
Hadden, Sally E. *Slave Patrols: Law and Violence in Virginia and the Carolinas*. Cambridge, MA: Harvard University Press, 2003.
Hacking, Ian. *The Taming of Chance*. Cambridge: Cambridge University Press, 1990.
Hall, Stuart, Charles Critcher, Tony Jefferson, John Clarke, and Brian Roberts. *Policing the Crisis: Mugging, the State, and Law and Order*. London: MacMillan, 1978.
Hallett, Michael, and Dennis Powell. "Backstage with 'COPS': The Dramaturgical Reification of Police Subculture in American Crime 'Info-tainment.'" *American Journal of Police* 14, no. 1 (1995): 101–129.
Hallin, Dan C. "Mediatization, Neoliberalism, and Populisms: The Case of Trump." *Journal of the Academy of Social Science* 14, no. 1 (2019): 14–25.
Haraway, Donna. "Situated Knowledges: The Science Question in Feminism and the Privilege of Partial Perspective." *Feminist Studies* 14, no. 3 (1988): 575–599.
Haraway, Donna. "A Manifesto for Cyborgs: Science, Technology, and Socialist Feminism in the 1980s." *Socialist Review* 15, no. 2 (1985): 65–107.
Harsin, Jayson. "Aggro-truth: (Dis-)trust, Toxic Masculinity, and the Cultural Logic of Post-Truth Politics." *The Communication Review* 24, no. 2 (2021): 133–166.
Hartcourt, Bernard. *Against Prediction: Profiling, Policing, and Punishing in an Actuarial Age*. Chicago: University of Chicago Press, 2006.

Hayes, Read. "Retail Theft: An Analysis of Apprehended Shoplifters." *Security Journal* 8, no. 3 (1997): 233–246.
Hayles, N. Katherine. *How We Think: Digital Media and Contemporary Technogenesis*. Chicago: University of Chicago Press, 2012.
Hayles, N. Katherine. *Unthought: The Power of the Cognitive Nonconscious*. Chicago: University of Chicago Press, 2017.
Hepp, Andreas. *Cultures of Mediatization*. Cambridge: Polity Press, 2012.
Hjarvard, Stig. *The Mediatization of Culture and Society*. London: Routledge, 2013.
Hodson, Hal. "AI Could Help Investigation of Boston Marathon." *New Scientist*, April 18, 2013. www.newscientist.com.
Hong, Sun-ha. "Technofutures in Stasis: Smart Machines, Ubiquitous Computing, and the Future That Keeps Coming Back." *International Journal of Communication* 15 (2021): 1940–1960.
Honovich, John. "2030: The Coming Dominance of Mega Cloud Physical Security Providers." *IPVM*, August 14, 2023. https://ipvm.com.
Honovich, John. "Hostage as a Service (HaaS)—Meraki, Rhombus, and Verkada." *IPVM*, April 5, 2021. https://ipvm.com.
Huberman, Jenny. "Amazon Go, Surveillance Capitalism, and the Ideology of Convenience." *Economic Anthropology* 8, no. 2 (2021): 337–349.
Iliadis, Andrew, and Amelia Acker. "The Seer and the Seen: Surveying Palantir's Surveillance Platform." *The Information Society* 38, no. 5 (2022): 334–363.
Jordan, Michael I. "Artificial Intelligence—The Revolution Hasn't Happened Yet." *Medium*, April 18, 2018. https://medium.com.
Kittler, Friedrich. *Gramophone, Film, Typewriter*. Palo Alto, CA: Stanford University Press, 1999.
Knepper, Lisa, Jennifer McDonald, Kathy Sanchez, and Elyse Smith Pohl. *Policing for Profit: The Abuse of Civil Asset Forfeiture*. Arlington, VA: Institute for Justice, 2020. https://ij.org
Kuchinskaya, Olga. *Networked Movements and Technological Innovation*. Forthcoming.
Kumanyika, Chenjerai. "Livestreaming in the Black Lives Matter Network." In *DIY Utopia: Cultural Imagination and the Remaking of the Possible*, edited by Amber Day, 169–188. Lanham, MD: Lexington Books, 2016.
Latour, Bruno. *Reassembling the Social: An Introduction to Actor Network Theory*. Oxford: Oxford University Press, 2007.
Law, John. "Actor Network Theory and Material Semiotics." In *The New Blackwell Companion to Social Theory*, edited by Bryan S. Turner, 141–158. Oxford: Blackwell, 2008.
Levin, Thomas. "Rhetoric of the Temporal Index: Surveillant Narration and the Cinema of 'Real Time.'" In *CTRL [SPACE]: Rhetorics of Surveillance from Bentham to Big Brother*, edited by Thomas Y. Levin, Ursula Frohne, and Peter Weibel, 578–593. Cambridge, MA: MIT Press.
Lewis-Kraus, Gideon. "The Great AI Awakening." *New York Times Magazine*, December 14, 2016. www.nytimes.com.

Linnemann, Travis. *Meth Wars: Police, Media, Power*. New York: New York University Press, 2016.

Livingston, Julie, and Andrew Ross. *Cars and Jails: Freedom Dreams, Debt and Carcerality*. New York: OR Books, 2022.

Loader, Ian. "Plural Policing and Democratic Governance." *Social & Legal Studies* 9, no. 3 (2000): 323–345.

Loader, Ian. "Consumer Culture and the Commodification of Policing and Security." *Sociology* 33, no. 2 (1999): 373–392.

Loader, Ian. "Policing and the Social: Questions of Symbolic Power." *British Journal of Sociology* 48, no. 1 (1997): 1–18.

Low, Setha, and Mark Maguire, eds. *Spaces of Security: Ethnographies of Securityscapes, Surveillance, and Control*. New York: New York University Press, 2019.

Lundby, Knut, ed. *Mediatization of Communication*. Berlin: De Gruyter Mouton, 2014.

MacDougall, Ian. "Police Say Seizing Property without Trial Helps Keep Crime Down. A New Study Shows They're Wrong." *ProPublica*, December 14, 2020. www.propublica.org.

MacKenzie, Donald. *An Engine, Not a Camera: How Financial Models Shape Markets*. Cambridge, MA: MIT Press, 2006.

MacKenzie, Donald. *Inventing Accuracy: A Historical Sociology of Nuclear Missile Guidance*. Cambridge, MA: MIT Press, 1993.

Madrigal, Alexis C. "#BostonBombing: The Anatomy of a Misinformation Disaster." *The Atlantic*, April 19, 2013. www.theatlantic.com.

Manovich, Lev. "Separate and Reassemble: Generative AI through the Lens of Art and Media Histories." In *Artificial Aesthetics: Generative AI, Art, and Visual Media*, edited by Lev Manovich and Emanuele Arielli. 2024. https://manovich.net.

Manning, Peter K. *Policing Contingencies*. Chicago: University of Chicago Press, 2003.

Manning, Peter K. "Producing Drama: Symbolic Communication and the Police." *Symbolic Interaction* 5, no. 2 (1982): 223–242.

Mawby, Rob C. *Policing Images: Policing, Communication, and Legitimacy*. Uffculme, UK: Willan, 2002.

McCarthy, Anna. *Ambient Television: Visual Culture and Public Space*. Durham, NC: Duke University Press, 2001.

McCosker, Anthony, and Rowan Wilken. *Automating Vision: The Social Impact of the New Camera Consciousness*. New York: Routledge, 2020.

McCulloch, Jude, and Dean Wilson. *Pre-crime: Pre-emption, Precaution and the Future*. New York: Routledge, 2016.

McKay, Carolyn, and Murray Lee. "Body-Worn Images: Point-of-View and the New Aesthetics of Policing." *Crime Media Culture* 16, no. 3 (2020): 431–450.

McLuhan, Marshall. "The Medium Is the Message." In *Understanding Media: The Extensions of Man*, 23–35. New York: Signet Books, 1964.

McQuade, Brendan. "World Histories of Big Data Policing: The Imperial Epistemology of the Police-Wars of U.S. Hegemony." *Journal of World-Systems Research* 27, no. 1 (2021): 109–135.

Mearian, Lucas. "As Police Move to Adopt Body Cams, Storage Costs Set to Skyrocket." *Computerworld*, September 3, 2015. www.computerworld.com.

Mirzoeff, Nicholas. "Artificial Vision, White Space and Racial Surveillance Capitalism." *AI & Society* 36 (2021): 1295–1305.

Mitchell, Timothy. "Uber Eats: How Capitalism Consumes the Future." In *Critical Zones*, edited by Bruno Latour and Peter Weibel, 84–88. Cambridge, MA: MIT Press, 2021.

Mnookin, Jennifer. "The Image of Truth: Photographic Evidence and the Power of Analogy." *Yale Journal of Law and the Humanities* 10 (1998): 1–74.

Monahan, Torin. *Crisis Vision: Race and the Cultural Production of Surveillance*. Durham, NC: Duke University Press, 2022.

Moore, Kelli. *Legal Spectatorship: Slavery and the Visual Culture of Domestic Violence*. Durham, NC: Duke University Press, 2022.

Morozov, Evgeny. *To Save Everything, Click Here: The Folly of Technological Solutionism*. New York: Public Affairs, 2013.

Moses, Lyria Bennett, and Janet Chan. "Algorithmic Prediction in Policing: Assumptions, Evaluation, and Accountability." *Policing and Society* 28, no. 7 (2018): 806–822.

Mowatt, Rasul A. "Black Lives as Snuff: The Silent Complicity in Viewing Black Death." *Biography* 41, no. 4 (2018): 777–806.

Muhammad, Khalil Gibran. *The Condemnation of Blackness: Race, Crime, and the Making of Modern Urban America*. Cambridge, MA: Harvard University Press, 2010.

Mukerji, Chandra. *Impossible Engineering: Technology and Territoriality on the Canal du Midi*. Princeton, NJ: Princeton University Press, 2009.

Mukerji, Chandra. "The Territorial State as a Figured World of Power: Strategics, Logistics, and Impersonal Rule." *Sociological Theory* 28, no. 4 (2010): 402–424.

Müller, Nina C., and Jenny Wiik. "From Gatekeeper to Gate-Opener: Open-Source Spaces in Investigative Journalism." *Journalism Practice* 17, no. 2 (2023): 189–208.

Muniesa, Fabian, Yuval Millo, and Michel Callon. "An Introduction to Market Devices." *The Sociological Review* 55, no. 2 (2007): 1–12.

Nadler, Anthony, Matthew Crain, and Joan Donovan. "Weaponizing the Digital Influence Machine: The Political Perils of Online Ad Tech." *Data & Society*, October 17, 2018. https://datasociety.net.

National Research Council. *Strengthening Forensics Science in the United States: A Path Forward*. Washington, DC: National Academies Press, 2009.

Newell, Bryce. *Police Visibility: Privacy, Surveillance, and the False Promise of Body-Worn Cameras*. Berkeley: University of California Press, 2021.

Nhan, Johnny, Laura Huey, and Ryan Broll. "Digilantism: An Analysis of Crowdsourcing and the Boston Marathon Bombings." *British Journal of Criminology* 57 (2017): 341–361.

O'Connor, Daniel, Randy Lippert, Dale Spencer and Lisa Smylie. "Seeing Private Security Like a State." *Criminology and Criminal Justice* 8, no. 2 (2008): 203–226.

O'Mahony, Niall, Sean Campbell, Lenka Krpalkova, Daniel Riordan, Joseph Walsh, Aidan Murphy, and Conor Ryan. "Computer Vision for 3D Perception." In

Intelligent Systems and Applications: Proceedings of the 2018 Intelligent Systems Conference (IntelliSys). Vol. 2, edited by Kohei Arai, Supriya Kapoor, and Rahul Bhatia, 788–804. Cham: Springer, 2018. https://doi.org/10.1007/978-3-030-01057-7_59.

Oppal, Wally T. *Forsaken: The Report of the Missing Women Commission of Inquiry*. Victoria, BC: Missing Women Commission of Inquiry, 2012.

Osnos, Evan. "Can Mark Zuckerberg Fix Facebook Before It Breaks Democracy?" *The New Yorker*, September 10, 2018. www.newyorker.com.

Owens, David B. "Violence Everywhere: How the Current Spectacle of Black Suffering, Police Violence, and the Violence of Judicial Interpretation Undermine the Rule of Law." *Stanford Journal of Civil Rights & Civil Liberties* 17 (2022): 476–514.

Parenti, Christian. *The Soft Cage: Surveillance in America from Slavery to the War on Terror*. New York: Basic Books, 2003.

Parisi, Luciana, and Steve Goodman. "Mnemonic Control." In *Beyond Biopolitics: Essays on the Governance of Life and Death*, edited by Patricia Ticineto Clough and Craig Willse, 163–176. Durham, NC: Duke University Press, 2011.

Parks, Lisa. "Earth Observation and Signal Territories: Studying U.S. Broadcast Infrastructure through Historical Maps, Google Earth, and Fieldwork." *Canadian Journal of Communication* 38 (2013): 285–307.

Parks, Lisa, and Nicole Starosielski, eds. *Signal Traffic: Critical Studies of Media Infrastructures*. Urbana: University of Illinois Press, 2015.

Peirce, Charles Sanders. *Charles S. Peirce: The Essential Writings*. Edited by Edward C. Moore. Amherst, NY: Prometheus, 1998.

Peters, John Durham. *The Marvelous Clouds: Toward a Philosophy of Elemental Media*. Chicago: University of Chicago Press, 2015.

Petersen, Jennifer. "Ubiquitous Video, Objectivity, and the Problem of Perspective in Digital Visual Evidence." In *Law and the Visible*, edited by Austin Sarat, Lawrence Douglas, and Martha Merrill Umphrey, 17–41. Amherst: University of Massachusetts Press, 2021.

Peterson, Joseph L., and Matthew J. Hickman. "Census of Publicly Funded Forensic Crime Laboratories, 2002." *Bureau of Justice Statistics Bulletin*, February 2005.

Poli, Joseph A. "Development and Present Trend of Police Radio Communications." *Journal of Criminal Law and Criminology* 33, no. 2 (1942): 193–197.

Reeves, Joshua. *Citizen Spies: The Long Rise of America's Surveillance Society*. New York: New York University Press, 2017.

Reeves, Joshua, and Jeremy Packer. "Police Media: The Governance of Territory, Speed, and Communication." *Communication and Critical/Cultural Studies* 10, no. 4 (2013): 359–384.

Ristovska, Sandra. "Open-Source Investigation as a Genre of Conflict Reporting." *Journalism* 23, no. 3 (2022): 632–648.

Ristovska, Sandra. *Seeing Human Rights: Video Activism as a Proxy Profession*. Cambridge, MA: MIT Press, 2021.

Richardson, Allissa. "Bearing Witness While Black." *Digital Journalism* 5, no. 6 (2017): 673–698.

Richardson, Allissa. *Bearing Witness While Black: Smartphones, African Americans and the New Protest #Journalism*. Oxford: Oxford University Press, 2020.
Richardson, Rashida, Jason Schultz, and Kate Crawford. "Dirty Data, Bad Predictions: How Civil Rights Violations Impact Police Data, Predictive Policing Systems, and Justice." *New York University Law Review* 94 (2019): 192–233.
Rosenblatt, Daniel N., Eugene R. Cromartie, and John Firman. *The Impact of Video Evidence on Modern Policing: Research and Best Practices from the IACP Study on In-Car Cameras*. Alexandria, VA: International Association of Chiefs of Police, Community Oriented Policing Services, and U.S. Department of Justice, 2004. https://bja.ojp.gov.
Rossiter, Ned. *Software, Infrastructure, Labor*. New York: Routledge, 2016.
Rowley, Laura. *On Target: How the World's Hottest Retailer Hit a Bull's-Eye*. Hoboken, NJ: John Wiley & Sons, 2003.
Rule, James. *Private Lives and Public Surveillance: Social Control in the Computer Age*. New York: Schocken Books, 1974.
Sacharoff, Laurent, and Sarah Lustbader. "Who Should Own Police Body Camera Videos?" *Washington University Law Review* 95, no. 2 (2017): 269–326.
Scannell, R. Joshua. "This Is Not *Minority Report*: Predictive Policing and Population Racism." In *Captivating Technology: Race, Carceral Technoscience, and Liberatory Imagination in Everyday Life*, edited by Ruha Benjamin, 107–129. Durham, NC: Duke University Press, 2019.
Schrader, Stuart. *Badges without Borders: How Global Counterinsurgency Transformed Modern Policing*. Berkeley: University of California Press, 2019.
Schuilenburg, Marc. *The Securitization of Society: Crime, Risk, and Social Order*. New York: New York University Press, 2015.
Schüll, Natasha Dow. *Addiction by Design: Machine Gambling in Las Vegas*. Princeton, NJ: Princeton University Press, 2014.
Schulz, Winfried. "Reconstructing Mediatization as an Analytical Concept." *European Journal of Communication* 19, no. 1 (2004): 87–101.
Schuppli, Susan. *Material Witness: Media, Forensics, Evidence*. Boston, MA: MIT Press, 2020.
Schwartz, Louis-Georges. *Mechanical Witness: A History of Motion Picture Evidence in U.S. Courts*. Berkeley: University of California Press, 2009.
Siegel, Greg. *Media Mediation: Reconstructing Accidents in Accelerated Modernity*. Durham, NC: Duke University Press, 2014.
Sekula, Allan. "The Body and the Archive." *October* 39 (1986): 3–64.
Seo, Sarah. *Policing the Open Road: How Cars Transformed American Freedom*. Cambridge: Harvard University Press, 2019.
Sharma, Sarah. *In the Meantime: Temporality and Cultural Politics*. Durham, NC: Duke University Press, 2014.
Shapiro, Aaron. *Design, Control, Predict: Logistical Governance in the Smart City*. Minneapolis: University of Minnesota Press, 2020.
Shapiro, Aaron. "Predictive Policing for Reform? Indeterminacy and Intervention in Big Data Policing." *Surveillance and Society* 17, 3/4 (2020): 456–472.

Shedd, Carla. "Countering the Carceral Continuum: The Legacy of Mass Incarceration." *Criminology and Public Policy* 10, no. 3 (2011): 865–971.
Sheehey, Bonnie. "Algorithmic Paranoia: The Temporal Governmentality of Predictive Policing." *Ethics and Information Technology* (2019) 21: 49–58.
Sheers, Julia. "Video Forensics: Grainy to Guilty." *Wired*, January 30, 2002. www.wired.com.
Smith, Brian T., and Ronald V. Clarke. "Shoplifting of Everyday Products That Serve Illicit Drug Uses." *Journal of Research in Crime and Delinquency* 52, no. 2 (2015): 245–269.
Sorin, Gretchen. *Driving While Black: African American Travel and the Road to Civil Rights*. New York: Liveright, 2020.
Spiegel, Lynn. *Make Room for TV: Television and the Family Ideal in Postwar America*. Chicago: University of Chicago Press, 1992.
Spitzer, Steven. "The Political Economy of Policing." In *The Political Economy of Policing*, edited by David F. Greenberg, 568–594. Philadelphia: Temple University Press, 1993.
Srnicek, Nick. *Platform Capitalism*. Cambridge: Polity, 2016.
Sterne, Jonathan. "The MP3 as Cultural Artifact." *New Media & Society* 8, no. 5 (2006): 825–842.
Sterne, Jonathan. *MP3: The Meaning of a Format*. Durham, NC: Duke University Press, 2012.
Sterne, Jonathan, and Elana Razlogova. "Tuning Sound for Infrastructure: Artificial Intelligence, Automation, and the Cultural Politics of Audio Mastering." *Cultural Studies* 35, no. 4–5 (2019): 750–770.
Sterne, Jonathan, and Mehak Sawhney. "The Acousmatic Question and the Will to Datafy." *Kalfou: A Journal of Comparative and Relational Ethnic Studies* 9, no. 2 (2022): 288–306.
Stewart, Garrett. *Closed Circuits: Screening Narrative Surveillance*. Chicago: University of Chicago Press, 2015.
Steyerl, Hito. "In Defense of the Poor Image." *e-flux Journal* 10 (2009). www.e-flux.com.
Stillman, Sarah. "Taken: The Rise of Civil Forfeiture." *The New Yorker*, August 5, 2013, www.newyorker.com.
Stork, Benedict. "Aesthetics, Politics, and the Police Hermeneutic: Online Videos of Police Violence beyond the Evidentiary Function." *Film Criticism* 40, no. 2 (2016). https://doi.org/10.3998/fc.13761232.0040.210.
Sturken, Marita. "Advertising and the Rise of Amateur Photography: From Kodak and Polaroid to the Digital Image." *Advertising & Society Quarterly* 18, no. 3 (2017). https://doi.org/10.1353/asr.2017.0021.
Tagg, John. *The Burden of Representation: Essays on Photographies and Histories*. Minneapolis: University of Minnesota Press, 1988.
Thorpe, James. "The Rise of Video Surveillance as a Service." *ISJ: International Security Journal*, February 14, 2022. https://internationalsecurityjournal.com.
Towns, Armond R. *On Black Media Philosophy*. Berkeley: University of California Press, 2022.

Trottier, Daniel. "'Fear of Contact': Police Surveillance through Social Networks." *European Journal of Cultural and Political Sociology* 4, no. 4 (2017): 457–477.
Trottier, Daniel. "Policing Social Media." *Canadian Review of Sociology* 49, no. 4 (2012): 411–425.
Trottier, Daniel. "Vigilantism and Power Users: Police and User-Led Investigations on Social Media." In *Social Media, Politics, and the State*, edited by Daniel Trottier and Christian Fuchs, 209–226. New York: Routledge, 2014.
Turow, Joseph. *The Aisles Have Eyes*. New Haven, CT: Yale University Press, 2017.
U.S. Bureau of Justice Assistance, *Public Safety Primer on Cloud Technology*. Washington, DC: U.S. Department of Justice, October 2016. https://bja.ojp.gov.
U.S. Bureau of Justice Assistance. *Video Evidence: A Primer for Prosecutors*. Washington, DC: U.S. Department of Justice, October 2016. https://bja.ojp.gov.
Vatulescu, Cristina. *Police Aesthetics: Literature, Film, and the Secret Police in Soviet Times*. Palo Alto, CA: Stanford University Press, 2010.
Virilio, Paul. *War and Cinema: The Logistics of Perception*. New York: Verso, 1989.
Wacquant, Loïc. *Punishing the Poor: The Neoliberal Government of Social Insecurity*. Durham, NC: Duke University Press, 2009.
Wakefield, Alison. *Selling Security: The Private Policing of Public Space*. Portland, OR: Willan, 2003.
Walby, Kevin, Randy K. Lippert, and Alex Luscombe. "The Police Foundation's Rise: Implications of Public Policing's Dark Money." *British Journal of Criminology* 58 (2018): 824–844.
Wall, Tyler, and Travis Linnemann. "Staring Down the State: Police Power, Visual Economies, and the 'War on Cameras.'" *Crime, Media, Culture* 10, no. 2 (2014): 133–149.
Wang, Jackie. *Carceral Capitalism*. South Pasadena, CA: Semiotext(e), 2018.
Weizman, Eyal. *Forensic Architecture: Violence at the Threshold of Detectability*. New York: Zone Books, 2017.
Williams, Brandt. "Target's State-of-the-Art Forensics Lab Catches More than Just Shoplifters." *MPR News*, October 21, 2011. www.mprnews.org.
Williams, Raymond. *Television: Technology and Cultural Form*. London: Collins/Fontana, 1974.
Williams, Rosalind H. *Dream Worlds: Mass Consumption in Late Nineteenth-Century France*. Berkeley: University of California Press, 1991.
Willis, James J., Christopher S. Koper, and Cynthia Lum. "Technology Use and Constituting Structures: Accounting for the Consequences of Information Technology on Police Organisational Change." *Policing and Society* 30, no. 5 (2020): 483–501.
Wilson, Christopher. *Cop Knowledge: Police Power and Cultural Narrative in Twentieth-Century America*. Chicago: University of Chicago Press, 2000.
Wilson, Dean. "The New Platform Policing." In *Automated Crime Prevention, Surveillance, and Military Operations*, edited by Aleš Završnik and Vasja Badalič, 47–68. New York: Springer, 2021.
Wilson, Dean. "Platform Policing and the Real-Time Cop." *Surveillance & Society* 17, no. 1/2 (2019): 69–75.

Wilson, Dean. "Predictive Policing Management: A Brief History of Patrol Automation." *New Formations* 98 (2019): 139–155.
Winner, Langdon. "Who Will We Be in Cyberspace?" *The Information Society* 12 (1996): 63–72.
Wise, J. Macgregor. *Surveillance and Film*. London: Bloomsbury, 2016.
Wood, David Murakami. "A New 'Baroque Arsenal'? Surveillance in a Global Recession." *Surveillance and Society* 6, no. 1 (2009): 1–2.
Wood, David Murakami, and Kirstie Ball. "Brandscapes of Control? Surveillance, Marketing and the Co-construction of Subjectivity and Space in Neo-liberal Capitalism." *Marketing Theory*, 13, no. 1 (2013): 47–67.
Wood, Stacy. "Policing through Platform." *Computational Culture* 7 (2019). http://computationalculture.net.
Wright, Jordana, Robert Heynen, and Emily van der Meulen. "'It Depends on Who You Are, What You Are': 'Community Safety' and Sex Workers' Experience with Surveillance." *Surveillance and Society* 13, no. 2 (2015): 265–282.
Završnik, Aleš, ed. *Big Data, Crime and Social Control*. New York: Routledge, 2018.
Zimmer, Catherine. *Surveillance Cinema*. New York: New York University Press, 2015.
Zuboff, Shoshana. *The Age of Surveillance Capitalism: The Fight for a Human Future at the New Frontier of Power*. New York: Public Affairs, 2019.
Zuboff, Shoshana. "Big Other: Surveillance Capitalism and the Prospects of an Information Civilization." *Journal of Information Technology* 30 (2015): 75–89.

INDEX

Page numbers in *italics* refer to images.

addiction and drug use, and shoplifting, 70
adolescents, and shoplifting, 69
ADT, 16
aesthetics, police, 145–47, 175n7
AI (artificial intelligence), 5, 25; and electricity, 122–24; imaginaries, 139; imaginary-infrastructural ontology of, 122; and large-scale systems for automated video processing, 30; and machine learning (ML), 123, 124; scale of, 147–48. *See also* video AI
algorithms, 130–133, 151–152
Allen, Rob, 63–64
Allied Universal, 16
Amazon, 47, 68–69, 120, 128–29, 147; Just Walk Out, 79; Rekognition, 128–129; Ring, 16, 47; Amazon Web Services (AWS), 128–29
American Apparel, 78
American Civil Liberties Union (ACLU), 128
American Society of Crime Laboratory Directors/Laboratory Accreditation Board (ASCLD/LAB), 65
Amoore, Louise, 7, 151, 152, 155–56
antitrust law, 112–113
Appeal, The, 69
Apple, 3, 20, 79–81
Apple Store (San Diego), 79, *80*, 126
application programming interfaces (APIs), 120

Arora, Sanchit, 130
artificial intelligence (AI). *See* AI (artificial intelligence)
audio. *See* sound
Aurora (CO) Police Department, 113
Aushana, Christina, 13, 91
automated redaction, 134–35
automated reporting, 135
automated transcription, 135
avalanche. *See* video avalanche
Avigilon, 113
Axis Communications, 17, 54, 64, 77–78, 84
"Axon Accelerate 2017" (conference), 3–4, 132, 133
Axon Cloud, 109
Axon Enterprise (formerly Taser), 3–4, 18, 24, 47–48, 88–89, 96–99; and "complete analytics" of video, 133–36; and Dextro, 121, 132, 134; imaginaries, 112; obstacles to growth, 112–16; "Officer Safety Plan," 107–108
Axon Evidence, 109
Axon Investigate, 47–48
Axon Network, 89, 101, 154
Axon Records, 109–110

backend information technology (IT) networks, 85–86. *See also* body cameras
Baidu, 122
Ball, Kirstie, 56
"banality of security, the," 57

189

Bank of America, 75
Bay Area Rapid Transit (BART) Police, 93–94
BBC, coverage of Bento case, 42
BBC Newsnight, 41–42
Bedford (U. K.) and Bedford Police, 40–43
Benjamin, Ruha, 153, 156, 164n32, 172n70
Benjamin, Walter, 154
Bento, Nico, 40–43, 49, 164n23; Bento case, 40–43
Big Data, 52, 122
Big Tech, 122–24; and surveillance capitalism, 15–16, 52. *See also* Target; and vision APIs, 127–28
BJA. *See* United States, Bureau of Justice Assistance
Black communities, poor: and video analysis, 46
Bloomberg Businessweek (magazine), 75–76
Black Lives Matter protests, 21
body cameras, 85–89; and image-risk management, 92–95; and police logistical mediatization, 89–92; and Taser (*See* Taser)
Bogard, William, 138
Boston Globe (newspaper), 61
Boston Marathon, bombing, 27–29
Bourdieu, Pierre, 11
branding, 97, 103; and brandscapes, 55–57; and memory, 105
Breaking Bad (television show), 12
Brickstream, 78
Brown, Michael, 21, 94
Browne, Simone, 46, 126

Caché, 78
Caldwell, John, 11
California, prison-building boom in, 111–12, 153
Canal du Midi, 148
Canon Inc., 17–18, 64, 77
Cara, 78

Caudle, Casey, 40, 41–42
ChatGPT, 155
Chicago Police, 112–13
Citizen Spies (Reeves), 16
Citizens United v. Federal Election Commission, 155
civil forfeiture, 114, 152–53
Clarifai, 130
Clinton, Bill, 19
closed-circuit television (CCTV), 2; as a "baroque arsenal," 17
Cloud Ethics (Amoore), 7, 151, 155–56
COBAN, 95
Cohen, Julie, 15, 122
compression, of video, 34–36
computational thinking, 7
computational perception, 29–30
Computerworld, 87, 118
Condemnation of Blackness, The (Muhammad), 6
conducted electrical weapons (CEWs), 88, 95–96, 99
COPS (television show), 91–92
Counterforensics, 50
Crawford, Kate, 7, 147
crime, and statistics, 5, 33; and "the crime problem," 50
Crisis Vision (Monahan), 155
CSI: Crime Scene Investigation (television show), 36
"CSI moments," 35–36
Curalate, 130
CVS Health Corp., 68

DALL-E 2, 139
Dayton Company, 55. *See also* Target
Dayton Hudson Corporation, 55. *See also* Target
deepfakes, 121, 138–40
deep learning, 130
Dextro, 3, 10, 120–21, 129–32, 134, 143; *See also* Axon Enterprises
Digital Ally, 95

digital compression, of video, 34–36
digital multimedia forensics, 23. *See also* video forensics
Disney World, 56
Dreyfus, Hubert, 119
drug use and addiction, and shoplifting, 70
dTective, 1
Dugan, Ben, 68
Duhigg, Charles, 52, 54

Eagleton, Terry, 145
Eastman Kodak, 107
Edmond, Gary, 45
electricity, and AI, 122–24
EmTech, 122
enhancing, video. *See* fidelity, of video
Ericson, Richard, 93, 110
Evidence.com, 97, 109, 132

Facebook, 150
Facebook Live, 21, 130
Facebook Video, 20
facial recognition technology, 126–29
Fan, Mary, 87
FBI (Federal Bureau of Investigation), 65–66; and the Boston Marathon bombing, 27–29; Uniform Crime Reporting data, 69
Fei-Fei Li, 124–25
fidelity, of video, 34–35
Floyd, George, 104; murder of, 75–76
Forbes (magazine), 66
forensic analysts, 39–41
forensic sciences (forensics), 33; as aesthetic practice, 175n8; and counter-forensics, 50
forensic turn, in video news production, 50
forensic video analysis, 23. *See also* video forensics
"Forensic Video Analysis and the Law" (course), 12

formats, proprietary video forensics, 46–48
Foucault, Michel, 26
frame averaging, 35
frame rates, 37–38
framed slices, of spatiotemporal ranges of perception, 34
fraud detection, 125–27
Fredericks, Grant, 41–42
Friedberg, Anne, 91
Fuqua, Antoine, 13
Fusion Center (Minneapolis), 64
"Futurist Manifesto" (Marinetti), 154

Galton, Francis, 5
Garner, Eric, 21, 94
Garsztka, Kamila, 40, 41–42
gender violence, 45
generative video AI, 138–41
Gilmore, Ruth Wilson, 111–12, 153
Goldsmith, Andrew, 21
Goodman, Steve, 105
Google, 3–4, 15, 47, 120, 121–22; Bard, 139; and video AI, 124–25
Google Brain, 121–122
Google Cloud Platform, 124
Google Nest, 16, 47
Google Translate, 121–22
Google Vision API, 124–26
Goold, Benjamin, 57
GoPro, 3
Grant, Oscar, 93
ground truth, 38

Hacking, Ian, 5, 9
Haggerty, Kevin, 93, 110
Hall, Stuart, 69
Hayles, Katherine, 11, 123
Hearst, Patty: kidnapping and bank robbery, 23
heat maps, 77
Hickins, Michael, 76
Home Depot, 68
Hong, Sun-ha, 140

Honovich, John, 47
"How Companies Learn Your Secrets" (Duhigg), 52

Iannelli, Jerry, 69
IBM, 18
image comparison, 36–37
image management, metaphorical and literal, 88
ImageNet, 151
imaginaries, 22, 89, 97, 116, 121–22, 141, 169n8
IMRSV, 78
indexicality, 31–32, 163n18–164n18
iNPUT-ACE, 47–48
in-store security systems; and retail analytics, 76–81
interlacing, 34
International Association of Chiefs of Police, 75
Internet of Things, the, 17
inventory shrinkage, 57
IPVM, 47

Joler, Vladan, 147
Jordan, Michael I., 123
journalism, forensic turn in video news production, 50

Kakutani, Michiko, 29
KBS+, 130
Kennedy, John, 41
King, Rodney, 20
Kopper, Christopher, 109–110
Kuchinskaya, Olga, 20
Kumanyika, Chenjerai, 21

labor-saving technologies, 46, 85, 96, 102, 106, 116, 133, 139
Las Vegas, Nevada, 56
Latour, Bruno, 101–102
Law Enforcement Manpower Resource Allocation System (LEMRAS), 18
Linnemann, Travis, 12–13, 94

Lippert, Randy, 75
Loader, Ian, 57, 161n46
logistical mediatization, 13–15; police, 88, 89–92
logistical media systems, 82
logistical power, 13–14
logistics, 160n36
Los Angeles, City Council, 75
Los Angeles Police Department (LAPD), 75, 112–13
loss prevention, 57, 165n17
Luan, David, 130, 131
Lum, Cynthia, 109–110
Luscombe, Alex, 75
Lustbader, Sarah, 22
lynching photographs, 22

machine learning (ML), 124; and deep learning, 130; *See also* AI (artificial intelligence)
MacKenzie, Donald, 106
Mandel'shtam, Osip, 145
Manning, Peter, 14
Marinetti, Filippo Tommaso, 154
Marshalls, 68
McCosker, Anthony, 11
McCulloch, June, 170n35
McLuhan, Marshall, 122, 161n72
mechanical objectivity, 50
mediatization, 160n19. *See also* logistical mediatization
Medium (blogging platform), 132, 134
Miami-Dade Police Department, 113
Michigan Public Radio, 70
Microsoft, 3, 75
Milestone Systems, 17, 54, 64
Minneapolis, Minnesota, 63–65, 72–73
Minneapolis Downtown Improvement District, 64
Minneapolis SafeZone project, 64–65, 83
Minority Report (film), 98–99, 170n35
Mirzoeff, Nicholas, 126–27
Misfit, 132, 134

Mitarai, Fujio, 17–18
MIT Technology Review, 122
mobile privatization, 11
Mobile-Vision, 95
Monahan, Torin, 155
Motorola Solutions, 18–19, 110–11, 155
Mowatt, Rasul, 162n79
Muhammad, Khalil Gibran, 6, 159n8
Mukerji, Chandra, 13, 148
multiplexing, 33–34
Musk, Elon, 140

National Police Foundations Project, 73, 167n72
National Retail Federation, 69
natural language processing (NLP), 137
Newell, Bryce, 22, 88, 134, 170n31
New York Police Department, 112–13
New York Police Foundation, 63, 73
New York Times Magazine, 121–22
Ng, Andrew, 122
Nichols, Tyre, 104
Nike Town, 56
North Hampton, England: crime prevention program in, 63
Nvidia Corporation, 8

Oakland Police Department, 113
objectivity, mechanical, 50
Occam Video Solutions, 47
occluding vision, 134
Oklahoma State Bureau of Investigation, 65–66
open-source investigation, 49–50
optical character recognition (OCR), 135
Oracle, 76
organized retail theft, 68–70
Orlando (Florida), City of, 128–29
Orta, Ramsey, 94
Osnos, Evan, 149
Our Biometric Future (Gates), 127–28
Owens, David, 22

Packer, Jeremy, 14
Palantir, 75
panorama, 101–102
Parakilas, Sandy, 149–50
Parisi, Luciana, 105
Parks, Lisa, 102, 150
Pelosi, Paul (Nancy Pelosi's husband), 104–105
perception, 10, 145; computational, 29, 39, 141; selective, 132; technological, 138; spatiotemporal ranges of, 34; logistics of military perception, 13, 89
Periscope, 21, 130
Peters, John Durham, 13
Phoenix Police Department, 113
Photoshop, 140
platforms, 15, 24, 109, 114, 119–120, 127–28; cloud-based, 87; proprietary video forensics, 46–48, 81, 14; social media, 49, 93, 94; video-sharing, 88, 153
police and policing: aesthetics, 145–47, 175n7; and body cameras (*See* body cameras); budgets, downward pressure on, 114; and carceral perspective of video AI, 151–53
files, 147; logistical mediatization, 88, 89–92; media work, 31; organizations as "meaning production machines," 14; perception, logistics of, 88, 89–92; predictive, 150–51, 170n35; private, 15; records management systems (*see* records management systems); surveillance economy, 15–19; unions, 137–38; video and logistical mediatization of, 12–14
Police Executive Research Forum (PERF), 73, 74
predictive analytics, 69
Priory Lake. *See* Bento case
Prism Skylabs, 78

prisons: and carceral perspective of video AI, 150–52; challenges of scaling back, 152–56; and prison-building boom in California, 111–12, 153
privacy, 15, 22, 81, 135, 155, 168n93
private crime labs, 83
private policing, 15–16, 153; and market research, 76
probability, 5
ProPublica, 75
prototypical whiteness, 126
Publix, 68

racial surveillance capitalism, 126–27
racism, post-slavery, 6
rape kits, untested, 45
records management systems (RMS), 18–19, 109–111
redaction, automated, 134–35
Reddit, 67
Reeves, Joshua, 14, 16
Rekognition, 128
reporting, automated, 135
retail analytics, 24, 54, 84, 126; and store security systems, 76–81
RetailNext, 78–79
retail theft, organized, 68–70
reverse logistics, 67
reverse projection, 41–42
Richardson, Allissa, 20
Ristovska, Sandra, 49
Rossiter, Ned, 13
Rule, James, 91, 148

Sacharoff, Laurent, 22
Safariland Group, 113
Safe City program, Target's, 63, 83
SafeZone project (Minneapolis), 64–65, 83
samples and sampling, video, 34
scale, 57, 73, 122; of video surveillance infrastructures, 62, 147–50
Schrader, Stuart, 19

Schüll, Natasha Dow, 141
Schwartz, Louis-Georges, 163n18–164n18
science and scientists, 2
securitized brandscape, 24
Security Executive Council, 71
Security Technology Executive (magazine), 61, 64
selective perception, 133
sensemaking, 4, 5, 31–40, 50, 145
Sexton, Jared, 12
Shapiro, Aaron, 14
shoplifting, 57, 67, 68, 69, 70, 167n61
ShopperTrak, 78
Siegel, Greg, 33
Sight Sound and Motion (SSM) platform (Dextro), 131
Smith, Rick, 134, 136
sound, 9, 135, 137; MP3 as container technology for, 159n14
Spielberg, Steven, 98
Spitzer, Steven, 15, 16, 161n46
Srnicek, Nick, 109, 118
Starbucks, 75
Sterne, Jonathan, 159n14, 174n56
storage, video. *See* video storage
Stream (Dextro product), 130–131
surveillance capitalism, 15, 84, 125, 168n93
surveillance systems, in-store video, 57–62. *See also* Target

Taming of Chance, The (Hacking), 5
Tampa Police Department, 127
Target stores and Target Corp., 24, 51, 52–55, 81–84, 128; branding and brandscapes, 55–57; charitable activity, 70–76; corporate command center (C3), 62; early years of, 55–56; as a high-tech company, 52–53; in–house crime lab, 53, 65–70; in-store video surveillance systems, 57–62; integrating store security, with law enforcement,

62–65; large-scale video infrastructure, 62; philanthropy, 54, 70–76, 93; and police foundations, 54, 70–75; public safety grants, 71–72; and retail analytics, 76–81; Safe City program, 63, 83; security stand, in store, *59, 60, 61*
Target & BLUE, 71–72, 76
Target Investigations Center (Westborough, Massachusetts), 62–63
Taser International, 88–89, 95–96, 98–99. *See also* Axon Enterprise (formerly Taser)
Tasers, 88, 95–96, 108
Taser Technology Summits, 96, 98
Tassone, Anthony, 137
televisuality and the televisual field, 11–12
temporal indexicality, of video recordings, 30–31, 37–38
temporal infrastructure, of modernity, 37–38
Tesla, 3, 140
Thiel Fellowship, 130
threshold of detectability, 35
Thumala, Angelica, 57
time-date stamp, 37. *See also* temporal indexicality, of video recordings
TJ Maxx and TJX Companies, 68
Training Day (film), 13
transcription, automated, 135
Truleo, 137
Turow, Joseph, 56, 77
Twitter, 130
Two Sigma Ventures, 130

Ulta Beauty Inc., 68, 78
"Unexpected Career: Target's Forensic Services Laboratory, An," 65
United Kingdom: Bento case in, 40–43; moral panic about muggings in, 69
United States: Bureau of Justice Assistance (BJA), 31, 43, 46, 87; Capitol, riot on January 6, 2021, 105, 140; Congress, 45, 69; Federal Bureau of Investigation (*See* FBI)
Federal Communications Commission (FCC), 34; Federal Trade Commission (FTC), 113; Justice Department, Office of Community Oriented Policing Services (COPS), 73
National Academic of Sciences, 45; Securities and Exchange Commission (SEC), 95–96; Supreme Court, 113, 155
upvoting (Reddit), 67
user engagement, 141

Vatulescu, Cristina, 145–46
video: digital compression of, 34–36; image management, 88; quality, 34; sampled, 34; scale of surveillance infrastructures, 147–50; as unique, 5–12
video activism, 20–23
video AI, 30, 118–21, 124–25, 129, 141–43; carceral perspective of, 150–152; and "complete analytics," 133–34; Dextro and, 129–132, 134; generative, 138–41; imaginary, 120; infrastructure, 120; *See also* AI (artificial intelligence)
video analytics, 118
video avalanche, 1–5, 49, 147–50
Video Evidence: A Primer for Prosecutors (BJA), 31, 32
video forensics, 27–31, 49–51; Bento case, 40–43; proprietary formats and platforms, 46–48; selective use of, 43–46; and video evidence, 31–40
"Video Forensics: Grainy to Guilty" (*Wired* magazine), 35
video news production, forensic turn in, 50
video recordings, temporal indexicality, of, 30–31
video recovery, 2, 27, 44
video storage, costs, 87–88

video surveillance systems, in-store, 57–62. *See also* Target
VieVu, 95, 113
Virilio, Paul, 13, 88
Visionics, 127
voiceprints, 174n56

Wacquant, Loïc, 11
Walby, Kevin, 75
Waldman, Peter, 76
Wall, Tyler, 94
Walgreens, 68
Walmart, 68
Wall Street Journal (newspaper), 68
Wang, Jackie, 152–53
War and Cinema (Virilio), 88
Washington Post (newspaper), 52, 63, 66, 72
WatchGuard, 95, 113
Weizman, Eyal, 50, 146, 175n7
Wells, Ida B., 159n8

"What Privacy Is For" (Cohen), 155
Wilken, Rowan, 11
Williams, Raymond, 11
Willis, James, 109–110
Wilson, Christopher, 13
Wilson, Dean, 90–91, 161n45, 162n66, 169n8, 170n35
Winner, Langdon, 29
Wired (magazine), 35, 129–30
Wolfcom, 95
Wood, David Murakami, 56
Wood, Stacy, 169n8
workers, and in-store surveillance, 78–79

Yale University, 130
Ybor City (Tampa, Florida), 127
YouTube, 20

Zapier, 139
Zuboff, Shoshana, 15, 84, 86, 115, 125, 150, 168n93

ABOUT THE AUTHOR

Kelly Gates is the author of *Our Biometric Future: Facial Recognition Technology and the Culture of Surveillance* (New York University Press, 2011) and has contributed significantly to the field as the editor of two collections: *The International Encyclopedia of Media Studies, Vol. VI: Media Studies Futures* (Wiley-Blackwell, 2014) and *The New Media of Surveillance* (Routledge, 2009), co-edited with Shoshana Magnet. She is currently an associate professor of communication and science studies at the University of California San Diego.

www.ingramcontent.com/pod-product-compliance
Lightning Source LLC
Chambersburg PA
CBHW020028040426
42333CB00039B/589